Theories of Psychology

Psychology for Human Development

I0454604

Dr. Eduard Schellhammer
Founder and President of Schellhammer Business School

All rights reserved. No part of this publication can be reproduced, stored in a retrieval system, or transmitted in any form or by any means, electronic, mechanical, photocopying, recording or otherwise, without the prior permission of the publishers and/or authors.

While every precaution has been taken in the preparation of this book, the publisher assumes no responsibilities for errors or omissions, or for damages resulting from the use of information contained herein.

1st Edition in English, 2020, translated from the German Edition
© Copyright 2020. Dr. Eduard Schellhammer. All rights reserved.

ISBN:

www.SchellhammerBusinessSchool.com

Construction of the Psychology Programs

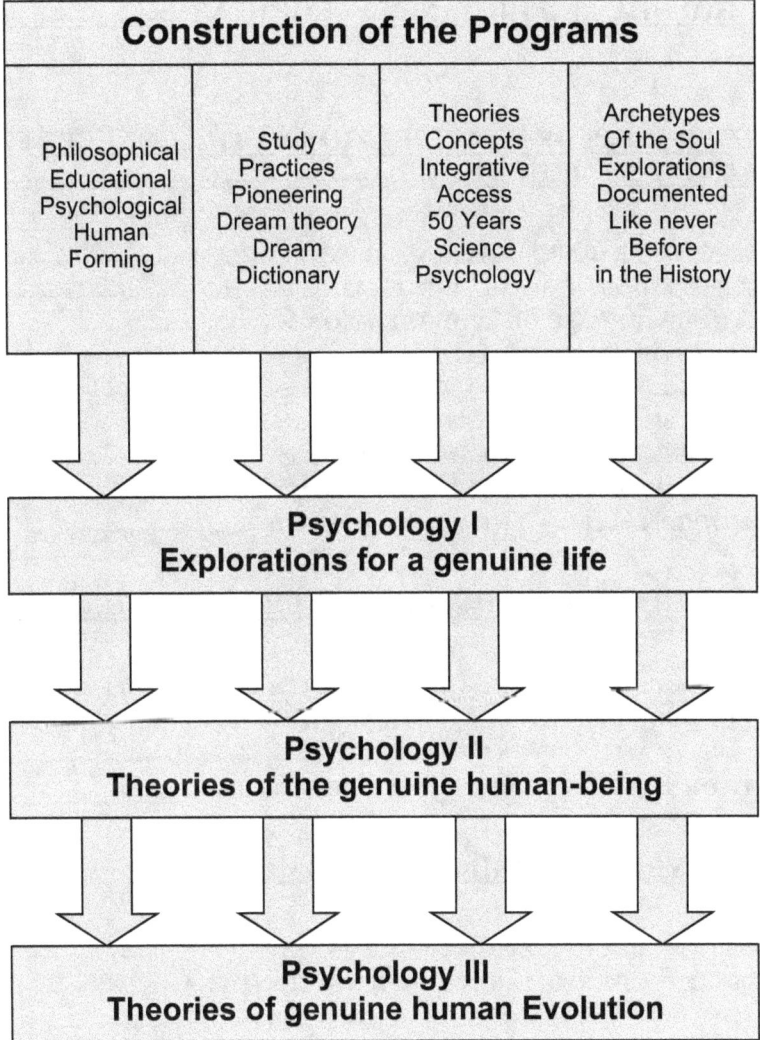

Construction of the Programs

Philosophical Educational Psychological Human Forming	Study Practices Pioneering Dream theory Dream Dictionary	Theories Concepts Integrative Access 50 Years Science Psychology	Archetypes Of the Soul Explorations Documented Like never Before in the History

**Psychology I
Explorations for a genuine life**

**Psychology II
Theories of the genuine human-being**

**Psychology III
Theories of genuine human Evolution**

Table of Contents

The Study Program:	All books contain:
Practical Psychology	Countless Practical Examples
Psychology I (1)	Multiple Choice Tests
Psychology II (2)	Short Exercises
Psychology III (3)	Working Units
Modern Dream Theory	General Theses
Dream Dictionary	Countless Lists covering Topics
Theories of Psychology	Notes and Perspectives
	Theoretical Aspects

Introduction:
Psychology and Human Development

Those who want to understand other people, require knowledge of human nature. Anyone who wants to form, and lead people cannot avoid studying (thoroughly) psychic life. Those who deal with people professionally, be it in teaching, in pastoral care, in social work, in caring, in nursing or in counseling, cannot work sufficiently or professionally without comprehensive, and basic awareness of human knowledge. In many professions, knowledge of human nature is more than helpful.

The knowledge of the 'inner man' is a prerequisite for successful and satisfying work, as well as a basic condition for understanding human life in all its depths. Those who seek answers, to the basic questions of existence, will hardly find them from outside of psychic life. Those who want to recognize and educate themselves need psychological knowledge. Thus, our topic revolves around human action and intrapsychic interdependencies. We explore the psychic powers and their formations.

We search into all depths of psychic life and ask many questions, such as: What do we recognize from human action in different life situations? What does a person do with his patterns of action in his environment? What moves him to act the way he does and not differently? Which internal and external forces control man's actions? What makes a person, with his life experiences, to live and think like that? What does the psycho-spiritual biography mean for the future of a human being?

How do the various psychic systems of forces (such as psychodynamics, intelligence, feelings, love) affect daily behavior? What can man gain with dreams and meditations? How do the needs press the ego? What is "consciousness extension"? How does self-education happen?

Where does a systematic comprehensive self-education lead? How are the buzz words such as "emancipation", "self-actualization", "self-development", "happiness", "life success" and many more in the connection to the many individual psychic forces to interpret?

Finding the answers to such questions ultimately means self-knowledge. These is achieved through reflection on oneself, one's own actions and one's own life. Thorough and systematic psychological knowledge of human nature is the prerequisite for every conscious lifestyle and in-depth self-education.

For self-education and for human education, as well as for human management and care, we want to work up knowledge that can help to reflect one's own actions at work, in their personal life, in the psychological interrelations, and thereby gaining a better understanding oneself. This is a prerequisite for being able to grasp other people psychologically and profoundly. We want to draw paths, develop instruments, and construct models that make it possible to understand the individual and social life as holistically as possible psychologically and spiritually. We refer to this area of psychological knowledge, under such viewing perspectives, as "Andragogical Psychology". Our goal is a difficult one in many ways.

Firstly, there is a harsh social reality: a few people who have hundreds of billions of dollars have more power and influence on the individual's daily life than many hundreds of social scientists. The big capital decides the welfare of the citizen in the industrialized countries, and not by the knowledge of the personality. Unemployment is a tough job. It is often about the survival of relationship happiness, and family happiness. What should be the formation of personality here?

The daily reality of poverty in Europe (and generally worldwide) is the face of wisdom and love. A gigantic massification of people make every scientific research - be it action-oriented in the interest of Andragogic - a ridiculous stewardship of big business.

Worldwide criminal systems (mafia) in trade, energy, economy, real estate, drugs, weapons, and corruption, determine the mental well-being of many millions of earth's citizens. This is more than all research results of social science. If some want war and "play" politics until they have this war, then they do not ask the social scientists to do so.

Those who control the world and therefore the masses do not speak in a "client-centered" way. This kind of domination and power in social life begins in smaller dimensions. Lying, cheating, playing games to procure a pleasure or a well-financed place in the transmission of the giant machinery of our industrial society come before the formation of personality. Politics is also stage play. Everyone can project fatherhood and motherhood desires, or early childhood wishes for prenatal oneness.

Happiness is the having and experiencing of the object. The object is the ego extension and thus the self-realization. Pedagogical and andragogical educational ideals do not have enough power to shape the social gears. We must keep an eye on these "um systems" and characteristics of basic social forces when we look at the human being in his inner life.

Another critical problem is the awareness of the individual citizen in industrial societies. He does not have the clarity. He has no overview. He does not see through it anymore. He is completely dependent on facts and social-psychological forces. Reality is what the television channels (with symphonic introductions) show daily in their messages to people's eyes. The newspaper and magazine journalists go to where something is "running". This is needed, but it is only a small part of reality.

Man does not know what his reality is. He has no idea of his intrapsychic functioning. Above all, he knows images and idols, unreal ideals, or the hardness of hell in the struggle for credit and recognition. That is the outer side of life. He is through and through trained and washed by the maxims of ideologies, the zeitgeist, and the dogmatism of his environment, pluralistic and liberal today. Man believes he is free and can think critically and acts responsibly. But no one can (or will?) see that the waves of maturity and emancipation have long since corrupted the mind.

At the same time, everything that man believes to be true, is nothing other than what he has absorbed in his life from the time before birth or has himself (often in opposition to it) conceived himself. He lives joy, lust, and sex, as far as his purse, environment, and ideology allow. After intoxicating love comes everyday life. Examples include, if money is missing, then more money is needed. Goods must be bought for the support of happiness. Children restrict liberal love. Cleaning, cooking, shopping, washing and other some small things take over. Chocolate and sunbathing by the sea reconcile the daily fight. If nothing worse happens, that's luck. Man does not see through all the projective contexts of his actions.

The "secret everyday life" behind the facades and backdrops of more than two-thirds of all people is suffering weakness of character, value indifference, instinctive archaic behavior, and enormously much destruction. Andragogic psychology has psychologically captured these dimensions and explored them educational processes.

If the science of the psychic man feels committed to the truth, it cannot communicate the actual psychological reality of human existence to the citizen. Man does not want that truth. He. Duty, solidarity, and faithfulness (if they exist at all) are tied to peer pressure, ideologies, dogmas, money, and personal gain, and never to the truth of inner psychic being. This is the "prison" in which the one is trapped.

Personality begins with the mirror of self-knowledge. Everyone is encouraged to first look at who (what) he is and how he lives. Self-reflection requires truthfulness. It requires that methods be used to systematically investigate one's own life; however, many avoid this mirror. Some, therefore, sell "colored mirrors". Examples of such "colored mirrors" are: "It is easy to find happiness, love, wisdom and transcendentalism". "Man… just look at the positive side of life". "With the power of the subconscious, you become successful".

Personality is traded like a market article, and as psychologically sedative as a "gentle drug". At best, the knowledge of personal development can mean for some, "How do I form and present myself for my career?" and for another, "how do I shape the masses to consume even more?". It may even be, "how do you have to talk to the people, so that they "join in", be it in the party or in the church?".

Real personality development, however, demands that one remembers oneself, uses all the knowledge and methods that help one understand one's own humanity and existence down to the inner depths: Why? How so? What for? Self-knowledge and self-education require laborious and extensive work. Andragogical psychology provides the scientific basis for this.

In this study, we want to develop concepts for self-reflection, for self-knowledge and self-realization of the individual in the gigantic company of society.

Personality education, as an education, requires systematic educational achievement. Those who want "redemption" and "enlightenment" must set themselves up. "Andragogical psychology" creates the "maps" and "instruments".

The first key question that accompanies us again and again is: "What is the human being?". This is the basic theme of philosophical anthropology (Landmann 1969, Gadamer / Vogler 1973, Diemer / Frenzel 1968, Schöpf, in Roth 1991). Our viewpoint is predominantly psychological, but achieves psychological depth, and parapsychological and transcendental dimensions. The goal of our statements is to essentially understand the human being. Every person at any time in the past, in the present and in the future (as far as anticipated) essentially has psychic and transcendental characteristics (psychic powers and subsystems). These are shaped differently depending on the environment and are evaluated differently.

This is the starting point for questions and statements that are constitutive for the educational theory of andragogy and for its practice. A comprehensive theory of philosophical anthropology cannot be developed here. We consider this a department that must be dealt with separately. Therefore, in andragogical psychology we largely leave biological, medical, sociological, and cultural aspects open.

Here we can only hint at her philosophical treatment as a starting point.

The psychological formability of man, and in particular the unfolding tendency of individuation, as well as the spirit principle, which can be worked out from the dreams and the dynamics of the imagination, lead us to a second key question: How should man be formed? As an empirical statement, Andragogical psychology can explain the variety of given variations and their effects on humans and the environment. As a normative statement, it can propose setpoint judgments as a formulation or linguistic description.

However, such value judgment formulations cannot be concluded from a Description. However, according to the principle of objectivity (Hengstenberg, in: Rocek 1972, 66) we can explain the context of argumentation and make the theoretical formulations arguable. This is a section of "Andragogical Psychology". However, the systematic development of a normative statement system is the subject of ethics and thus part of philosophical anthropology. In general, for us, what we formulate as a nominal sentence (for example, education goals, norms, values, action appeals), we put up for discussion, even if the one's values (the author) make a clear statement.

To write about the psychic life requires looking in all directions and positions. A survey of the most important fifty models of personality is also required. In addition, there is little manageable literature with individual themes, overall concepts, summaries, and critical appraisals. Psychology today is a barely comprehensible subject, with many branches and varied specific application interests. Furthermore, there are many topics in psychology, which are subjective, and thus problematic. There are always different factors that have been viewed as important, and what should be edited or basically omitted. The main criterion we have defined as the "andragogical reference".

This in turn is tied back in our educational theory (Schellhammer: Evolutionary Human Education, 1998). During the years, we have developed a first model of personality. We then corrected it; then, expanded it; then, corrected it again, and finally (while considering our own practical experience) designed a "last model". So, we already assume today that our personality model ("the psychic organism") must be renewed occasionally for objective, systemic and didactic reasons.

The terms "personality", "education" and "structural model" were discussed in our study "Visions for Human Education" (1998). Our definition of "personality" includes various concepts, including, but not limited to: "(Personality is) ... the totality of the psychological characteristics of a person" (Meili / Rohracher 1978, 143). In principle, this definition captures all psychic forces or psychic subsystems that can be recognized and described as such, emphasizing the individual character of the form (Meili / Rohracher 1978, 142). The aspect of the formation of psychic powers can be described in many ways.

In addition to the above-mentioned study, we would like to add a few key words, as they have already formulated neo-psychoanalysis. These are: undeveloped, largely latent, degraded, disturbed, blocked, weak, incomplete, and so on. (Schultz-Hencke 1950, 70-71). In contrast to psychotherapy (this should be emphasized here) we do not call such psychic powers shaped as pathological, but simply as what the words mean. If such property words refer to impulses (according to Freud, Adler, or Jung), this does not yet mean for Andragogy that they must be interpreted and evaluated as "neurotic" in the pathological sense. For Andragogy this gives rise to the educational mandate: the psychic powers are to be formed for life and for human beings according to what they can do in their own way.

Nevertheless, we claim the relative completeness of the essential psychic powers, which cannot be traced back to other psychic forces. For us, the power of love and the system of dreams, with the imagination (as conscious dreaming), is an independent psychic system, such as the intelligent functions, the needs, and the unconscious.

We will justify why we define just these "subsystems" as one entity. The whole system of the psyche, as presented here, is very dynamic and open. It is closely related to the "actions" in the habitat; however, it is different in an untold amount of ways. What is defined in our model as "subsystems" and as individual psychic forces are living realities that every person around the globe has as his own living psychic powers. The formations are infinitely different, and never identical to another person.

The whole system of psychic life is not a mechanical machine. It is neither manageable nor controllable by an experimental situation. No experimental design will ever capture this life complexity as a unit. Man can never be reduced to "safe factors", with this model. The experimental situation is never a reality. It is not even realistic. But that must be the "Andragogical psychology": close to life and close to the human being. The psychological experiment can never be grasped by a subject because of many uncontrollable variables. The theoretical contribution, from this direction, is confined to narrow sections of reality. In most areas, even a modest systematization of the relevant statements has not even been achieved (Brezinka 1978, 142).

The Behavioristic approach, for the description of personality, we consider to be far too narrow, and particularly (intra-psychically) motivated by obsessive and fear-filled attitudes towards life- with a concealed need for power. Which scientist could claim, and with what right, that only an empirical reality- in the sense of natural science- could be the object of science and of systematic research?

In our work "Visions for Human Education" (1998) we have stated that there are different realities of man, and that every reality must be explored with their own methods.

For example, if a scientist asserts, "There is not the unconscious"; or, "There is no psychic energy", then we cannot respect them as a conversation partner, as he would be fundamentally and psychologically conditioned to be closed to these realities.

To find some order in the multiplicity of things we have defined the following aspects:
1) Critical development of knowledge (concepts, theories) and applications.
2) Compiling of constructs for models (see: Schellhammer, 2000).
3) Decomposition of facts to link to the need for action of adult education.
4) Theses and critical questions, as well as networked reflections.
5) Educational achievement for andragogy.
6) Positive, and constructive aspects for people and society.
7) Critical aspects in the context of disturbances, conflicts, crises, and suffering.
8) Philosophical-anthropological reflections.
9) Ethical-moral considerations and guidelines.
10) Connections to the reality of life.

In the experience of the unconscious and the mode of action of dreams or the mind, but also in the experience of the power of love as a psychic reality, and especially in capturing the process of individuation, the principle is ultimately: Those who do not go through the individuation process has nothing to say, just to ask. There are psychic realities and processes that are almost only communicable with symbols. The individual finds his way through the inner reenactment.

Predictability and prediction prove to be myths of misunderstood enlightenment (Vinnay 1993, 60, 43-79). Planck sees in the quest for domination by exact science: "... and if he (the man) does not satisfy religion, he seeks a substitute for it in exact science." (Planck 1971, 5). We want to free ourselves from this "yoke", so that the scientific work can realize a realistic and life-practical goal - and so that we can also experience a little real joy in the "living" work.

Creating understanding about the psycho-spiritual foundations of human education is, on the one hand, the task of the educational theory of andragogy. We worked on this aspect in Visions for Human Education (1998). On the other hand, the "andragogical psychology" is responsible for this. This technical term is unusual.

The science of adult education does not have its own psychology for human education. This is the same for German-speaking countries. In this respect, the term "Andragogical psychology" is indeed unfamiliar.

However, the term "educational psychology" is known in the field of pedagogy. According to dictionaries and corresponding publications, this means the following:

1) the psychological components of school and non-school (educational) behavior.
2) Psychological teaching and learning processes.
3) Psychological education methods.
4) Psychological teacher behavior (leadership styles)
5) Forms of instruction and assessment of performance.
6) Diagnosis and Therapy of Learning/Educational Disabilities.
(Böhm 1988, 451, Horney et al., Vol 2, 540-544).

Educational psychology sees itself as the basis for pedagogical action.

"Educational psychology" is an interdisciplinary science (Herzog 1994, 425). The problems of this science are formulated by Herzog at various levels: there is a wealth of concepts. Educational psychology is more than "applied psychology". It helps to educate theories, and to research the psychic side of education. But it is also the psychology of educational practices that are relevant to practice, immediate, and influence.

A human being encompasses more than applied psychology. In this respect, "Educational Psychology" is an interdisciplinary science that open the perspectives of pedagogy (Herzog 1994, 442). Being transferred to the "Andragogical psychology" means that this is an interdisciplinary science which has researched those perspectives that determines Andragogical as areas of human education.

If pedagogical psychology is to be useful as an aid to decisions, instructions, and reflections (Weidenmann, in Mader 1991, 125, 128), then personality, the living-world, habitats, and individuation are central topics of andragogic psychology.

Like pedagogical psychology, it cannot deal with performance appraisals, grades, forms of interaction in the classroom, teaching and learning, and the like. It would also be completely wrong if the Andragogic wanted to use psychology as a "data quarry" (Siebert 1987, 150) for adult education.

Andragogic psychology must ask and answer questions on biographical research, the crises of the senses, environmental behavior, ideological "search movements", identity formation, (Tietgens 1986, 21, 114-115) and individuation.

This implies teaching as well as counseling aspects that cannot simply be delegated to psychology. Developmental psychological considerations (Gloger-Tippelt 1993, 98-118, Whitebourne / Weinstock 1982) become educational-theoretical problems and action-oriented concepts. Incidentally, personality education is much more than the "processing of reality", and "socialization" (Hurrelmann 1993, 155-175).

With our study on Andragogic psychology we can put some "substance" into a rather embarrassing gap for pedagogy. It says, "Is it only a modest limitation of scientists, or the condition of contemporary Pedagogical psychology, if there is no chapter on Personality psychology in a four-volume work entitled "Psychology in Educational Science "(Heller / Nickel 1976-1978)?" (Mader 1991, 14). The "Educational Psychology" by Gage / Berliner (1986) leaves much to be desired in this respect. The "psychology of the adult", as e.g. Olechowski rolls up (Zdarzil / Olechowski 1976), is far behind what the personality theories today can present to knowledge.

We want to emphasize the following critical remark, as it meets our central concern, "... depth psychology and psychoanalytic concepts are still being given too little consideration and reflected on their transferability into the andragogic field" (Kürzdörfer, in: Dewe 1988, 166). Becker (1992, 187-196) also calls for "psychoanalytic forms of thinking" in human formation (and in politics), with a focus on defense mechanisms, fears, desires, and the unconscious. He harshly criticizes: "Traditional psychology is not only insufficient for the recognition of mental disorders and the responsibility to act, it is not at all able to adequately describe the complexity of human action.", and, "Even within psychology there are the strangest and most dangerous simplifications." (Becker 1992, 190 and 195, respectively).
We hope that with our "Andragogical Psychology" we will be able to contribute to the understanding and practical education of all depths and complexities of the psycho-spiritual man so that practical human education is not taught, researched and practiced as "strangely and dangerously simplified". However, we cannot theoretically work up a theory about adult mental development or the variety of biographical development processes. This requires research and interdisciplinary (university) collaboration that we do not have. The spectrum of concepts has been worked up (see Kruse 1990, Flammer 1988, Olechowski 1974, Roszak 1994). To bridge the gap to individuation as a psycho-spiritual evolution and as a concept of human education, we leave to the academic community.

Based on Educational psychology, but without taking over the contents equally, we outline what the "Andragogical psychology" should contain:

1) The psychology of personality and individuation, insofar as it is relevant to the education goals of andragogy.
2) The actions under psycho-logical and educational aspects.
3) The psychological description of educational goals in the context of formability.
4) The description of the forming processes and their interdependencies in the overall human-environment system.
5) social-psychological and sociological connections with the psychic life of man.
6) The psychology of spiritual experiences (meaning, value, transcendence), including their symbolism.
7) The methods and tools that provide access to the mental life and active educational achievement of the individual.

In the interest of a clear division, we classify the aspects of concrete educational events in andragogic teaching, particularly, teaching methods, learning psychology, Andragogen teacher behavior, group dynamic processes, performance assessment and the like. The "andragogical subject didactics".
We group life topics, in particular, "conflicts, crises, difficulties, disorders and suffering", as an independent andragogical subject. For example, the term "andragogic life issues" is suitable for this. We see the "consulting methods" of Andragogen as another independent department.

As far as our human education is concerned, we can say that we can present a concept anchored in the highest ethical values of the occidental history of human education. We are at the demanding level of the philosophical-pedagogical tradition of European culture.

We therefore take the right to warn against all those concepts of human education, the "happiness", "success", "money", "career", "lustful and easy life", "reputation" and "attention" as central goals to promise human education.

Anyone who teaches this, and in addition says, "without health, everything is nothing", is not only discriminatory and cynical, but also racist. There are far too many "fraudsters" in human education who offer fairness, seriousness and even God as a mask. Therefore, we emphasize: problems, crises, conflicts, and difficulties are part of life. Suffering, illness, and strokes of fate are also part of life. We can accept that and deal with it constructively because we know the "mystery of man".

Finally, let us look at the characteristics of our "postmodernism." The sociologist Vester describes this "ambience." There are some key words (1993): mixing things and ideas (of everything and everyone), juxtaposition and confusion of fictions and facts there are no boundaries between culture, commerce, consumption and production; "Cultural values are not simply internalized but must be brought to the man or woman through marketing and promotion" (ibid., 35); "Shifting the weight of a statement to its packaging "... etc

Where this postmodernism leads each individual and the entire collective, we see every day wherever we look.

"Human development" is our "solution". For this we want to develop the basics here.

1. The Process of Individuation as the Concept for Human Development

1.1. Steps of transformation and its processes

The three phases and the main characteristics

In this book, we roll out the psyche as a complex system and break down the individual subsystems according to theoretical elements. We make it clear that this psychic organism, with the many psychic individual forces, represents the human being. "The psyche is life" shows up in many concrete contexts. The psychic system is the living thing. Psychic powers are the tools for shaping life and managing the world. But the psyche- as a whole- is more. It is the value and goal of human life. All questions of being human can only be formulated, sought, and answered within this psychic organism. Where else?

The psyche shapes life. But the opposite also applies: Life forms the psychic organism, from the moment of conception. Every single force in every psychic system is shaped by the outer life, by other people, and by self-education. The enormous abundance of forces, which have a shaping and determining effect on the human psyche, has the consequence that in every psychic system there are many opposing and contradictory forces.

It is probably not wrong to say that this diversity represents an almost unmanageable chaos of forces. Even between the individual systems, the forces often interact in opposite and incompatible ways.

No subsystem can work "reasonably" without the others. The ego stands in an enormous field of forces, as it were as a control center. The ego has the task to mediate between all forces. The actions should be the result of this comprehensive inner mediation.

The fact is that the abundance of "chaotically ordered" forces often pushes the ego into strange compromises. The ego must declare individual forces and subsystems as non-existent, for example the unconscious, the love power, and the mind.

Every human being has his or her own dynamics of allowing or blocking, using or leaving behind individual forces. Thinking is neglected or misused. The emotions "play" many variants of melodies, usually less harmonious, often loud, and powerful.

We state that all psychic powers can be fully absorbed into consciousness and consciously formed or changed. Only a few people practice this education. Most people do not know that this is possible. They have never learned that this is necessary for a constructive life. They are all afraid of turning to themselves. They think the unconscious is a "black hole without a bottom", and perhaps with "whimsical animals and devils" in it. Or, the dreams are "stupid stories", or the feelings are just disturbing forces. Or, love is sexual pleasure and satisfaction of needs, which may have to do with self-sacrifice. Or, thinking correctly works automatically. This is all completely wrong. All psychic powers can be limited, are aware of consciousness, can be reflected, changed, and integrated into the lifestyle by the ego.

Just as a person is psychically shaped, so he lives with himself, with other people and with the living space. Dealing with one's own psyche manifests itself in dealing with nature, with the water, the air, the earth, and the animal world. Just as the psychic powers are formed, so does man form his own world, and so does he affect the basic conditions of life.

The enormous damage and dangers that have arisen worldwide cannot be dissuaded away. The damage is enormous, even in individual and social life. Some of the most striking effects of psychic chaos the damage include: mental suffering, psychosomatic illnesses, accidents, destruction, divorces, social suffering, aggression, crime, violence, and war.

In psychology, school life is usually discussed in the context of the conscience or the superego. We must expand the debt issue. Man owes it to the integration of his own psychic inner world. Above all, this includes the formation and reformation of this disordered "growth" of forces. The effects of his actions in individual life, as well as in society, broaden the debt issue. The individual has his individual guilt in the collective situation, even if he cannot be identified as the direct cause. He is in solidarity in the lie of life, which negates the psychic life or at least handles it as insignificant value. As long as man remains in this guilt, and does not turn to his inner education, then he participates in education and socialization in this collective guilt. Forced from the inside, the person with hatred and defense must master the world and his life. Hatred and all forms of defense cover up this guilt.

We call the transformation and growth of the psychic system into a new, harmoniously functioning whole "INDIVIDUATION". Transformation means: changing, correcting, balancing, developing growth, unfolding, shaping, strengthening, differentiating, becoming richer and creating something new. By "unity" we mean that every psychic force and every psychic subsystem lives and works in many ways, and balanced with all other psychic subsystems and individual forces. The ego is the center of this balanced unity. This process is guided by the mind through dreams and imagination.

There is a misconception in psychological circles that this process cannot be realized to its goal. We want to emphasize with clear clarity that this goal is achievable, and that many women and men can achieve this goal. The process, however, takes a long time. The duration depends on the life lived, on the basic conditions of the person and of course on the mission. The decisive factor is not the goal. Rather, it is crucial that man learns to live more and more consciously in this "connection" to his own psychic life. From this inner orientation - we have called self-love - life becomes constructive and progressive. In this "back-bonding" man finds his true value and his sense of being. To experience and to live this way is much more important than always to keep in mind the rather distant goal.

It should be emphasized once again that the term "individuation" should not be equated with individualization or "ego-determination". Nor does the term belong in an orthodox psychoanalytic conception.

The historical tradition of the process of individuation has been curated by C.G. Jung in many of his works. Who deals with the process of individuation, does not come around these works, even if many of the theories constructed there today are in need of revision. We have further developed this conception and worked up didactic (educational theory) for human education in our works.

We divide the process of individuation into three phases. Of course, one can also determine ten or thirty phases, as has been repeatedly imaginatively constructed, for example, in esotericism. But that would be too complicated and would have its pitfalls. We cannot present a sequence program that would be the same for all people in every step of the order. Our classification criteria are quite formal. Nevertheless, this subdivision can be clearly and unambiguously described operatively.

In a sense, the individuation process is like a tree: one can recognize certain growth steps and define them in their order. But much of this growing tree of life can never be set exactly. In general, it seems to us that man with his intellect cannot control and determine this process in detail. There is the spirit in the psychic system for that. This is the only force that always knows what needs to be worked on and how the individual forces can be brought together to form a whole. Incidentally, one cannot "do" the inner processes of change or simply "learn" them. They happen when the individual carries out the necessary work in a comprehensive and committed manner. That is why people's education is not reduced to learning processes.

Can man go through this process alone? The answer is no, unless the inner mind directs a person to it and it is his destiny, as it were, to walk the path completely alone. Otherwise, this leads to all sorts of peculiar life constructions, and depending on the one-sidedness of the aspirations in a disaster. For orientation, we first give an overview of the three phases of individuation:

The beginning:
Basic education as "general personality education"

1st phase: affirmation of mental life: discover, dissect, and understand the forces; Rebirth of the inner man.

2nd phase: recognition of the spirit as a guiding principle, changes of all mental powers, and unification (dissolution) of opposites.

3rd phase: From the old psychic government principle to the new intellectual principle of government, to create harmony between inside and outside, and the completion of wholeness.

The goal: to achieve individuation.

The process of the individuation process cannot be imagined simply as an additive linear. The path is dynamic: "three steps forward and two back", sometimes "ten steps back and then eleven ahead", or a "descent for a long time and then a powerful upward". In the first phase of individuation, one can completely transform certain forces, while in the third phase, other forces only really come to the fore. You can save time by being systematic.

Whoever has a plan of the landscape of the psyche, can define his journey quite accurately, while without plan, the personality formation and the work on changes and conversions mainly means a stepping in different places. Daily life is always part of psychological occupations. You cannot stop time and leave the living space to some extent. The practical work always happens on the time axis present-past-future. Often you must look at a piece of the past every day, take a closer look at the present and look with one eye into the future (the next days or weeks or months).

A universally valid didactic for all learning and conversion steps is theoretically and practically producible. There are some typical progression characteristics that are directly grounded in psychic systems and can be objectively plausibly argued, for example, "knowledge comes before transformation," or "no change without the previous learning of the practice of handling the psychic powers!" The nine main changes in our phase model are only executable in the given order. The reason is in the thing itself.

From the archaic human to the evolutionary human

Our review makes one thing very clear: Individuation does not lead to "self-dissolution" (as in Zen Buddhism, for example). Individuation makes man, in all his psychic powers, more meaningful and constructive when coping with life. Individuation is also not self-centered, such as Kegan's concept of "step development of the self": "Our survival and development depend on our success in attracting the attention of others" (Kegan 1994, 39). The development and survival of the "self" cannot be evolutionarily anchored with either Kohlberg's stage theory, Piaget's developmental psychology, or the American philosophy of experience according to Rogers or Maslow. Kegan's conceptual use of the "self" - for example: the impulsive, the supra-individual, the interpersonal, the institutional, the sovereign, and the incorporated self ", as these do not grasp what constitutes as our concept of individuation in possibilities or the dimensions of our understanding of "development":

From the phase model of individuation arise two human images:

☐ THE ARCHAIC HUMAN

☐ Negation of the psyche
☐ Rejection of the inner mind
☐ Fixation on dogmas, ideologies
☐ Pressured by internal stress
☐ Without interior experience
☐ Defense and repression

☐ No holistic growth
☐ Life in unconsciousness

☐ THE EVOLUTIONARY HUMAN

☐ Living consciously with the psyche
☐ Communication with the inner spirit
☐ Individuation as a life orientation
☐ Order and freedom in the unconscious
☐ Systematic interior experience
☐ Integration and editing
☐ Growth holistically balanced
☐ Life in full consciousness

The "self" is Rogers' key word. The self is the individualized pattern of perception, consisting of what identifies the ego as "mine." The self is the configuration of perception and experience about oneself. The ideal self is then what the ego wants or wants to own. The ego wants to update, preserve, and increase what contains the self. This tendency pushes for differentiation and integration, for independence and change. That is Roger's "self-realization." The self-actualizing person has confidence in himself and others, is open to experience, spontaneous, flexible, creative, and able to genuinely respond to others (Rogers 1971, Pervin 1993).

Rogers describes the basic experiences in the process of development (1973, 114-129). Let us look at the keywords: false facades and behind the mask. Recognize what is behind the masks, make the decision to be yourself, and fully experience your own attitudes. Recognize dependencies, and to turn to: pain, anger, desire, grief, pride, etc. Recognize the inner wealth, find the inner pattern, and be open to living experiences. Reduce defensive posture and rigidity, endure uncertainties, experience your own organism, and find confidence in it. Recognize your own source of decisions and value judgments and be accepting of yourself as a unique being. Experience your development and take responsibility for personal growth. Rogers describes seven stages of personality change (ibid., 136-162).

This conception of Humanistic psychology is different from that of Analytical psychology. The "self" as the archetype of wholeness and as the goal of individuation achieves qualities quite different from humanistic construction. We cannot do much with the definition from Rogers. It does not provide a comprehensive psychological depth. It is narcissistic from the beginning.

There are some banal wisdoms: trust the other, only as much as he can trust himself. Capital interests, power needs and neurosis make many people unpredictable. Anyone who turns to it openly and confidently can suffer "total loss". Responding to others "real and spontaneous" often means the same as stepping on a "banana skin".

The climate of "emotional warmth" emphasized by Rogers as vital is in many ways an expression of the desire for symbiotic unity and expression of fear of life. This is not love and, according to Fromm, the opposite of growth. You can also carry out an andragogic consultation with a normal amount of attention, without having to radiate heat. "Emotional heat" all too often creates illusions, covert dependencies, and group dynamic constraints.

Also, we cannot share the positive judgment of such self-actualizing tendencies. Life shows the opposite. And love cannot grow by itself either. This assessment of man's growth powers is unworldly. It testifies to a lack of realistic life experience. Above all, the "spirit" is missing in this self-concept. Nowhere in the accessible literature on humanistic psychology have we found a construct that structures this organized perceptual material as individual psychic forces or psychic systems of forces. Rogers also avoids entering the world of the unconscious, be it Freud or Jung. It is here that the inner reality of man begins to become really exciting. We do not consider the concept of the "self", from Rogers, to be suitable for a comprehensive theory of personality, let alone for a conception of psychic-spiritual development in the sense of individuation.

The individuation occupies a large space in the works of Jung. Jung means "individuation" in general, "self-development of the individual" (1971, 65). He divides these into two types. The first type of individuation is the biological and psychological maturation process. He calls this the "initiation into adulthood and into external reality" (Jacobi 1971, 42). The ego becomes autonomous and moves away from the inner self. The "persona" is formed and the consciousness functions (thinking, feeling, intuition, feeling) unfold. Accordingly, the consciousness expands outside-oriented.

The second type of individuation is a process that is to be settled in the second half of life. This is the affection to the inner reality. In-depth self-knowledge and "accomplishment of one's own person" are central goals here. The "self" is new and expanded to attain. Characteristic in this process is the integration of the opposite sex function (Anima, Animus). Furthermore, Jung writes about "The Relationships between the Ego and the Unconscious", and, "How the self is to be liberated from the false envelopes of the persona on the one hand and the suggestive power of unconscious images on the other" (Jung 1971, 66). The "shadow" is to be integrated in this process. Thus, Jung means the "dark sides of the person" in different places. Shadowing is a moral problem. Individuation is "exploration of the numinous", and Individuation is "self-realization".

The individuation of the second kind (according to Jung) becomes a process of realization of individuality in which the opposites to a higher unity ("the self") are to be brought together. In this context, Jung means "the wholeness of personal disposition", whether consciously or unconsciously. Individuation is differentiation from the collective psyche, expansion of consciousness, dissolution of opposites, expansion and development, unification of self and self. This happens through the confrontation with the "archetypes".

The archetypes have a key role in this process. Mandalas represent this higher unity and wholeness, creating centering and reorientation (Jung 1977, 1987, 118-126). In his work "Aion" Jung analyzes "Christ" as a symbol of the self. "The individuation process ... subordinates the many to the one. The one, however, is God. And it is to whom the correspondence in us represents. The image of God, however, expresses itself ... in the mandala. "(Jung 1977, 75) The historical source is gnosis:" Gnosticism is undoubtedly psychological knowledge whose content comes from the unconscious "(Jung 1976, 239) so that the archetype of wholeness (circle, square, cross) can be opened up through dreams, visions and imagination (Jung 1976, 241; 1977, 115-117) .We will return to the main archetype, the circle-cross-mandala.

It should be noted critically to Jung that some terms are used undifferentiated or ambiguously (for example, self, archetype, animus, anima). The entire conception also lacks a comprehensive theory of learning psychology.

The model of the psyche presented by Jung (Jung 1975, 51 and 1935) (consisting of feeling, thinking, intuition, memory, subjective components of functions, affects, burglaries, collective unconscious, etc.) has long been scientifically outdated and must be regarded as an historic pioneering achievement.

The natural (biological) process of personality growth, in the first half of life, and the pedagogy or educational psychology (developmental psychology) with "socialization and enculturation" is much further developed. The individuation as an "inner process after the middle of life" may in fact correspond to a certain client population of analytical psychology but is neither socio-psychological nor developmental psychological justifiable. To declare individuation as a method of psychotherapy lacks the scientific basis.

We set the counter-thesis here: A person with severe neurosis or psychopathy does not have the necessary psycho-psychological prerequisites to go through this mental-spiritual process. Individuation is much more than "damage repair" (trauma clearance) and "correction of education".

Jung's individuation lacks any well-defined goals, like those generally known in humanistic psychology. The steps to the goals are not operational. A control of the course is objectively not possible. The ultimate goal is unattainable, and maybe sometimes, for a few at the end of life approximately, detectable. Methodological aids are not defined, except for the psychoanalytic conversation. In fact, it is not possible to directly grasp the ideas of individuation by Jung and analytical psychology. Such a one has not been developed by Jungians.

Constructively, the following aspects should be emphasized. The great achievement of Jung is in the collection and analysis of images of the unconscious and intrapsychic processes of alchemy, mythology, religions, archeology, rituals, fairy tales, legends, and cultural objectifications of all kinds. The "principles" of individuation derived from these investigations have a temporal validity: the inner purposefulness of growth, the pursuit of balance of all mental powers between inside and outside, an inner (spiritual and intelligent) source of power, the urge for comprehensive development of all psychic powers, the dissolution of opposites, the process from unconsciousness to consciousness, the conflict pregnancy (neurosis) of inner "tornness", and liberation through creation of the harmonic inner wholeness.

We want to try to describe clearly and unambiguously the process of individuation in the context of psychic systems.

In the conception of Jung's individuation, almost everything revolves around the unconscious. However, we will explain how all psychic subsystems must be included in this process, how the process in the third phase leads to transcendental experiences, and to God is not our "guilt" nor a "metaphysical derailment".

Jung (and many others) pointed out: "Individuation is creation of wholeness, but it is God" (Jung 1976, 46-80). In that sense, individuation is more than mere self-realization, and more than a "basic need". Campbell also calls the highest goal "finding God" (1978, 31). If you want to know something, you must set yourself up to do so. Individuation can ultimately, and only be, experienced by the one who walks the path (Jung 1971).

It should also be noted that individuation is not the same as "individualism". This would be pure egocentrism! Individuation as a way of life. It also means "mindfulness", in relation to psychic life (Kerényi 1971, 194). This is "religion" in the true sense of the word: re-attachment to the being and growth of the psychic life and thus restoration of the original (Eliade 1961, 165).

The term "self" also characterizes Jung's goal. But we want to avoid this term. There are too many conceptual usages and meanings here, for example, the lower self, the higher self, the true self, the mental self, the pseudo self, the self as the center, the self as the goal, the human being as the self, and even as an archetype, etc...

With such a variety of meanings you cannot work seriously anymore. What in Indian (Atman, Brahma) means "self" is what we call "mind." What can be meant by archetype, we explain exemplarily with the life symbol as the highest archetype.

In the chapter about dreams, we have delineated pictures, symbols, and archetypes. The archetype has the function to say something about the mental-spiritual reality, which is difficult to grasp in words, but can be experienced imaginatively.

This is our definition of "archetype". We want to emphasize that Jung's various studies on individuation contain a rich diversity to the mental-spiritual process.

Likewise, Campbell (1978) describes individuation in an almost unbeatable variety. The "hero" actually has a thousand figures. And we think that our exposition of this process can be presented in many other forms, and can be linguistically caught and lived. But if the psychic subsystems and their wholeness are missing, it is no longer individuation, but imagination, beauty, illusion, fraud, lies or baubles. The world may indifferently and uncomprehendingly look to those who have lived this way and even reached the goal (Campbell 1978, 42). No inquisition, no bondage, and certainly not a positivistic understanding of science, can belittle the truth of individuation.

The rootedness of the theory of individuation captures two realities:
1. The psychic system with all the individual subsystems.
2. The main archetypes of individuation.
The "self" is neither a sufficient theory nor an archetype for our conception.

In this chapter, we talk about dreaming, and how the images and the symbols in the dreams and in the imagination convey to man everything that there is to say about him and about humanity. This world of images is created by the spiritual intelligence - the inner spirit. Inner pictures and symbols are the language of the soul and the keys to the "mystery of man". Inner pictures and symbols are the "seven seals" (Hartmann o.Jahr, Horneffer 1979, Kessler 1977, Poeppig 1972).

From this we conclude that the formation of personality and individuation, without this source of knowledge cannot possibly lead to the comprehensive, complete wholeness of psychic life. Decisive consequences also arise from the evaluation of values, attitudes, convictions, and dogmatic teachings.

The more people understand this inner language, the easier it is for them to use dreams and meditations to open ethical questions, religious topics, and transcendental dimensions. The interpretation of these inner experiences depends on what the person knows about the psychic life and the inner process of development or growth through experience.

This concept of introspection is for us an indispensable source of knowledge and relates to the formation of personality in general and individuation.

We want to pick out two symbols that have occupied a central position in Western history for the representation of the inner psychic-spiritual evolution: the "holy grail" and the "circular cross mandala" (also called "life symbol"). We have studied these symbols in detail in "Being Human in the Future" (1987) and here we only want to capture the essentials.

The "Grail" is the "philosopher's stone" ("lapis philosophorum"). The esoteric and Gnostic also speak of "chalice", "emerald" or "jewel". Mysticism interprets the Grail as a "vessel of change". Grail also means "the spiritual man" and "the inner Christ". Grail is, according to several authors, the greatest mystery of mankind (Boron 1980, Bosshart 1970, Campbell 1978, Chrestien de Troyes, Jung 1975, Jung, E. 1980, Ravenscroft 1982, Schäfer 1983).

Grail stories tell of the "mystery of man". It basically contains the following scheme: At the beginning is a country that is in chaos with a sick king of decomposition. The suffering king is always a tyrant. The "hero" in this story wants to heal the sick king. He does not realize that salvation has another purpose. Therefore, he must go on a long adventure, where he must overcome many obstacles, overcome dangers and pass exams. Gradually, the hero realizes that he cannot heal the sick king, but himself to be the successor; thus, the savior of this country. A spirit helps the hero master all dangers. He finds the "big secret", receives supernatural powers and becomes a "Grail King" himself. He becomes in the land (in the epic) what he was before in the spiritual world.

Psychologically, this schema can be interpreted as an internal process of change. The "land in chaos" is the inner land of the psychic life (the unconscious). The figure that leads the hero is psychologically the inner mind or dreams and imagination. Some figures in such heroic epics represent intrapsychic powers, others real caregivers. The hero loses everything on his journey. He even must leave his homeland. His friends are not good enough. But he gets everything back in a new form. This is the process from "die and become" to the new inner wholeness.

The Grail is a symbol of the highest mental and spiritual development. The "Grail" can be understood as the highest spiritual force and as the goal of this process. In his analysis of alchemy (1975), Jung has comprehensively explained the psychic processes of the path to the grail (goal): from unconsciousness to consciousness, from the opposites to reconciliation and unity.

Beyond an interpretation in the context of individuation, Grail history can also be interpreted as a process of social renewal.

If a state - and its religion - is sick and in a chaotic state from the inside out, then the "cure" can never be created from within. This also applies to Andragogy as a science. The solution is a rebuilding of the "Grail", whereby the hero (for example, King Arthur) first must perform the psychic-spiritual process on his own.

No psychological theory can capture in words what this archetype "Grail" captures. From our understanding of theories about symbols, we conclude that the inner experience of a symbol reveals its reality to everyone. However, the highest experience does not come from meditation, but from the inner workings of the process. Meditative experience of archetypes does not mean their completion. You can not confuse that.

The Kreis-Kreuz-Mandala has a history going back to the Egyptian high culture (Eggebrecht 1984). The sun wheel is probably the first symbolic representation of the "mystery of man" (Bauer 1982, Herder 1978, Schwarz-Winklhofer et al. 1980).

The cross also includes the symbolism of quaternity (Jung 1975), which in turn mentions mental-spiritual processes. Shoot and mind, earth and sky, wholeness and centering, and the masculine and feminine are dimensions or realities that address this symbol.

The wheel is according to ancient esoteric tradition, the circular movement of rebirth, and the inner rebirth. This archetype also represents the sun and thus the transcendence.

So here we have depicted two realities in one symbol: the wholeness of man as the living image of the spiritual sun, the circle-cross mandala as an image of God.

This makes this symbol the highest archetype of all. For it is the most abstract form of representation of a psycho-spiritual reality in the highest stage of evolution. What God is can hardly be put into words. Likewise, the wholeness of the inner process can only be limited to language. The characteristic of a symbol is precisely that the meaning can be experienced through inner experience. The symbol of life becomes a symbol of the process of individuation. The archetype is the symbolic representation of the "theory" of this psychic-spiritual process.

Is the symbolism - knowledge through symbolic experience - science or belief, religion or psychology, andragogy, or esoteric philosophy (gnosis)? We think: Faith does not. That is not a dogma either. Even less can one speak of mythology here. When a hundred people meditate on this symbol of life and all experience an aspect that captures parts of meaningfulness, without knowing anything about it, it means that this inner experience captures a reality that all human beings can find through the power of the mind.

Jung speaks here of the collective unconscious. We find this assignment linguistically unfortunate and mean: The inner mind is the source of information that everyone in meditation and in dreams can experience.

The history of gnosis (in all variants of doctrine and practice) confirms the fact that in all of us knowledge is hidden about our origin, our goal, and the process leading to this goal. That is why we said in the introduction that we do not recover something through (natural) scientific education. Reality can be found within every human being and can be the object of scientific employment. Depth psychology-hermeneutic methods open this inner reality or experience.

The scientific exploration of this inner spiritual reality is still largely broke. We have undertaken approaches of a non-dogmatic systematic exploration of these inner realities. So much has been shown from the practical professional activity. The experience is based on the state of the psychic inner world and the thinking of the meditating person.

In addition, there are psycho-energetic techniques that allow clear experiences. The life symbol is also an operative force that activates psychic energy and their sense affects the entire psycho-energetic system. We have described these phenomena elsewhere (Schellhammer 1986 and 1987) and do not want to continue this here.

The Grail and the symbol of life both contain essentially the same theme, which is: the inner psycho-spiritual man in the highest stage of this evolutionary process. We elevate the symbol of life because, through its abstract form, it is intercultural all over the world and more appropriately represents wholeness. We can adequately grasp the process and goal of individuation only in reference to this archetype. Where words, and especially psychological concepts, are scarcely able to capture facts, this symbol continues. Who then closes his eyes, looks inward, and sees this archetype, learns more than words can say. The Andragogic has to include this step in methodology and theorizing.

The many levels of enlightenment, such as the history of esotericism, are examples of imaginative aberrations and delusions (Miers 1980). "Self-realization" is even interpreted "without consciousness". The "ascension of Kundalini to the seventh chakra" was the highest goal: "self-realization" (Johari 1979, 36).

Through the liberation from all earthly bondage man experiences the "highest eternal grace and divine wisdom". Dreams are just a "tool for fulfilling repressed instincts" (Johari 1979, 29, 35). We regard such ideas as an aberration, for expressing a denial of life, for thinking without a mind.

In many psychological movements, in all esoteric orders, and in psycho-or pseudo-religious systems of ideology, one finds again and again the same illusion: they all mean that man reaches some higher stage of development and consciousness. However, this is without the clarification of his unconscious life, and without his inner mind, without "hard" work of the systematic, and without a profound and comprehensive self-knowledge and psycho-catharsis. All these ideas are full of life-hatred, and deeply harmful to people and threatens democracy. Thus, a "sudden breakthrough" (Dürckheim 1976) may in a way mean the moment of the turn from Saul to Paul. But then begins the first phase of the individuation and thus a long journey. Campbell describes the model of this "heroic journey" in all the colorful images of possibilities (1978, 237). We strive to set the path free from mythical images.

It is not worthwhile to look in the many esoteric books for the living truth of individuation. For sexual ecstasies, it is better to turn to corresponding services, as we know in relevant columns of advertisements. The abundance of maternal and patriarchal educational ideas in the field of esotericism, including Masonic, Rosicrucian, and Christian communities, contains a lot of frighteningly incompetence about depth psychological realities. Movements of all kinds, which want to establish the "new divine order" on earth, have to do with power and illusions, and nothing with individuation and hardly anything to do with God and his spirit in the human being. They are dangerous to a pluralistic democracy because they consist of emotive ideologies and muddled dogmas.

The reassuring thing in this fatal situation of the many teachings about the inner way is that God will not redeem people. He cannot. Man must redeem God within himself. Whatever his theory of salvation, it only happens when theory and practice agree. Not a single scripture says how the sun and the earth move, but life itself teaches man the position of his ego to himself, to the world and to God. Those who are never redeemed look for it, because they are always on the lookout for short ways and do everything to avoid life, and to be able to deny the eternal in man, in order not to admit the ego's arrogance towards God and the Spirit , The way to this salvation is not a matter of faith. One cannot wait for grace in the room and hope for forgiveness. There is a lot to work on. Humanity is still at the beginning of this psycho-spiritual evolutionary process. People first must realize that the outer world cannot be understood without the inner world (Jung 1957).

Individuation creates evolutionary humanity. Jung has proved this in extensive research (1971, 65-122) We have emphasized and discussed this already. "Individuation" is self-development ... which, on the one hand will liberate the self from the false envelopes of the persona (masks, shadows), but on the other hand, it is the suggestive power of unconscious images... It is also the dissolving of the contrasts between the unconscious and the consciousness ("putting them together into a whole"), finding a relationship with one's own unconscious (also anima / animus), and creating unity and centering inside (inner center) .

Elsewhere Psychologically, the self is defined as the psychic wholeness of man. Since man knows himself only as an ego and the self as a totality is indescribable and indistinguishable from an image of God. Therefore, self-realization, in the religious metaphysical language, means the incarnation of God. Furthermore, "The image of God is expressed in the mandala." Central is: "Consciousness is far from embracing the whole of the psyche."

The 'self-realized human being' is characterized by the following characteristics, which are associated with the concept of individuation (Maslow 1973, 160):

1. A clearer and more effective perception of reality.
2. Having a greater openness to experience.
3. A stronger integration, wholeness, and unity of the person.
4. A greater spontaneity and expressivity, fully functioning, and liveliness.
5. A real self, a fixed identity, autonomy, and uniqueness.
6. A greater objectivity, and transcendence of the self.
7. Recovery of creativity.
8. The ability to combine the concrete and the abstract.
9. Having a democratic character structure.
10. Ability to love.

What man has created on the outside is an image of what is living in the psychic inner world. If people would live with individuation, war would not be possible. For it is the repressed and externally projected that creates the psychodynamics of the wars (Neumann 1980, 47).

This psycho-spiritual evolution of man does not happen by itself. People must want to explore, to plan, and to work on it. Self-knowledge, personality-building, and individuation are works for human evolution. Andragogy as the scientific and practical authority of this psycho-spiritual development has much to do here.

1.2. The first phase of Individuation

Processes of transformation: Affirmation of the psychic inner world, discovery and understanding of the powers, and rebirth of the inner man.

Before the practical work of individuation can begin, the individual must have found individuation as a means of life. At first, human beings live, so to speak, without a conscious focus on their psychic inner life. Man does not know that he must discover and change the inner world. There is a lack of knowledge.

In the general state of their consciousness, humans do not realize that they live unconsciously, which means that certain ego forces are not interested in integrating the psychic life into consciousness.

Usually, the approach to this inner reality begins in small steps. You read a book, attend a course, and get to know people who report on experiences in the field of personality development. Therefore, the entrance begins timidly and imperceptibly. We call this affirmation of the "first process of change".

The basic question of "Who am I?" leads through all psychic subsystems. Our system model "the psychic organism" is a kind of map. From this work units for self-knowledge can be developed in which the orientation always remains clear. Systematically you can ask:

What are my daily feelings? How do I think? How do I perceive the outside world? What are my daily needs? How do I deal with it? What is my psychodynamic? How do I experience my will? How do I experience myself? How do my defenses work? How do I experience my love power? How is my dream life? How do I experience my conscience? What is still unrecognized in my inner (unconscious)?

Discovering, understanding, and dissecting the diversity of psychic powers is the basic work in the first phase. The attitudes to the mental inner world are thereby increasingly fundamentally changed.

Man is always also past. One can grasp a person only if one looks at him in the perspective of his life experiences.

The life story does not just characterize one person. It is always part of its present existence. The near past may be the "yesterday". How does it work? How are the last days and weeks moving in daily consciousness? Which memories often come into the present? How does the first overview of life live back to early childhood? Which distinctive life experiences shape the identity? Which future perspectives are already alive today? That may be the next trip. These can also be wishes of all kinds: a friend is missing; a new car should be bought; professional goals are planned.

Every human being is in a psycho-social network. He has friends or at least acquaintances. He has his parents, family, and relatives. Maybe they died already. Then they are part of his story. The relatives may live near or far. In the inner life, they are part of existence. Everyone has their reference systems in the field of work, leisure, and in the household.

Some are already married and have children when they start individuation. This complex network is his freedom of movement. All dynamic relationships determine what everyone can live with. They reflect psychic powers.

Then certain crises, conflicts or disturbances may be current. These too are always a part of life. One experiences constant stress. Another has just the usual tensions in his relationship, or problems in the workplace with the supervisor or with work colleagues are current. Leisure time may feel like empty time. What to do? The small disturbances of the psychic forces can be quite annoying, and result in inhibitions, lack of concentration, feelings of inferiority, or difficulties in dealing with one's own sexual needs. Some smoke or eat too much. Alcohol consumption may be "on the edge" of the rational. Disagreements with one's parents can also have a significant impact on daily life. The job situation is perhaps unsatisfactory. There is a lack of ideas and especially of initiatives to lead one's life out of the rut. If you have children, you can create a whole list of daily trifles. Over the months and years, it can be quite significant. Overall, these small and larger burdens, are an overview, which provides an introduction to practical individuation.

Dily life always is always filled with obligations. These include the financial and administrative obligations, such as taxes and insurance. In addition, we also count on personal property such as car, furniture, hobby items, home ownership and so on. The daily care (maintenance) of one's own living conditions is also part of the life commitments, such as household bills, food, media consumption and so on. Dealing with these facts reflects psychic powers.

Another approach to self-knowledge is the analysis of critical event situations. In addition, you can put together the life-relevant situations in an overview. For example: food, body care, living, driving, working, household, leisure, sexuality, communication with the life partner, dealing with money, holidays, weekend, being alone, chatting, contacts and so on. These keywords can be used as a list. It is certainly renewable. For each keyword, a "critical event situation" can be searched and noted. The overview of the different actions is already knowledge. Furthermore, individual situations should be addressed critically. This creates bridges to the psychic forces and subsystems: Why am I doing this? Why do I experience this and that situation as critical? Why does the same pattern always run through like a red thread?

Many people dream a lot. Others must first wish for dreams to come true or remember dreams. Writing down dreams in a dream diary is essential for foundation work. It makes little sense to start with interpretations altitude flights immediately. It is enough to first get an overview over a few months. You can learn what are the main characters and main themes in the dreams? What are the objects and actions? How is the dreamer involved in the dreams? What connections to everyday life and the past can be made? A first overview gives directions to where to continue. The elements in dreams are like the beginning of a red thread. Who pulls it automatically comes to the heart of the thing in the dream.

Only then should one deal with the relation to the psychic subsystems or individual forces. The deepening approach to the content of a dream offers the imagination. Dream elements and questions about individual psychic powers can be approached with imagination.

The inner view shows the external reality with its own point of view and a different logic than the thinking is able to do. It should be kept in mind that there is no doubt about the diversity of one's own life and psychic powers. The implicit theory of personality determines the scope and content of the interpretation of the processes of imagination. Gradually, one learns to interpret one's dreams and deal with imagination.

The daily activities- with these aspects- make it clear to everyone what he knows and what he does not know. Knowledge and skills are needed. Education continues there. However, everyone increasingly recognizes how the ego works with defense and repression, with projection and integration. Sometimes you must admit, "I do not want to see that. It's embarrassing, unpleasant, annoying, laborious and expensive". The dynamic between consciousness and unconsciousness is slowly becoming a controlling theme of the ego. "I want to know; I want to bring the realities into consciousness and no longer work outside".

With these first practical works, the picture of oneself and of one's own life forms: "That's me and that's my life". Thus, the need to consciously live and care for the psychic inner life as part of the everyday reality grows. Psychic powers become important. They are increasingly getting their life value. This is the premise that the power of love can build. The other person (the life partner, one's own parents, friends and acquaintances or colleagues in the workplace) are increasingly being perceived with their psychic reality.

It is becoming increasingly clear that psychic life is real life. Therefore, movement comes into the psychic inner life. Unrecognized strangers become an important part of one's own life. The neglected gets care. The weak receive protection and strengthening. The inner life is no longer the "black box" and the dark unreachable 'numinous'. There is light in these rooms.

The forces are approachable and are increasingly becoming a natural part of ego management. It forms a first order in the overview. Signs of change are becoming increasingly clear. The process of individuation begins to receive a systematic dynamic. Correspondingly constructive effects can be recognized in daily life.

The inner orientation receives a vital meaning from the end of the first phase. Psychic life becomes a great value for the person. At this stage, there is always a dream in which the person has a birth, which is important to the person, or a newborn is suddenly there. Sometimes the baby in the dream is already several months old, and the dream may want to draw attention to the fact that it should be cared for and looked after. This is the beginning of the new inner life. The first phase is about to be completed.

The practical individuation causes the following emotional experience:

☐ Experience exciting and discover of the psychic reality.
☐ Increased self-esteem, by turning to oneself.
☐ Being challenged inside, with concentration and alertness.
☐ Inner anchoring of life and increase of ego strength.
☐ Relief from inner pressure and burdens from the subconscious.
☐ Confidence in yourself with positive feelings of life.
☐ Life with the body, with the psyche, and with nature.
☐ Being touched, by the inwardly experienced truths of life.
☐ Self-responsibility in the consciousness: "Nobody does it for me".
☐ Positive body and pleasure feelings, free of guilt.
☐ Objectivity and sobriety in dealing with the psyche.
☐ A matter of course in integrating the psychic reality.
☐ More and more versatile psychic powers.
☐ Joy and healthy pride in one's own achievements.
☐ Healthy self-love and differentiated philanthropy.
☐ Being anchored in the experience of the intelligence of the mind.

1.3. The second phase of Individuation

The processes of change: initiation as recognition of the inner Spirit as a guiding principle; Changes of all psychic powers ("die and become new") as well as dissolution of all opposites.

Only a few months after this "birth", of the inner new man, comes the time where it becomes clear that there is a force in the dreams and meditations that controls this process. The inner mind gives advice and analyzes the situations and sets forces in motion towards a life-building future. This is a special challenge: does the ego want to acknowledge this spirit as a higher guiding principle or not? This requires humility, cooperation, responsibility, and duty. Once you have decided, it is not easy to turn back to the unconscious, without taking long-term damage. To deny the experiences with the psychic inner life requires an immense repression force. This causes self-guilt, which then also must be repressed.

Those who now want to move forward in the individuation should increasingly integrate their ego and the way of life into this life-giving instance, which is experienced in dreams. The ego must admit that it is "smaller" than this spiritual power.

The ego can no longer spread itself in its own world, with great beautiful words as powerful and knowing. In the regular study of dreams and imaginative meditations it becomes clear that this mind is transcendental, and not sensual, not brain-physiologically and not empirically trained.

In dreams, the spirit will ask the ego, "Do you want me, do you want to live with me and your life, do you want to know the secrets of life, do you want to become what is in you as an archetype?" The gradual growth into this inner reality is a condition for the main transformations in the second phase of individuation. That is what we call "initiation". The experience of this execution can esoterically be called a "life secret".

It must be clearly stated that this basic decision is far from being stable. The ego does not like such an "insertion". The ego always wants to break out, preferring ideologies, dogmas, goods, and recognition. After all, man first must learn to voluntarily commit himself to the spirit. The "wave of emancipation" and the proclamations of "self-realization" do not have such a commitment in mind. The self wants to be independent and bigger than it is. The ego does not want to give up the rule. The deepest dream experiences and many moving meditations and also ritual experiences on the power of the archetypes (see: Schellhammer 1987) cannot yet establish this stability, because the unconscious powers are still too little worked on and the power of love is still too weak.

In difficult situations, where it depends on whether one says "yes" to the reconnection with the inner spirit, the ego with all registers of the defense can twist everything to escape this classification and obligatory cooperation. Consequently, the dreams and inner experiences are "bent over" until they are acceptable to the ego.

The ego is afraid that it can no longer live "freely", and that it can no longer "freely" have and give up the external pseudo-unity with people and goods. Truthfulness and genuine love also mean abandonment of the unconscious way of life. The ego has a certain arrogance towards the mind, which is not easy to solve.

In addition, the cooperative communication with this inner power depends on how the person becomes competent to understand the language of dreams. This means that man must learn a lot and assumes full responsibility for his skills and actions. Also, the ego almost wants to shun at all costs, including living truthfulness. The initiation is really a big challenge.

After initiation, the field of the psychic landscape needs to be tilled deeper and completely rebuilt. All psychic systems, including actions, are to the very bottom. The work is like a total renovation. The well-formed forces are to be further promoted. Unfocused forces are to be developed. Wrongly made powers must be corrected. Time and again, the forces from the individual subsystems must be compensated with forces from other subsystems. Many powers can be traced back to the roots.

The whole psychic landscape is mostly full of weeds and wild growth, full of long and deep rooting. Again, and again, the effect in daily life is to be included. Conversely, the new formation always has consequences for daily life. Genesis on the one hand and growth on the other hand, become a conscious experience. Some may find this a ridiculous exaggeration. But who wants to storm a high summit, must pay attention to the smallest details in his expedition, and must not overlook or forget anything.

The second phase of individuation is a true journey. With the initiation, the captain can start and steer with his ship to the open sea. The inner mind- to a certain extent- is the compass, and the now familiar system of psychic powers its map.

The second phase of individuation is as challenging as a big expedition. It is understandable that most psychologists and educators flee this journey. The attitude of the behaviorists is understandable. In their world, one can control, master, never dare, and can always stay away from commitments and responsibilities.

Individuation is now definitely becoming a way of life. It leads something away from the outside-oriented life. But in the third phase, it will be brought back to life. The literature describes this journey in many ways. Homer has drawn a magnificent picture of this adventure with his odyssey. The grail stories and heroes of all kinds are stories that describe this journey (Jung Emma 1980). Mythical stories, made tangible in some films, also relate to this journey. The fights of King Artur are not exaggerations (e.g., movie Excalibur). The ego, with its many powers resembling a ship's crew, must cope with enormous tasks.

The people in the habitat of the one who lives in this realistic "epic" play important roles. Some turn out to be friends in difficult hours. Others put obstacles in the way. Many are there as hostile figures. The collective unconsciously undertakes everything that is possible to prevent a person from traveling, as if the earth were flat and did rotate the sun.

A person's network of relationships always acts as an unconscious collective dynamic against this journey. We cannot prove that "scientifically! Experience shows, however, that opponents participate daily on the stage of events. Because it applies to the people of the "secret oath", "Never cover the mental inner world and never go this way." This is the unconscious rebellion of man against his psychic inner world, against the spirit and thus against God, as we will explain in the third phase.

The "journey" itself, first turns out to be a banal educational event of a very psychological nature. The individual psychic systems are to be examined to the furthest corners. Again, and again the same questions are at the beginning.

These questions include: What is there? How does it work? How did it happen? How do I use these powers? How do they interact with other forces? How do you "make" daily life? How should they be shaped and transformed? How do you want to grow out of yourself and become one?

Like the magnifying glass, the ego must look at the smallest life in itself and shine through. For this purpose, we have already opened a series of doors in the individual chapters and illuminated individual rooms in detail.

Psychoanalysis is primarily in the subconscious and the defenses, in the basic needs (or the instincts) and the associated feelings. This is a vast country where many "wild animals" and dark figures are at work. Those who turn to these forces soon find them friends. They only scare because they cannot control them, and because they drive their mischief out of the dark ambush. First, you must break a taboo, that means: "Do not look there, that's all right". It is nothing but the taboo of patriarchal society. Never question your father and your mother critically. But there is no holistic growth without accurate transillumination, and transformation of the unconscious.

The unconscious can certainly be systematically illuminated. We have divided the areas of this inner imagery into four groups. The one access is rational. The other and always necessary access is provided by dreams and imagination. Rationally, one can outline one's own landscape through memories. These include: What kind of a mother image has formed life in me? Which father pictures have been emotionally structured? Which women have made a memorable appearance in life? What do I imagine a "good man" to be? Which men have left impressions during my lifetime? How do I see myself as a child? Which images about being a child shaped life in me?

With such questions you can set up a living museum about your own life experiences. Another question is how the characters interact with each other. For example, the mother does not let the daughter become a wife; the father is the best; The former friend is a role model and a guiding idea for his own attempt to be original. The mother has an image that turns out to be a "witch" and the father adores some unreal image of women.

The inner images give enormous pressure on the ego in the overall dynamics, whether man or woman. What the man lives outside is the result of this inner power game. The same applies to the woman. Real inner images and ideals create opposing tensions. Every human being is subject to the powers of projection who seek out what is inside.

The woman then finds a man who is, on the one hand, a boy, on the other hand, the "macho". What is outside the woman, for example, a little girl and an excellent mother, has a dynamic inside and in the partner, which is, as it were, the psycho-energetically charged pattern of the realization of life.

The superego also moves in a dynamic, sometimes with contradictory variety. What the child has heard a thousand times from parents and teachers, from birth to the twentieth year of life, influences the ego for a lifetime, if it is not changed. Some reproduce this voice compulsively for a lifetime.

Others find themselves in a rigid opposition. Norms, prohibitions, punishments, and judicial conduct are not strong, because they are thought through, but also because the life experiences have anchored these emotionally memorable in the unconscious. The punitive- and at the same time benevolent God- to whom some pray, is only the picture taken, but never God. The image inside is worshiped, and fear is the fear of the psychic dynamics of this image.

This is the reality of the widely practiced religion. Much must be refurnished in this room. It is not the goal to sweep all the idols from the pedestal. Rather, it is about replacing them with new, appropriate images. Some things may turn out to be good and right. It is important to preserve and promote this. The dreams show the way. The power of love shapes this normative world. This is what we call conscious conscience formation.

Everyone has their prejudices, opinions, attitudes, and beliefs. Some may show in one's thinking and other in what is spoken. Why can these prejudices not be changed by analyzing and rationalizing? What appears outwardly has a living, and emotionally charged image in the unconscious. Many attitudes are not the result of a thinking process, but simply an impression of life experiences. Some have learnt from his parents. A lot has put the daily life in this inner space of experience. The school, the church, the parties, the social life, the workplace, the leisure time and, above all, the television channels are the main creators of such images. Colors, clothing, music, and soulful expressions are the forces that have a formative effect. Impressive images, films, events, and circumstances are anchored pictorially in the unconscious, from earliest childhood.

General life experiences determine and shape the entire life course if nothing is changed in these pictures. The images want to be reproduced in the outer life. This is a principle of the psych energetic dynamics of the unconscious. In doing so, we disregard the so-called "complexes".

Psychoanalysis is based primarily on these complexes. Because they have a particularly disturbing or ill-making influence. In individuation, however, it is always fundamentally about all pictures. The ego must decide which furnishing it wants. Deeply hidden, almost in secret rooms, man can discover many of his own strengths, good wishes, and valuable opportunities. These are to be liberated from their "moth boxes". They are to be cared for, protected, and grown.

The processing of the unconscious inventory also requires thinking. Feelings are to a certain extent a measuring instrument of the meaning of such pictures. The processing of painful experiences strengthens the love power. The integration of basic needs is often the result of reconciliation with one's own history. This work with the unconscious is also called "psycho-catharsis".

Speech is an expression of thought and perception. Many people talk so fast that one must doubt whether they can actually think so fast, especially in new territory. Everyone can recognize this when making a phone call. Small protocols about one's own speaking and listening can lead to "aha experiences". Thinking about psychic systems is slow because that is new territory. Likewise, the perception is to be maintained slowly and critically concentrated. Only then can you see what you have not seen before. This is especially enriching for interpersonal relationships.

It can be an embarrassing experience, which probably everyone has experienced, which moves the ego. But only a "glowing iron can be forged". Suddenly, a lot of fog goes away. You can clearly see how people do not see or think, or think wrongly and above all talk rashly.

You do not want to talk that much anymore. Because what people talk about when they are together is usually empty. Why are they talking about this and that? Why are they telling each other this or that story? What is the content of the discussions at Stammtisch in the pickling? What is man talking to woman about? Or woman to man? Dandruff falls from the eyes, observing for some time and writing protocols as a participant!

Emotions are activated by other various psychic subsystems. The outside world also creates many feelings. Man is mostly helpless. He have his feelings. The satisfaction of "quasi-needs" is an attempt to mask and calm emotions.

Feelings are the most important barometers to identify forces. Like the pain that always wants to say that something is not good here or there. If people were to hear their daily feelings as music, then they would want to turn this CD off. It would make them crazy!

Emotions are an indication of other certain powers. Obviously, it is time to grasp and examine one's own feelings. Why am I sad? What made me aggressive? Where does this mood of emptiness come from? Why am I happy now? What makes me dissatisfied? Why do I not have any hope? What has been bothering me so much for months or years? Why do I experience feelings of embarrassment when I feel sexual pleasure? Why do I always show everyone the same feelings? Why do I let myself be infected by feelings of others? Such questions open the door to a clarification. Over time, feelings become lifelike, real, deep, balanced, and positive.

Who wonders "What are my basic needs?" Or, "How do I deal with my basic needs?"

Everyone will be able to recognize that they satisfy "quasi-needs" daily but pass on much deeper needs. How does everyone fulfill their need for love? That is a "hot" question! It quickly makes the iron glow, who honestly and unconditionally investigates those depths. This need must be shaped and requires a differentiated consciously well-groomed approach. The basic needs allow many questions to be formulated.

Even in dreams, the needs are reported. Mostly, it shows how the human satisfies needs. A key need is self-updating. We can also refer to this as being "all about ourselves" and the life that wants to live from the inside out, with the power of love. It is also very invigorating if you take a closer look at which "quasi - needs" are dominant. Such as: holidays, visits, going out, alcohol and food in abundance, driving by car, sensational experiences, talking about others, television consumption, capital production, power, ambition and much more. In order to understand the powers hidden here, you must look at your daily life for a long time in the evening. Thus, the fulfillment of basic needs can be learned.

The self can reflect itself: how do I see myself? How do I want to be (ideal-me)? Am I really the one I mean to be? "Clothes make people" and capital can magnify the ego. The tricky question for the self is not "How weak am I?", But, "What did I really accomplish in life, and what is important for love and the mind?" It is a completely wrong orientation of many psychotherapeutic efforts to strengthen the ego by emotional attention.

The ego should learn to strengthen itself by learning to accomplish something. It appears that man sees it correct for his I to objectively have a small value. Yet, people feel guilt when they have an objectively small ego. Psychotherapy should take this seriously and not collaborate with this "oath of obscurity". It is a fact that the ego struggles against God, obstructs life, is less capable of adulthood, lives a lie about life and adores many idols. Down there, in these depths, man must rise, if he wants to master the process of individuation.

The ego first must acknowledge that it rejects, represses, transgresses, projects, acts, regresses, disfigures, and blurs, only to not face its reality of life. Daily, the television channels report clearly and vividly about consequences. Health insurance premiums and tax burdens are also an indicator of the damage caused by the ignorance of the people. It can easily be proven that the enormous damage list has to do with the psychic powers of everyone. The churches as "haven of peace" do not have the keys to solve this situation.

The power of love confuses most people with the degree of their pleasure-feeling. However, the capacity of love proves to be rather weak in the individual and the social life. Some believe that fidelity to ideology and dogmatic doctrine is an expression of love. However, almost all mental subsystems are missing, especially in the mind. Only in combination with all forces can love really grow. It is therefore a somewhat simplistic idea to locate this power in the heart. Symbolically, however, the picture is completely true: the heart is a crucial organ for the life of the body.

Therefore, love brings nothing without thinking. It is of little value if the unconscious acts as an adversary and lacks substance because the mind must be silent. Every step on the path of individuation strengthens the power of love. This is a principle, and this is necessary. Without the power of love man never makes this journey. He must reconcile and process. He must learn to understand and accept. He must go beyond his pride and stop accepting his self just as it is. He must learn humility and take his psychic life more seriously than idols. This grows love. And at the same time, this process is only possible through the power of love.

Dreams lead one through all these experiences. Dreams not only inform, but also directly transform the psychic material. They draw the path to the future. Dreams make the main changes. In the esoteric this is called "to die and to become new".

With these occupations, a new person gradually begins to develop from inside. That is hope. Through all the educational processes, socialization and enculturation, the psychic system "above all" can be rebuilt. This is the purpose of individuation.

This is the key. Thus, this process goes far beyond what humanistic psychology conveys to growth messages.

When all the psychic forces have come into transformation through the process of "dying and becoming new", the next major transformation process follows. This consists in the dissolution of the inner opposites. In every subsystem these opposites must be resolved in interaction with the ego. However, the opposites in the unconscious prove to be extremely strong and thus a central task. It means: "inside, outside." This is especially true for the unconscious. The inner pictures about man and woman form the outer person. Again, opposites are to be resolved. The process of dissolving all opposing forces takes place in small steps.

Over, and over again, the old forces want to gain the upper hand. The new forces are constantly "nourished", nurtured, protected, and strengthened. This happens through training in everyday life. What is worked out on the outside must be trained and implemented in life. The rebuilding is always centered in what the mind designs and builds through dreams. At some point, then, the pictorial material in the unconscious, the power of love, and the powers of the other subsystems are to a certain extent brought into the mix.

The union of opposites is complete. The ego can now shape life in a balanced way, and with all psychic subsystems. Feelings are no longer in opposition to thinking. The unconscious is no longer a disturbing counterforce to the ego. The male is balanced dynamically to the feminine (Jung 1972, 175, 473). The basic needs are integrated and, as far as possible, considered in everyday life. The power of love has grown.

It goes without saying that the dissolution of the inner opposites dissolves the destructive forces. Man can now live without the play of forces of the unfolded life, such as: instincts, validity, domination, struggles, object fixations, as well as "incestuous" longing, having the strength to assert themselves. This constructive dynamic is the dynamic of a fully sound mental life.

So, the second phase is about to be completed. Dreams can "confirm" the result of your efforts in many ways. Sometimes in the dream, this union is represented by a wedding, or by becoming one with the sun. There are many pictures of the extensively harmoniously functioning forces.

Man has found his inner harmony with the conclusion of the second phase. Various yantras reflect this harmonious interaction. Mandalas of all kinds can also be regarded as an expression of the dissolution of all opposites (Jung 1968).

Each psychic subsystem has found its own centering and all individual systems have found their appropriate place in the living psychic reality.

But the forces are still young and not well established. The consequences of this state is that it is not yet fully aware of the ego, or it has not yet received any comprehensive relevance to life. The harmony of the power game must first consolidate.

If life in the second phase is strongly centered, then man can gradually open more and more to the outside and live what he has become.

1.4. The third phase of Individuation

The transformation processes: from the old to the new governmental principle, harmony between inside and outside, as well as the completion of the unity of all psychic powers to the wholeness.

The ego has achieved the multifaceted integration of psychic powers with the completion of the second phase. But that does not mean that the psychic powers have completely changed. Also, the increasing orientation towards the outside life will revive some old forces. For many, habits and old patterns have a strong effect, and can be determining factors, on the outer habitat and conditions for humans. Some individual forces are to work through again.

The inner being is confronted with the reality of life. This reality of life can seem like a shock: people are far from this inner state. Religions teach myths. They teach by what man is inside. Politicians pretend to be human leaders, without one having created his complete humanity. Psychology is the science of the psyche. But there is little that corresponds to the second level of individuation. Philosophy has long since lost its inner humanity. And pedagogy is superficial in this regard.

Humans build Babylonian towers, but inside they build nothing. People "nourish" themselves on the outside. They get their food for life in objects, ideologies, and dogmas. They build structures; yet they do not know the communication with the inner mind. People live their whimsical constructions. They are making their life full of lies and more and more complicated then they need to be. This threatens the ego in individuation and places enormous strain on the newly developed harmonic integration of forces.

The new harmonic dynamic of the interaction between the different psychical forces contains something like an inner "governing principle". It is characteristic that the "boss" of the psychical subsystem "sits at a round table with the other systems and subsystems". The ego ('I') is the "boss" and must take the lead. It is always decided together how the mental forces must operate. The "boss" of every system (sub-system) has his right to have a say about its active operations.

No psychic system can be neglected and even suppressed. Old forces keep coming back, especially from the 'Über-Ich'. Old thought patterns and behavioral habits can also return and want to dominate. The battle of the powers is not yet completed here. No one can completely transform what has lived for thirty, forty or fifty years, within days. The ego must also compromise with the conditions of daily life.

In this field of tension, the ego must learn how the inner "democracy" works and can come to fruition in life. The new principle of government has yet to be consolidated. This force must be differentiated. Then comes the time when, even in difficult and stressful situations, this new principle of government can master life from its own patterns. This completes the first step in the third phase. The new captain has the rudder in his hand and leads the way safely on his life's journey.

After this step comes the actual enforcement of the new man in daily life. The Inside and outside are reconcilable. This has clear consequences in all areas of life. The personal relationship to the life partner or friend is mutually formed from this inner life. Leisure is the space where many creative forces can find a personal expression. The profession is not next to humans.

The work itself and above all relationships in the workplace receive an internal resonance. The relationship to work is alive. It is not just about "earning money" or prestige or career. Whether worker, employee, businessman or freelancer, work is always a part of the life expression. There are many forms possible. We cannot fix this here.

Everyone who lives in the third phase of individuation will learn to shape his or her expression. Social and political work, too, has a new depth and, above all, new forms of expression.

You cannot really want anything more valuable for a society than politicians who take their responsibility out of their inner roots. Scientists, especially in the field of social sciences, as well as teachers- of all grades and types of schools- could work in this kind of human centering. The design of the personal living space, as well as holidays, get a completely new expression. Over many months, this new principle of government will prevail in one's personal life. Life becomes a comprehensive expression of the new man. This is the second step.

In the final section of the third phase, man increasingly experiences himself as an internally centered wholeness and unity. The circle is closed and yet always open to the outside. Man experiences himself as a living image of the highest archetype. He has become the realization of his originality. He has found everything in himself and shaped what life is inside. Man is in it the realization of what religions teach in words and portray many myths about man. There is nothing to believe. There is the truth about man's living incarnation. That is the true enlightenment. But the individual does not shine. He cannot do miracles. He does not want power to rule.

This new being can be called the true experience of God. Only in this condition and consciousness can man really understand what it means to be a "God-man", to live the "truth" or to be a "living image of God". Such experiences about the original humanity cannot be "made" by humans. He has a way to go until he has become this psychic-spiritual state of oneness and oneness. What is offered to "enlightened ones" in the world proves to be empty pods to such experiences.

You do not have to go to a monastery to reach this level of humanity. The highest experience of the (real) mystics does not have to be sought in lonely forest huts, free from sex and without giving up goods. This may have been a form of reaching this stage. Today, however, these processes are to be accomplished in the world and carried into the world with the possibilities of today. The scope of this being and knowledge is enormous. Where are the people who want to live?

It is not possible to outline the experiences in the third stage so concretely that they could be valid for all people who go through this process.

The growth goes in the direction of the life symbol until the goal is reached. As a living image of the highest archetype, the individuated human being is to live. If he can do that after years of training, then he has reached the goal. He has been able to clarify all essential questions through his inner mind.

Now the third phase of individuation is complete. Man is an "individuated person". He has found his self-fulfillment in full. The life of the individual remains what the life of man is: earthly. These include everyday trivial things. No crown crowns the individual. No dress presents him powerfully. No share package makes him the "maker" of economic policy. No political competences give him the opportunity to pass laws for the people. He cannot fight.

It is the ultimate argument that the completion of individuation is the only path to humanity. Although the psychological foundations are clear and unambiguous, the individual processes are self-evident and arguable. But the transcendental meaning cannot be scientifically "measured", as it is only accessible to humanity. Living out the goal of individuation may well be called the highest form of love. Whoever does not go on this inner path, always only has external ideas about these processes of change and about the psycho-spiritual man.

Through the inner fulfillment of individuation, it can be comprehensively determined what is meant by "transcendence". Any attempt to interpret or define transcendence, outside the experiences of all processes of change, remains purely metaphysical and thus speculative to illusionary. We can distinguish different dimensions of transcendence.

A first central experience is that of the mental system. Mental intelligence works through dreams and in the imagination.

Only this spiritual power knows how the process of individuation must proceed. This spirit has its own values and language. The mind is more than a psychic force, such as intelligence. The spirit transcends the earthly life and thus has access to the otherworldly reality. The mind is an aspect of God. The systematic dream work leads to this experience. That is why this is the first fundamental transcendental experience.

A second experience of transcendence results from the growth of the power of love. Love exceeds thinking about utility. Love overcomes the logic and dynamics of psychic powers. Love is oriented towards "higher" interests, namely the integration of all life into a unity and wholeness. Through all hate and envy, this power of love can rediscover, protect, nurture, and unfold life. In that sense, the power of love is transcendent. (Otherwise it would just be the "drive" and would have to be classified in the subsystem of needs.). Those who experience and live this kind of love experience "transcendental experience".

The third kind of transcendental experience can be called "experiencing archetypes." The way to do this is contemplation, such as, putting oneself in a basic archetype. The life symbol is considered the main archetype. Ritual practices with this archetype, including other archetypes, are further inner experiences of this reality. The archetype is- to a certain extent- the door that leads to another reality (see Schellhammer 1986 and 1987).

The fourth type of transcendental experience is the main processes of individuation. Anyone who does this not only experiences a mental procedure, but a different reality. He learns the "secrets of life" that reveal themselves only through the completion of individuation. We can illustrate this with a picture: the unconscious is like a vessel full of water. The content obscures the view and is at the same time a bad elixir of life. The catharsis of this water is then not only an experience, but after completion a clarified water. This is another reality. We also call this experience a transcendental experience. The "clarified water" is the being of this transcendental experience.

The fifth type of transcendental experience is the goal of individuation. Anyone who has achieved this goal experiences in himself a completely new humanity, which does not consist merely of the "renovated psyche" but results from the experience of the all-round connection. Through individuation man becomes a living image of the highest archetype. But this, on the other hand, is also an image of God. No one can be closer to God. Only the accomplishment of individuation makes it possible to experience so closely what God is and to be so close to God. The contemplative experience alone never reaches this depth. That which man has become here is part of the transcendental divine being.

A sixth form of transcendental experience is the experience of one's own psychic-spiritual location in the otherworld, as well as the experiences of the organization of the "soul-world". Spiritualists claim they have contacts to the hereafter. The author has carried out many hundreds of such spiritualist sessions as a medium, experimenting with numerous out of body experiences and examining experiences in the context of individuation. It cannot be the place to step closer.

Our implications are that most, the so-called "media" experience, which has nothing to do with transcendental experiences, but with the personal and collective unconscious. It seems to us that the only guarantee for reliable information about the eternal being of man, and possibly about the organization of the spiritual realm in the cosmos, are dreams. But these only report when it has a special meaning for this person to have such knowledge.

The fact is, of course, that all these transcendental experiences convey neither "delight", "ecstasy", nor "bliss." In fact, in the spiritual, transpersonal, and transcendental enlightenment scene, there are a variety of concepts that are hollow and pompous. What is the "All-Consciousness"? Or the "essence of bliss"? Or the "essence of the miracle"? Or the "transcendence of the ego"? Or "sanctification of everyday life"? Or "the highest heightened sensory perception" (see Tart 1975, Assagioli 1992, Dürkheim 1976). We think such terms are dangerous. They pretend something with their superlative forms. They are purely emotional. They activate dispersed expectations. They are not tied back to the mental subsystems. They express an extremely narcissistic and infantile ego.

Individuation does not lose itself in inflation since no ego is "inflated" and certainly not something compensated or postponed. The experiences in individuation are deep and life-like human challenges. They demand a high intellectual and emotional effort for their processing and integration. Is there perhaps another reality, unknown to us, that conveys the experiences of which some "enlightened ones" report from the "trans scene"? No; At least we have found nothing of the same kind, with all the meticulousness of our research efforts.

Therefore, we say decisively, there is no "higher" transcendental consciousness beyond the experience of individuation. The third phase of individuation is the path for the so-called "highest" transcendental experiences. Everything else is only illusion, beauty, delusion, or fantasy, and at best, metaphysical speculations and gnostic "search movements".

These claims - we recognize as a personal statement - have enormous consequences. Much on the psycho-esoteric market proves to be a neurotic misorientation. The sectarianism falls completely off the table as a true path to humanity and to God.

And, the most sensitive question is, how can a religion "represent God on earth" if it does not integrate the entire psychic organism and thus the individuation process into its teachings and practices? What is religion anyway if it does not comprehensively comprehend this psychic organism? Or, how can someone be a "priest" without having completed the individuation? But these are problems that cannot be further developed here.
With the completion of the individuation, the person is "released" from this process. He has everything in him that life can give. The "psyche" is then what Jones tried to clarify under the question, "Is there a normal psyche?" (1978, 260). With the completely "normal" psyche the individual must live. He must implement it. He always stays in development. Growth certainly does not stop with this day. Again and again he has to do mental hygiene, renew his unconscious and refresh the power play of the psychic subsystems.

After all, external life also demands the completion of everyday things. Sartre says, "Man is condemned to be free" (1977, 16). There is no freedom outside of this daily self-care. There is also no freedom outside of the psychic system. Individuated man has attained the highest form of freedom that a human being can have and live.

Some may think, "And now away from this earthly chaos and away to an oasis or an island". But that cannot be. The individual has carried out the psychic-spiritual evolution in himself. That is the theme of all humanity. There is no change of mass without change of the individual (Jung 1977, 71).

The time comes for each INDIVIDUATED PERSON, where he must go back to the people. This is so that: other people can draw from this power of love for their own individuation; for politics to be conducted out of individuation; in order to build a society that organizes from this inner centering; so that philosophy, psychology and pedagogy expand their image of mankind; so that a new hopeful humanity gets a chance.

The andragogy is centrally concerned with the comprehensive formation of personality. Individuation is their educational concept in the future. In it, the individual steps of self-knowledge and self-education are embedded. Thus, Andragogy assumes the highest responsibility in human education.

However, the Andrologies must first be formed and shaped so that they can bear this responsibility and be able to practice it professionally. Many can seize this opportunity for a great pioneering work: for a hopeful, people-centered, pluralistic, democratic society.

The modern Hero – The modern Heroine

The modern hero and the modern heroine who set out from their daily lives are motivated, and, invited or voluntarily embark on an adventure. First, they meet the gatekeeper, who does not let anyone through who does not want to reveal the lies of life. Humility and determination are the keys that open the gate. Then, beyond the threshold, the "battles" and the "trials" begin. Many shadow beings confront the hero and the heroine. To begin, everyone wants to only reproduce and believe what he has experienced. Many forces push back and want to disfigure everything and lure people in. Gentle voices call from everywhere: "We have the truth; the true gods are with us". The dark forces do not wear horns and the king does not wear a crown. Gloomy figures wave from everywhere: "Come, come ...". You look for changes and are spellbound by the magic of many beautiful words. Wisdom must be forged. Gates sell them as a market article. The instinctual and egotistical mind will never find true wisdom. The hero and heroine can only reveal the mystery of the Grail if they are always guided by the power of the Spirit. This requires competences: skills are to be learned. At the end of this adventure, the soul of the hero and the heroine is united: one with the sun. That is the real freedom. This is true "God-realization".

Ideas taken from old Literature and made new for the future.

2. The behavior oh humans in the living fields

Activities and their characteristics in the living fields

In the first decades of behaviorism, "behavior" has been defined as "any psychic activity," and thus, identifiable by other observers. Today, thinking, willing, experiencing and feeling are also called behavior. Today, even consciousness is understood as the subject matter of behavioral psychology (Dorsch 1987, Link et al 1986, Pervin 1993, Pawlik 1968, Kaufmann 1970).

Behavioral psychology is increasingly understood as social psychology and social research. Human behavior finds in "ecological psychology" an extended perspective, based on Lewin's field theory (Kaminski / Bellows 1981) as well as numerous multidisciplinary approaches (Kruse / Graumann / Lantermann 1990).

We use the term "action" here to avoid misunderstandings. Action was given as the ordinal meaning of "behavior." While behaviorists have considered behavior to be isolable, for our understanding, the action space and the psychic loop are constitutive of the term. The person acts in a habitat and always experiences the action together with the action result. The action is done in conjunction with the intrapsychic forces. Action as a psycho-logical concept - and not as a physiological concept - is a construct concept (system concept) and thus contains theoretical assumptions.

These theoretical implications are largely confirmed by social psychology, cognitive psychology, depth psychology, and ecological psychology. The principles of learning are characteristic of the structural dynamics of concept system "action". Classical conditioning, operant and instrumental conditioning, learning through rules and learning on the model (Hilgard / Bower 1971, I, II). Bronfenbrenner (1979)) comprehensively describes the dynamic forces of human action, human development and learning in ecological understanding, such as in the mesosystem, in the exosystem and in the macrosystem (Oerter 1987, 87-128).

The question of man begins with the fact that we perceive ourselves and others in this world as doers. There are people who are active and sometimes idle. They move on this planet as acting humans. Man cannot act in empty space. Man always acts in a more or less organized world, if we refrain from the natural world. Action is life; however, this activity looks and works well. In Fact, we can only grasp action as action in a living space.

If the habitat is specifically structured, we call this space "life system" (Katz / Kahn 1966, 39-47). If the habitat is relatively unspecific, we speak of "Lebensraum" (based on Lewin 1963, 99). Habitats usually contain different life systems. Without life systems, there is no human life.

Bronfenbrenner examines human development through the networking of life systems. He defines these life systems as: a) the microsystem. This is the sphere of life of the person in which he works; b) the mesosystem. This is the areas of life in which the person interacts; c) the exosystem. This is the areas of life in which the human being is not active (not involved), but in which events take place that influence what happens in the microsystem; and d) the macrosystem. This is the formal and content system (Bronfenbrenner 1989, 38, 41, 42, 59). A person's structures are set in this model in a correlation with the environmental structures. We simplify our analysis model, which is primarily for practical interests (self-knowledge and self-education).

According to Lewin, the current living space also contains views of the individual about his future and past. The expression of the experience of feeling, often forward-looking or bound by history, is part of human action: "The past and the future of the psyche are simultaneous parts of the psychic field." (Lewin 1963, 96). Elements are from the life story, as well as future-oriented hope and expectation, for example, how the individual sees the present and future state of the specific habitat and its action is part of every field of life. In addition, each action space, in addition to the time perspective, also has various micro- and macroscopic elements (Lewin 1963, 93). A life system also contains individual elements (variables) or subsystems. Only the factors that have a constitutive or causal function for the action itself are considered for the formation of theories, as well as for action strategies of innovation or action change.

According to Miller, Galanter and Pribram (1991 and 1964, 23-25, 116-120), each action is based on a picture (that is, a knowledge of the world) and a plan (anticipating the implementation of that picture). Image and plan become actions through evaluation (motivation, will, see Lewin's valence parameter).

The aspects of actions are: the origin of image and plan, time span, details, flexibility, speed, awareness, openness, stop commands, language (or variety of meaning), and the recognized or unrecognized alternatives. With all the decomposition of action into its parts we want to keep in mind what Miller, Galanter and Pribram stated (1991, 207): "Life is more than a thing ... it is also a process that is realized in doing." The dynamics of life itself causes action. This implies learning processes and instinctual aspects of behavior.

It is a concise, yet decisive fact, that every human being as a living entity, who is always acting in one and / or several life systems. Therefore, we can only grasp and understand man as a personality- be it is as a psychic-spiritual individual or as a "beast" in the sense of the highest level of organic life- if we perceive him as an acting individual in his life-systems (Lewin 1963) , 168).

By "action" we mean: a simple or complex sequence of movements that an individual performs in a life system (Dorsch 1991). Here we limit actions in the sense that non-specific action, such as the arms or feet moving, is not considered subject of investigative. The action can have an explicit goal or simply implicit effects. The action itself is tied back to intrapsychic forces such as thinking, judgments, feelings, needs, unconscious life patterns, love power, ego-control forces such as will and defense, dream power and psychodynamics. The intrapsychic systems are dealt with in the following chapters. With the individual intra-psychical concepts of the system, we create the bridge to this, without entering a theoretical and further differentiating approach.

Aebli (1993, I, 83) builds his action theory on the building blocks of action: "It is the building blocks of action, the action patterns repeatedly come into play ...

The repetition of an action occurs when two episodes have the same structure. Such action schemes include repeatable, and transferable to new tasks and to new situations. They are also defined by its structure invariant in repeated implementation. This includes the action situation, such as "Frame". Action is "an in-relation of elements to a goal" (ibid., Vol. II, 13).

From the work of Cranach (1980, 10-23) we find: "... action as a system of a subordination of larger and smaller units assigned to each other ...". These are in chronological order and referred to as the "action steps". For example, "a path from a starting point to an end point". Another level of analysis is "the hierarchical structure of an action". On a further level, the "subjective experience" is to be grasped as "the consciousness of the objective, the planning and control and the intention", "goals are reasons, which lie in the future", "planning presupposes goals", "Actions, set with a goal, is planned with strategies to control their execution", "People act purposefully". We supplement with Eckensberger and Silbereisen (1980, 23-26): "Action is a central psychological category". The term "action" presupposes that the human being is potentially reflexive and intentionally related to the environment ". For this, ten aspects are presented.

- ☐ Relatively steady and stable
- ☐ A limited variable
- ☐ Mainly long-term changeable
- ☐ Renewable
- ☐ Correctable
- ☐ Partly conscious and partly unconscious
- ☐ Censored by your own consciousness
- ☐ Actions as a maneuver for "secret" goals are concealable and defaced
- ☐ Predominantly complex
- ☐ Shaped in the dynamics of human life systems (learning processes)

Actions manifest intentions, directions, meanings, and expressions of mental state (Meili / Steingrüber 1978, 41-42). Filipp defines the following features in the "General Model for the Analysis of Critical Life Sources" (Filipp 1990, 10):

- ☐ Previous experiences
- ☐ Personal characteristics
- ☐ Context features
- ☐ Event features
- ☐ Characteristics of immediate conflict (instrumental, cognitive)
- ☐ Effect characteristics: person, context, interactions
- ☐ Timeline (subjective, objective, past, present, future)

Actions can also be analyzed at various levels, such as: "macro-, meso- and micro-level" (Belschner / Keizer, in Filipp 1990, 178). Human action can and must be understood in a complex network of different micro, macro, and subsystems. Each subsystem has its entirety, goal orientation, regularity, feedback, homeostasis, levels of change, limits, and its "internal model of experience" (Schneewind, in: Oerter / Montada 1987, 976-980). Aebli, with his 16 theses on the theory of actions, captures some specific aspects that we put aside here for practical personality development (problem-solving learning). We refer to this with keywords, such as: restructuring of all elements in the plot, laws of nature and causal relations of the elements, intermediate targets, and freely generated or reconstructed actions (Aebli 1993, I, 87-95). From a specific point of view, Aebli analyzes the actual problem solving for: action structures, thought processes, and the media of problem solving, such as the language (Aebli 1993, II, 13-82). A crucial element of the action is also the learning increase and its effect on subsequent similar situations.

A system model of action situations implies theoretical assumptions, such as:

☐ Every action happens in a life system.
☐ The life system affects the person performing the action.
☐ The life system directly influences action in the sense of determinants.
☐ The result or goal is also part of every action.
☐ Every action has a certain value with the result.
☐ The action is based on an action repertoire from earlier situations.
☐ The psychic system is involved in many ways in an action.
☐ Every action implicitly contains a future-oriented perspective.
☐ The time dimension gives past and future feedback.

If you want to make an action in humans or change a certain type of action, it is essential to consider all these components. Areas of application are marketing, leadership, innovation of institutions, as well as personality development. Political action can also be recorded in this system. Andragogy and pedagogy, as well as their diagnostics and counseling, cannot be solely oriented intra-psychically. Man and life systems are a composite that forms a whole in life. Self-realization and growth are not feasible outside wholeness. Heckhausen and Oerter (1987, 681) place an action in the context of the following systems: environmental structure, situation, action result, executive, target value, and person structure. Our model of the "action situation" includes these subsystems.

The analysis of the topic "human actions" developed here is subject-oriented. Our concept may appear to the experts as one-sided ("naïve"); however, this is because we have largely ignored various and significant aspects.

We refer to keywords such as "interaction", "roles", "communication", "socialization", "habit" (Bourdieu 1974, 1979, 1984, 279), "situational structural patterns" (pattern analysis, Arnold 1985, Dewe 1988, 184 ff.) As well as "social-scientific-cultural-theoretical approaches". In the interest of a manageable size, we must be modest here and would like to recommend these aspects of the science of Andragogy for educational work.

Our definition of the term "action" is characterized by the closeness to life, which contains the manifest process, the subjective experience, and the social meaning, as also Cranach (1980, 29) describes. Cranach determines further components which are also given in our model: Awareness, being focused on the aim, planning, with intention, beginning / end, personal and environmental components, effort and quality (motor ability), knowledge, information theoretic control loop, picture over the action, plan or structure in the picture, value, cognitions, personality-shaping effect, will, control, self-expression, rules, and roles (self-presentation). Every action is based on psychic processes, which we have integrated into the model of the system "psychic life".

Cranach lists the following components as a classification (1980, 77-99):

☐ Concrete action (course): purposeful, deliberately planned, intentional
☐ Interaction / communication: certain types of actions
☐ Organization of action: cognitive and subconscious self-regulation
☐ Objective and subjective phenomena: visibly, subjectively, experienced
☐ Adaptation function: inside-out regulation
☐ Knowledge
☐ Motivation and emotion
☐ Social control
☐ Values and Attitudes

We highly appreciate the importance of the unconscious and refer to this subsystem in the corresponding chapter. Cranach underestimates this subsystem if he only allows it to be considered pathologically (Cranach 1980, 29). The actions of humans are decisively influenced by the organized life knowledge in the unconscious, consisting predominantly of pictures. In general, we will build a bridge to action in all psychic subsystems.

There are many life systems and every life system have its subsystems. Sociology and political science may create systematic concepts for this purpose. For our interest, it is sufficient to make a rough classification of these life systems according to the criterion of the thematically closer connection of individual components. Every person has different personal interests in the individual systems. Each system offers elements with which each person shapes their personal living space. Moreover, every human being is widened in the whole system context, be it as a passive spectator, be it through occasional actions or through the extended conditional contexts of his personal living space.

Based on the book "ANNO 709 O.R." (NHG 1973) we can create the following list of major life systems (without specific order):

- Personal relationships
- Consumption, goods
- Peoples, groups of people
- Schools, educational institutions
- Job, work
- Knowledge, knowledge carriers
- Games, sports, hobby
- Art, culture
- Capital
- Living room
- Foreign cultures
- General Environment
- Built habitat
- Energy, raw materials
- Traffic, transportation
- Ethical or moral systems
- Wastewater, waste
- Welfare
- Nature and wildlife
- State finances
- Religion, spiritual institutions
- Party politics
- Healthcare
- International
- National politics
- Peace policy, military

Lewin refers to "Habitat" as the psychological habitat (i.e., person) and real human living space (1963, 99). In this way we open up the outer living space and emphasize the meaning in the sense of Schütz / Luckmann (1991, 27), who refer to: spatial conditions, physical existence of other people, things of the outside world, an articulated social and cultural world, as well as all possible interactions human-human and human-life-world.

According to Schütz / Luckmann (1994, Vol.2, 14, 37-134), actions are "experiences", they include: goal, motive, design, plan, time structure, meaning, will, limits of experience or action, interests, a social range and constellation of conditions, choice, decision, conditions of feasibility, a process structure, and a stock of knowledge. Actions are based on a historical (biographical) basis.

In social relationships, action is to be interpreted in the reciprocity of the individual components. Thinking and working are special forms of action. The various networks of individual psychic powers are discussed in the corresponding chapters. The sociological and socio-psychological consideration of action events can be opened here only with keywords. To what extent a transcendental dimension can be attributed to action, as the Schütz / Luckmann (1994, vol.2, 145) explains, is an interpretation question. We discuss the transcendental power in the context of love, mind, and the process of transformation of individuation.

The life systems of humans contain neither an "I" nor a "consciousness". The picture on the wall has no feeling when viewed. The waste mountain on the outskirts does not suffer as it grows bigger and bigger. The constitution is only printed paper. The church remains unmoved, whether it is full or empty on Sundays and whatever people do in it.

The consumer goods feel no desire when they are bought. Whether the TV is running or not, whether there is lived in the room or not, the apparatus does not care. A corporation can lay off a thousand people. Therefore, the system of movables and real estate does not have sleepless nights. For ten thousand years, a country can be nuclear-contaminated and deserted; no stone cries a tear. Laws, regulations, contracts and administrative regulations in state and companies are just stringed letters. A university can refrain from socially significant research and claim "value freedom". This does not interest the academic halls.

Fine food may do the mouth good and give the subject pleasure, but what does this plate of food take care of? Bombs and weapons of all kinds have no conscience. Money is known to be a means of buying almost everything, but it does not turn red with shame. Thousands of tons of gold bars on a soccer field cannot astonish the Universe. The gold itself remains unmoved. Whether the air stinks, is poisoned or is destroyed globally, this does not matter to the air itself. There may be many destructive products and institution: therefore they do not suffer. Castle and boarding houses cannot talk to each other, even if they stand side by side for a hundred years. Scriptures in abundance, including ideological teachings, never quarrel. The library holds all positions without flinching.

Again, it seems succinct: All this is only there because people have acted and acted. Everything receives only one function in the context of humans. The life systems and their subsystems or individual elements are related to human action.

Science has long since proven - and we know, even without research results - that man is born into these systems of life and without such systems - whether primitive or industrial - is not viable. Furthermore, we know that man is shaped by these systems of life. Man acts in the life systems, keeping them upright and changing them, creating new systems. Everyone creates their own living space within the life systems and their private life system.

Man uses these life systems for his interests. He binds himself according to his intrapsychic situation. He exploits the systems, urged by his inner powers. Instead of forming himself into a unity, he creates a symbiosis with institutions, people, or objects. Unsatisfied oral pleasure finds steady repetition in consumer behavior. Inferiority can be compensated in the exercise of power. Aggression is externally projected and tied to an object and lived.

Inner emptiness is stuffed with goods. Bonds to ideologies and dogmas or their representatives are repetitions of unbounded maternal and patriotic ties. In some life systems there is a hatred of life or profound humiliation- for want of experiencing love.

In many ways, humans can burden and damage life systems. Man can act as a "thief" in it! First and foremost, he wants to take as much as possible, without adequate consideration, while at the same time disadvantaging each other (Fromm 1973).

Conversely, life systems also affect humans. Money is a factor that is the decisive determinant in all life systems. You cannot live without money. Without money, almost nothing and nobody moves in the life systems. In life systems, people often experience loneliness, loss, and powerlessness. Much creates alienation. Freedom is illusory in some sectors. The life systems have their own dynamics and (material) constraints to maintain their viability. Imagine that from one day to the next, there are fifty percent fewer accidents and illnesses. This would have enormous consequences for the health service. Many thousands of doctors would stand on the street.

Or, Group A must expand capital and production, otherwise Group B displaces this from the market and ruined. Sixty percent of the product range, let us say, is not life-critical at all. One invents new products, creates with hypno-suggestive advertising the necessary need for replacement, and thus forces the people to act in this subsystem. He then needs the system to live and act accordingly as a consumer or a teammate.

There are also smaller and larger subsystems that have only one purpose: to raise capital. Such systems are actually "money machines". As a consumer, the human being is urged to act in away that does not fulfill the slightest basic need.

The purpose is in the system, not in the human being itself. In the life systems, there are many objects that have an idol function. Ideals, ideas, and their main representatives fix libidinous attachments, which are then considered to be a substitute for something more original in man. Life anxiety is covered with it. The whole thing then works like an automaton, where the subject freely believes in his actions and the "total manipulation" nobody thinks possible. Most believe that they hold the helm of their life-ship in their hands and steers on the right track. Life systems obviously have not only the function of enabling and promoting life. They often push people away from themselves, away from their real life, away from their personality as their central life theme.

The life systems have characteristics that constitutively characterize the action. Action is in the interaction of the human system. We formulate ten theses:

1. The life systems affect humans.
2. Man acts in life systems.
3. Man draws and profits from the life systems.
4. The life systems limit the human action.
5. Man creates his space in the life systems.

6. The life systems can cause damage to humans.
7. Man can cause damage in these life systems.
8. Man can suffer or rejoice through these systems.
9. The life systems are a fact; they are there.
10. The life systems are vital in the basic functions.

From this it can be concluded:

☐ We cannot grasp and understand people without life systems. Every action is tied to life systems.

☐ Happiness, joy, and every kind of subjectively positive experience or objectively positive state, are always related to life systems.

☐ Suffering, harm and any kind of subjectively negative experience, or objectively negative state, are always related to life systems.

☐ Man can only realize himself within the life systems; however, he imagines his self-realization.

☐ Personality forms, stagnates or grows in the interdependencies with the life systems.

☐ According to Leben, life systems determine what is a good and / or bad "reality" for humans.

☐ Man is existentially bound to these life systems and binds himself in many ways.

☐ Some life systems taboo themselves by their carriers and beneficiaries by mediating themselves as a goal and being used as such.

☐ Human action in these systems of life can be so systemic that one could run the risk of seeing "personality" in this conditional fabric as a purely mechanical construct.

Personality development without consideration of these complex interrelations and conditions remains without social relevance and reaches only a few with its humanistic goals. The theory about the personality is always one-sided, without this reference to the system. Any kind of solution or targeted action is already in the theoretical approach. This becomes a matter of fact, especially when the goal of science about personality is to create action knowledge and methodological concepts, for example, to politically solve social problems.

The problem list of the so-called risk society is large. It seems that the game of forces runs in a destructive spiral until life systems break down or destroy themselves. This then affects the people. First individually (as always), then many, and soon whole communities of peoples (as future predictions set out). Does man want total self-destruction through the destruction of life systems-by exploiting them and reducing their human-centered function to absurdity?

Since the life systems have no ego and no consciousness, the next steps must begin by examining the action and form them to allow the "inner man" to go further. The considerations that we take of the aspects of action, should primarily address the human being, and have for him a "critical" function and meaning.

Methods for detecting "critical event situations"

Flanagan (1954) has developed the "Critical Incident Technique". Behaviors that are critical in the context of success and failure, require a decision from the actor, are descriptively recorded, and an analysis of the content. For an analysis of the content, firstly, an identification of the elements of the field is requires, and the quality determined. As a second step, the dynamic qualities are recorded, for example, the constitutive and causal functions are to be identified and formulated as a hypotheses or provisional theory. This type of theory formation is generally called "structural analysis".

Following this procedure, we refer to an action to be investigated as a "critical event situation" ("KES"). "Critical" should indicate that the investigation of actions is based on a critical interest in knowledge, action, and happiness. "Critical" also means to want to look deeper, to be more conscious about it, to seek better variants, to consider other patterns as a possibility, to include a problem or conflict and more. Asking, "What is the case?" is the starting point in every field of research (Brezinka 1978, 146). We can also interpret "critical" as "significant" in the sense. For example, Pregnancy, success, or lotto profit, all indirectly open quite critical action perspectives (Thomae 1988, 14, 28).

In a sense, a "KES" can also be defined as a "problem". The features include the initial state, desired target state, and obstacles (Geue 1993, 11-13). A problem is an unsolved task situation or an unanswered question. Although the "critical" element, in our sense, is included here, the definitive goal-directedness (i.e., the "desired goal") is too restrictive for our interest. Likewise, we take the aspect of "critical" further than the meaning of "problematic". Die zentrale These von Geue im Zusammenhang mit Problembewältigungslernen in der Erwachsenenbildung ist jedoch auch unsere Leitidee: "Werden Informationen über Strategien des Problemlösens auf methodisch-didaktischem Weg vermittelt, dann verbessert sich die individuelle Problemlösungskapazität" (1993, 54, 142).

To improve individual problem solving, two aspects must be differentiated:

a) The solution strategy with the elements: specification, knowledge deficit, solution-oriented theory formation, practical solutions, and implementation.

b) The problem-solving capacity, that is: the ability to perceive, the overcoming of inhibitory factors, motivation, and the ability to apply strategies.
The "Critical Incident Technique" is a working tool.

The ability to emphasize is in our conception. In addition, the so-called "small things", which in their summation become a critical burden (Weber / Knapp-Glatzel 1988, 140-142) and not just age-specific and / or situation-specific are viewed as critical events. Here, subjective perception, interindividual experience, course characteristics and coping resources are research-methodologically and andragogical significant.

A "critical event situation" as an examination object can be limited differently. We can first define the critical action and then leave the possible situations open. We can also define a critical situation and seek and analyze the critical actions given in it. In the critical situation, the direct portion of the life field or life system in which the action occurs emerges. Therein, stands man. Goal and development opportunities are prospectively anticipated in the situation. Based on Lewin, the investigation unit "action" should thus include the time perspective and the extended macro range in addition to the narrower action situation. The actual reality is certainly more complex and nuanced.

The "Critical Incident Technique" makes it possible to investigate human action in a lifelike and system-related manner. In principle we can choose any action in any given habitat as the object of consideration.

We can look at action from different time perspectives, such as, a snapshot of a few seconds, an action over a day, or certain action over a longer period of time, or even as a time-limited unit of event (e.g., hard, session).

The selection depends on the specific interest. A researcher may choose to be flexible in their choice and have their curiosity co-opted, while a business consultant or conflict resolution officer will select specific actions. A marketing manager also choose other situations.

The main criteria for selecting "critical action situations" are:

☐ Cognitive interest
☐ Innovation intentions
☐ Training and education
☐ Conflict Resolution
☐ Problem reduction
☐ Products Planning
☐ Production processes
☐ Damage reduction
☐ Medical prevention
☐ Social prevention

- Damage repair
- Counseling
- Psych-agogics
- Reduction of suffering
- Dealing with suffering
- Breaking down crime
- Optimization of workflows
- Promoting political participation
- Quality improvement in everyday life
- Promoting quality of life
- Problem-solving strategies

The structure of the examination unit contains three systems:

1) The acting person
2) The action (the event)
3) The life system in which the person acts

The model "person-behavior-environment" also finds application in the interaction-related model of self-concept (Filipp 1993, 212). In the context of the "critical element" there are various investigations, reported by Filipp and others (1990). The "critical life events" are defined under the aspect of particularly drastic effects. Although different definitions are available (Hultsch / Cornelius, in: Filipp 1990, 74), the following general characteristics apply (Filipp 1990, 23-25):

Characteristics of "critical life events":

- Spatio-temporal sequence
- Stages of relative imbalance
- Emotional meaning (imbalance)
- Sudden (unexpected?) entry
- Stressful (challenging) experience
- Crisis / conflict life

Furthermore, such critical events can be classified from three perspectives:

1) age-related (life course)
b) time-related (incident)
c) non-normative (factual event)

(Hultsch / Cornelius, in Filipp 1990, 76).

For clarification, a selection of examples are presented (Filipp 1993, 12, 118, 255-256, Saup 1988, 125-127, Tress 1986, 50-70, Jungk / Mullert 1994, 69-70, Hurrelmann 1994, 142).

Examples of topics "critical or significant events" from biography, stressors and health research are:

▨ Transport	▪ Menpause
▨ Holiday	▪ Victim of theft
▨ Marriage	▪ Midlife Crisis
▨ Inheritance	▪ Puberty
▨ Birth	▪ Entrance of stepfather/mother
▨ End of school career	▪ Relocation to retirement home
▨ Early - / late retirement	▪ Exodus of the children
▨ Divorce	▪ Information overload
▨ Cancer	▪ Loss of sense of life
▨ Unemployment	▪ Moving
▨ Death spouse	▪ Unwanted procreation
▨ Remaining seated	▪ Remarriage
▨ License loss	▪ Negative parenting style
▨ Duty calls	▪ Departue of siblings
▨ Traffic noise	▪ Absent father
▨ Confrontation with boss	

Our definition of "critical event situations" is more specific in the case of everyday situations that do not change, as well as its uniqueness. The uses of this approach include what Filipp and others mention (Danish / Augelli, in Filipp, 1990, 156-171): education, primary prevention, competence enhancement, crisis management skills, assistance skills (social interventions), Coping with stress (Lazarus, in Filipp 1990, 216-229), recording a change in self-image (Mummendey, in Filipp 1990, 252-268), life event research, developmental psychological models (Filipp 1990, 303-306; Montada, in Filipp 1990, 272-289), and, improvement of counseling, care, facilities, prevention, and mediation (Montada, in Filipp 1990, 287, Belschner / Kaiser in Filipp 1990, 192).

Thomae (1988, 79-100, 110) has examined some typical forms of response to significant events in the biographical context. The reaction forms are: achievement, adaptation to institutional aspects of the situation, adaptation to the peculiarities and needs of others, foundation and maintenance of social contacts, reliance on others, evasive reaction, acceptance of the situation, depressive and/ or anxious reaction, deferment of one's own needs, identification with goals and destinies of others, asking for help, resistance, aggression and criticism, assertion, correction of expectations, taking up of opportunities, distancing, situation left to the circumstances, and hope. In these aspects, we see crucial approaches to self-critical reflection and the formulation of educational goals. Identity learning (Tietgens 1986, 21, 31) does not only permeate each other with job-related qualification learning, but above all with learning to live.

Hurrelmann (1988, 106-110) discusses the developmental capacity of the CV in his study. These gain outstanding importance in the context of the basic life risks and life chances. Formulated positively, this means: "Competences achieved in a development phase can be defined as prerequisites and consequences for the following stages of development. If the coordination and organization of personal resources succeeds in a phase of life, then coping well with future challenges is too expected. A competent individual can use the environmental resources and personal resources in such a way that there is a good outcome for personal development. " Before that, Hurrelmann says, "Through social and technological change, as well as mental and physical changes, it is necessary to constantly adapt the behavioral repertoire with the associated processing and coping capacities. This is to generate and coordinate flexible and adequate responses to environmental demands, and the opportunities for exploiting the action that the social environment offers. " In other words, skills are needed to meet real needs, and these form from the earliest childhood.

The biographical retrospective makes it possible to self-record development related capacities or their weak points. "In any phase of life, a mismatch between social, psychological and the physical demands one's own capacity for action. However, this can occur and be experienced as threatening or stressful." We refer to the list of factors of Hurrelmann (ibid, 108-109) and briefly summarize the conclusion for the personal life. The greater the vulnerabilities, the higher the life risks.

There are different events for every person over the course of life that, like certain actions, can be called "critical." Here is not the actual action, but the event in the center of the analytical consideration. Filipp has studied these phenomena together with several authors (1990, 74-82). Norbert Halsig and Annette Schröder examine the various coping strategies of critical events (1988, 42, 117).

The author has used the "Critical Incident Technique" in various research projects on both teacher education and home education (for young people). Isenegger (1971) introduced the technique in Swiss educational research. Roth and the author (1973) applied these for the first time as part of a research project to determine the educational needs of elementary school teachers ("BIVO project"). Incident was defined as incident and event: what happened? The event is the starting point: a situation or an incident. In the slightly modified procedure presented here, we refer the "critical event" to a situation in which the interviewee acts and want to record this "critical action situation". In addition, we introduce here advanced questions, which we have taken from another research project (then member): Study on Futures Research in Switzerland (NHG 1973). We call the method "KES method".

Analytical Protocol about Critical Incidents "Kritischen Ereignissituation" ("KES")
KES is the general description of what happened.
....

A) Proper activity in an event situation
A1. Quality of Action: What did you do (make)? How did you do it?
A2. Objectives / intentions of the action: what did you want to achieve? What happened to your story?
A3. Values in action: What is the value of the action for you?

B) Systems of life
B1. General context of the action situation: what was the situation?
B2. Limiting factors and influencing factors: what influenced the action of the environment?
B3. Effects in the surrounding system: What were the effects on the parts / persons in the surrounding system?

C) Acting person
C1. Self-handling of the acting person: How did you deal with yourself?
C2. Effects on the agent: What effects did the action have on you?
C3. Psychic powers (thoughts, feelings ...) of action: Which psychic powers were active?

D) Retrospective and prospective
D1. Similar event in the past: has such an event occurred earlier?
D2. Future with unchanged action: What is the future with unchanged action?
D3. Desirable act in the future: What action do you see constructive / positive in the future?

This analytical protocol contains crucial components for the research and counseling practice of Andragogy:

1. The material contains current experiences of those affected.
2. The material contains elements of life systems.
3. Problem-solving processes start with those affected.
4. Action and learning history offer operationalized solutions.
5. Learning motivation is promoted by the personal material.
6. Positive needs and wishes are prospectively integrated.
7. Innovative elements are put directly for discussion by the actor.
8. Value experiences are integrative components and thus arguable.
9. Action research or theory-practice feedback is guaranteed.

With these nine components, all conditions of action research and innovation strategy- in social systems- are fulfilled (Isenegger 1977, Lewin 1976, Hague 1972, Ulich 1980). The protocol is comprehensive and holistic. The reduction of reality or the action situation is taut, but not too comprehensive. The author has sometimes used the "critical event situation" protocol as part of deliberations on a comprehensive situation analysis. We do not want to give a research result, but only three impressions. These are: A person has the tendency to describe themselves, other people and different situations according to similar schemes. These ways of looking at things can differ considerably between individuals. Often, after completing 10 protocols, the subjects expressed themselves as follows: "Actually, in such situations and then afterwards, I have never thought so differently about situations of action". People also tend to respond to this kind of self-analysis: "I find that similar patterns (meaning actions and experiences) are repeated again and again in a variety of situations."

The cognitive approach to personality research provides further guidance for us. People evidently form categories for situations and for relationships between situations, feelings, and behaviors, as well as forming categories for individuals. With regard to different situation categories, each person seems to have a unique pattern of stability and change in feelings and behaviors (Pervin 1993, 472). With our protocol, we give the person a scheme and teach them that we create a confrontation with the usual schemes of the person. These schemas are cognitive generalizations of the self-image (always only particulate variable elements), past experiences (consistently "prototypes") and the processing of situational information (usually rather one-sided or subjective). With the cognitive errors in everyday life, as described by Nisbett and Ross (quoted in: Pervin 1993, 479), we can only confirm that sources of error are: observation, evaluation, categorization, assumption of causes and prediction.

This results in some conclusions, for the Andragogic practice. First, look more closely: what exactly was the situation and what exactly were their elements? Is the self-assessment of, one's own situation in the situation, correct? In which inner relationship are the emotive and the cognitive patterns? To what extent does the pattern of action deviate from this? In many cases, our KES analyzes revealed that people usually thought little to nothing before and during the action situation. Anticipatory consequences are rare in general reflection. The happening is a spontaneous reciprocal interaction between personal and habitat-related components. Bandura calls this "reciprocal determinism".

For personality education, in the beginning, one needs to perceive and to think (learning); then, to reflect on one's own schemata of cognitive functions. Finally, is the conscious cognitive examination of the action situation. This is action-oriented practical andragogic. In further steps, the learning history of the behavior patterns can be rolled up. The "prototypes" of the schemes usually lead to the central life experiences

The action analysis can also be understood as a "biographical method". The questioner is simultaneously a cognitive producer. In the retrospective, biographical questions about self-awareness will be asked: Which "critical life events" have imprinted? Which people, which places, which institutions, and which things, books, films, music, etc. have influenced me significantly? Our analytical protocol allows profound biographical reflection and can thus contribute significantly to the formation of identity (see Fuchs 1984, Gudjons et al., 1986, Kohli 1978, SVEB 1992/1). The analysis of KES reaches deep into the life story. Because a KES is rarely characterized by uniqueness, as it not only captures factual contours, but reflects the self-image and its history. KES editing in adult education is biographical communication (Fuchs 1984, 55, 93, 167).

Such retrospective and systematically guided biographical reflections or occupations, lead to increased cognitive competence and expand the competence to act. We also know that almost everyone does not reveal certain "big and small secrets". Andragogic consulting and training therefore integrate feedback that is feedback-linked in terms of location and learning history. This undoubtedly enhances intrinsic motivation, especially if the newly acquired competencies can predict a new future (action success) or systematically and purposefully strive for it.

From our professional practice, we have put together some salient topics of critical event situations.

Critical situations and critical topics are:

☐ Eating, drinking, and smoking	☐ Dealing with the inner life
☐ Shopping	☐ Suppressing others
☐ Communication between spouses	☐ Cheating
☐ Spending holiday season	☐ Sadistic torture
☐ TV	☐ Being violent
☐ Handling waste	☐ Handling money
☐ Phone calls	☐ Causing accidents
☐ Driving a car	☐ Design home decor
☐ Housework	☐ Dealing with the inner life
☐ Defining products	☐ Relationship/ looking for a partner
☐ Selling goods	☐ Education
☐ Spending your free time	☐ Play
☐ Sex life	☐ Getting sick
☐ Practice religion	☐ Dealing with the inner life
☐ Addiction live	☐ Suppress others
☐ Lies	☐ Cheating
☐ Drugs consumption	☐ Being at a party

☐ Dealing with the inner workings of others	☐ Speculation
☐ Punishing others'	☐ Doing office work at home
☐ Managing the daily routine	☐ Sunbathing for days
☐ Negotiating situations	☐ Listening to music
☐ Altruistic action	☐ Disrupted relationship
☐ Disputes	☐ Work situations of all kinds
☐ Make "blue"	☐ Anxiety behavior
☐ Praising someone	☐ Behavior in the feeling of loneliness
☐ Reading magazine	☐ Grief reactions
☐ Evening in a bar	☐ Self-dealing in being alone at home
☐ Chat with acquaintances	☐ Evening activities
☐ Celebrations	☐ Weekend design

Critical event situations allow a first approach to humans. The first point of view is from the outside: Human action is at the center of critical interest. The protocol can be used for various purposes.

Firstly, the logging of a diary can be a guide. However, a relatively high degree of self-motivation is essential. In addition, the autodidactic work requires a minimum of basic psychological knowledge.

Second, the protocol can serve as a tool in andragogic practice. The actor himself can fill out the protocol. Or, the adviser (as an interview partner) can use advanced questions to pinpoint the individual aspects in the protocol. In the analytic-counseling conversation, an action pattern can be rolled up and illuminated to the depths of the unknown. The idiographic content analysis takes place in an informative conversation, the result or the benefit depends essentially on the andragogy.

Third, such a protocol can serve as a pattern for homework in all manner of education and training in personality development. Theory can be discussed experientially in a course.

Fourth, one can work in the research with samples from a population. In action research, the actors can be involved in the process of theory building. In systematic theoretical and practice-oriented research, the content analysis, and the entire research planning, must be carried out according to appropriate rules. Specific personality variables may additionally be included as independent variables. Although a certain vagueness is given in cluster analyzes and semantic problems make an objective classification more difficult, the system human-action-life-system can be descriptively very differentiated and recorded realistically.

Fifth, in innovation projects of an institution, the actors can make a significant contribution, to the dynamization of innovation, by being involved in the process of innovation-oriented contract research from the beginning.

This technique of "critical event or action analysis" is the basic instrument for lively, life-oriented personality formation. The complexity of this system analysis has advantages and disadvantages. The disadvantage is the effort required. However, the everyday language, the "implicit personality theory", as well as attitudes of the protocols, can determine the collecting of the material. The problem can be handled as action research and lifelong advice on andragogy.

The following can be regarded as central advantages: avoidance of general social criticism, expansion of intervention strategies of all kinds, more realistic diagnosis of all kinds, "problem cases", clearer assessment of personality formation, constant feedback of theoretical analyzes of the lifeworld, feasibility of visions of a "better" society , dynamization of life systems through the involvement of the actors, objectification of ideological and dogmatic life assessments, centering all innovations in the combination of human action life system, evaluation of all components in renewal processes, evolutionary societal restructuring, manageable concept for individual self-reflection and planned life renewal in interest of improvement, the centering of all orientations in the human being as a life unit in the life systems, as well as clear assessment of the personality formation.

Innovative analysis of behavior

Imagine: We study certain critical situations (events, actions) of 500 people over a shorter or longer period of time according to the protocol pattern mentioned above. Or a person creates about 100 protocols for his own personal development. It is likely, we will find "typical patterns of action" that are constitutive for specific situations. This is a valuable approach for innovation or change and for new learning processes in individuals as well as in institutions. This is our hypothesis.

We assume that one can establish categories with common structural properties from the analysis of different "critical event situations". In contrast to these structures, structured solution processes can also be developed. Perhaps even a reference can be made to cognitive schemes (Sydow, in: Foppa / Groner 1981, 269). For the formation of personality, it suffices for the time being to heuristically analyze the critical event situations and their solutions or innovative strategies for change and improvement through reflection and dialogue (in class or in counseling) (Hussy, in: Oerter / Montada 1987, 509).

Let us introduce two examples according to this analytical protocol:

Example 1: Analytical Protocol about "critical event situation" ("KES")

KES indicator: General description of the event situation: What has happened? A car accident on the way home after work.

A) Actual action in the event situation:

A1 Quality of Action: What did you do (make)? How did you do it?
Not concentrating, tired, indifferent, or bored.
A2 Objectives / intentions of the action: what did you want to achieve? What happened to your story?
Wanted to get home quickly after work.
A3 Values in action: what is the value of the action for you?
Irresponsibility, indifference, gross negligence.

B) Life system:

B1 General context of the action situation: what was the situation?
Main street, dusk, and lots of traffic.
B2 Limiting factors and influencing factors: what influenced the action of the environment?

Wet road and winding.
B3 Effects in the surrounding system: what were the effects on the parts / persons in the surrounding system?
3 injured, major property damage, 2 months out of work, and physical suffering.

C) Acting person:

C1 Self-handling of the acting person: how did you deal with yourself?
False self-assessment and indifferent to risks.
C2 Effects on the agent: what effects did the action have on you?
Injuries, costs, feelings of guilt and strains in the family.
C3 Psychic powers (thoughts, feelings, etc.) of action: which psychic powers were active?
Sorrowful thoughts, aggressive mood, and lack of concentration.

D) Retrospective and Prospective:

D1 Similar event in the past: has such an event occurred earlier?
A year ago, accident at work, also out of negligence / indifference.
D2 Future with unchanged action: what is the future with unchanged action?
High accident risk.
D3 Desirable act in the future: what action do you see constructive / positive in the future?
No more accidents.

Example 2: Analytical Protocol about "critical event situation" ("KES")

KES indicator: General description of the event situation: What has happened? Quarrel with wife

A) Actual action in the event situation:

A1 Quality of Action: what did you do (make)? How did you do it?
Reproachfully talked about boredom and quite moody.
A2 Objectives / intentions of the action: what did you want to achieve? What happened to your story?
I do not know what I wanted to achieve
A3 Values in action: what is the value of the action for you?
Speaking unreflectively, no constructive communication, and somehow aimless.

B) Life system:

B1 General context of the action situation: what was the situation?
Under the kitchen door, my wife was cooking
B2 Limiting factors and influencing factors: what influenced the action of the environment?
Hectic environment, with the unpaid bills on the table.
B3 Effects in the surrounding system: what were the effects on the parts / persons in the surrounding system?
Have hurt my wife; she kept on cooking.

C) Acting person:

C1 Self-handling of the acting person: how did you deal with yourself?
Indifferent, and somehow helpless.
C2 Effects on the agent: what effects did the action have on you?
Frustration, aggression, sense of misunderstanding, and a bad mood.
C3 Psychic powers (thoughts, feelings ...) of action: which psychic powers were active?
Above all, a mixture of feelings, disinterest, and bored.

D) Retrospective and Prospective:

D1 Similar event in the past: has such an event occurred earlier?
We have quarreled every week, often over very little.
D2 Future with unchanged action: what is the future with unchanged action?
Repeated disputes.
D3 Desirable act in the future: what action do you see constructive / positive in the future?
Speaking differently, being cooperative, listening more, and less arguing.

The examples illustrate that many factors partly determine the action, and that the action cannot be detected by sufficient behavioral psychology. Man is to be grasped in his total system: human-action-life-systems. It is also clear that the actual ability to act alone is also not sufficient for the prevention of accidents. Necessary to Psycho-hygiene, improve relationship, clarify workplace situation, and have better management of the inner psychic powers.

The second example also shows how layering factors interact with psychic forces in situations. Behavioral psychological factors play a role as well as the mood. Finally, andragogy will emphasize that there are far more internal psychic powers involved.

The intrapsychic structural interdependencies are so diverse that they tend to be neglected in this way of capturing human action. This depends directly on the knowledge of the protocol or any extended references to the description of the facts. The concerned person can offer important approaches to understanding and change, which in turn can have a motivating effect.

The solution approaches are easy to recognize. Listening, starting with oneself and talking about problems properly are the first conditions for a solution in example 2. Learning processes are necessary. Both can practice how to discuss improving problems in a relationship. The system frame is controllable. The action can be better placed. Everyone has their own opportunities to contribute to change. Example 1 highlights, among other things, the importance of mental health. Furthermore, it is obvious that unfinished problems, even uncontrolled shreds of thought, determine the behavior in quite banal situations. Those who have an eye for the prospective, in such situations, can analyzes form motivations for new learning. The negative outlook for the future can promote the positive possibilities or the willingness to learn.

Several other KES examples (characteristics) are presented:

1) KES indicator: No more desire for sex with my husband.
2) KES mark: Search unsuccessfully a friend.
3) KES label: I always eat too much every day.
4) KES indicator: Had a heated argument with the boss.
5) KES mark: I do not dare to go out with colleagues.
6) KES license plate: I am lying in bed on Sunday until the afternoon.
7) KES license plate: The children annoyed me on Saturday.
8) KES label: I am tired of cleaning, washing, cooking ...
9) KES mark: My in-laws constantly criticize me.
10) KES indicator: I am disabled, looking for sexual experiences in vain.
11) KES indicator: Our neighbors no longer greet us.
12) KES mark: I am bored in my job.
13) KES mark: I cannot stand my colleague.
14) KES indicator: Holidays in Mallorca were a frustration, I was alone.
15) KES license plate: I do not know what to do after work.

Critical event situations of all kinds can be decomposed and examined according to our analytical protocol. Situations that are reported as an experience- without specific conflict - related action - can also be logged in relation to the action. A critical experience and action can provide approaches through dissection that can initiate a change. Basically, most critical event situations are not that easy to change because of their interconnections. Rarely, can someone quickly "flip the switch" or take away a system component to have the solution.

We assume that the action itself contains specific characteristics that must be integrated into a solution strategy. This in turn, is to be embedded in a comprehensive personality formation. Each solution variant contains different starting points, according to our model (see also Hoff, in: Oerter / Montada 1987, 920 f.). Are there any critical situations where no solution is possible? Firstly, it depends on what you mean by solution. The fact is that there are many situations in life, where flexibility is not possible, where the systemic determinants or mental conditions create difficult-to-change facts, for example, no work, psychopathic or criminal character structure, fanaticism, destructive dynamics of the unconscious, illness or disability, tragic events of fate, unforgiveness, lack of insight, constraints of corporate structures and their interdependencies, inviolable power behavior, narcissism, regressive psychodynamics, social taboos, greed, wars, incestuous fixations given facts (e.g. highway through housing estates, heavily polluted industrial area adjacent to residential areas, lack of capital, inflation, recession) etc...

Our interest here is focused on the personality; thus, on personal education. We cannot pursue social determinants here for reasons of space. Other methods are needed. The examples here illustrate that people within their private life, and in professional life, can grasp and clarify many critical situations. From one hundred own examples about critical event situations, everyone can learn to understand their actions in the most diverse life systems and thereby change themselves evolutionarily and progressively. Man can recognize the changeable quantities and himself as changeable unity. The reduction to elemental psycho-spiritual life is sometimes the only possible solution.

Those who cling to the outer life (and things) often find no solution to their critical situations. However, those who focus inwardly (focus on being human or concentrate and build the solutions on the inside) will be able to create changes. There are many solutions for many critical situations or actions. More than people want to admit. Those who understand humanity, as the highest good, can recognize this. This is where personality development begins.

In our model, we separate the human being, with his "psychic organism", from his actions. Firstly, action is an expression of what happens in individual psychic subsystems: the experience of anger manifests itself in cursing words; what is thought and still active in thought operations is presented in a linguistic discussion; an experienced need, for example after sexual encounter, leads to corresponding activity; an inner conflict (in the unconscious), which is repeatedly psycho-energetically active and can cause somatic reactions, urges actions that correspond to the conflict pattern; the power of love causes an inward processing of an earlier conflict; an intensively experienced warning room leads to a change in the holiday planning; a clear value-expectation disposition increases the urge to action, etc.

Action is, secondly, an expression of the form of the psychic powers: if love is little developed, it can do little; If someone does not know the interpretation of dreams and does not know about the possibilities, then he cannot do anything with dreams; if the needs are not consciously taken care of, then they act instinctively and often outside of the ego control; whoever never exercises the willpower, has hardly the "push" for a (let us say "necessary") "fiat" ("it happens") in difficult situations with considerable counter-forces; Anyone who never reflects on his language use hardly recognizes the ambiguity and the associated sources of conflict; he who does not form his feelings is easily overwhelmed by them in his actions; Who does not train in dealing with a stress syndrome, for example learning psycho-hygiene and relaxation techniques, is overwhelmed by his psychodynamics, etc...

Thirdly, we can put action directly related to the skills that we have learned, emphasizing "performance", as a special form of action: Driving (as an action) depends on how well someone can drive; Communication, in business as well as in a personal relationship, depends on learning processes; dealing with the environment is related to knowledge and ability; the parenting behavior of a father can vary considerably, depending on the skills learned in dealing with educational situations (and with oneself); The design of leisure time is also subject to many different skills, some social (communicative), some instrumental type and so on.

Many difficulties in life from nutrition to specific conflict management - and many other types of actions - are closely related to learned, incorrectly learned, or not learned skills. Professional - and everyday actions of all kinds - contain different qualities, which are subject to learning processes.

Fourthly, all actions are part of a life system embedded in higher life systems. Here are a variety of conceivable factors that influence the action, perhaps even force, or trigger the opposite of what was intended with the action. Man's actions are always to be seen in psycho-social, economic, ecological and health contexts. Implementation options can be limited.

The "right time" (the Kairos) is often crucial in life. Political news, the "Zeitgeist" of the environment, the daily subliminal advertising, and the hidden suggestive effects of all sorts of elements of the life system can decisively influence the action.

Fifthly, people's actions are to be considered from the point of view of the European masses of people - and not an experimental laboratory situation. Many people lie, steal, cheat, act, intrigue, and behave cunningly cleverly to obsessively, to achieve certain goals or to be able to live out of their unconscious inner life. Very few people are ignorant, arrogant, and aggressive-stupid. More than half of all people have a less educated character and a particular sense of differentiated values, and a distinctly undeveloped conscience.

This results in a tremendous violent and destructive potential for action, and not least a collective susceptibility to the repetition of the history of horror. This is not moralized but descriptive of the development of a realistic educational concept of Andragogy.

Sixth, we do not want to overlook the fact that the personality theory, the attitudes of the Andragogen, and educators, decisively influence the judgment of the actions of another person. One should not underestimate the state of psycho-spiritual development and the current fulfillment of life of Andragogen and teachers as covertly cooperating forces.

This means that the assessment of a person's actions is subject to many conditions and aspects of consideration. To develop a theory of action, nomothetical theory would want to "reach for the stars". The research on motivation and action clearly shows us that from concept definition, to concept constructions - of all kinds and, including rat, among others - there is a greater theoretical consensus today (Heckhausen 1989).

Andragogical psychology, therefore, must focus on those areas where fruitful educational conceptions can be developed. This may bring the reputation of a "naive action psychology" or a non-value-free science. But that is at least lifelike, close to the human, realistic, and a concept with optimal instrumental human action- where the education can lead to action changes in the sense of quality both subjectively and. We cannot go on discussing the problem of value-free or evaluative opinion in andragogy. The embedding of the "actions" of man in the various networks, also leads to significant epistemological and methodological problems. In addition, this topic is excluded here since it would exceed the unity of the topic of this study considerably.

Behavior skills – Example 'Health'

Laaser (1987) presents new aspects to the definition of health: "Health is the culture of all food, the occupation of the body, and the environment in social action. Health is a path that is formed by walking it" (ibid., 54) ... "Health factors are also methodical principles, such as' striving for appropriateness', 'emotional world,' and closeness to life '..." (ibid., 56).

Hurrelmann describes health as (1994): "Self-responsibility and self-determination are regarded as important components of healthy personality development ... Health is understood as part of the individual development of life history, as a process that is only possible if an individual is flexible and purposeful in each case, optimally achievable, and the state of coordination of internal and external requirements, while ensuring a satisfactory continuity of self-identity (identity) ... "(ibid., 16-17) ..." Health is defined as the high adaptability of man to physical, psychological and social pressures understood and associated with the whole way of life. " (ibid. 126).

Homfeldt and co-authors (1993) give practical suggestions and reflections on the topic. Here are some theses: "Perception training or sensitization means developing a greater sensitivity, precision, and differentiation for external and internal processes" (ibid., 78). "Perception, and design, impression and expression are all part of the circle".

They affect each other. Intensity and variety of perceptions and their individual processing belong to the preconditions of creative design (Ibid., 83). Holistic perception results from the harmonious interplay of sensory and spiritual powers "(ibid., 61).

Homfeldt describes practical health in the areas of feeding, moving, dressing, and experiencing nature (1994). According to Homfeldt, "We understand health education as the effort to build a personally healthy lifestyle that incorporates social, economic and ecological aspects of human behavior. Responsible behavior, in the sense of Health education, aims at an expansion of personal competence in a concrete sociocultural world of life with its requirements, and open spaces "(ibid., 4). "Similar to illness, it can be said to nourish, to move, and to dress, are biographically motivated." (ibid, 20). "Consciousness is the prerequisite for creating a program for the right personal health action" (ibid. 20).

Becker examined the "Psychology of Mental Health" and presented a list of mental health factors (1982, 143). Obviously, health is much more than "absence of illness." Sommer writes, "Health is not something you 'have' or 'do not have', what you 'lose' or 'regain', and health is not something that adds to the life of man and makes it more beautiful and enjoyable. "Health is the way of life, the realization of life itself, and the way of coping with life." (ibid 1994, 37). And, "Used and known is ... the system of risk factors." Sommer faces the "construction factors" (for health) against them.

"They ... allow health - at every stage and moment - to be experienced as something beneficial. It motivates oneself to further efforts for health, and thus, promotes self-initiative and self-responsibility." These include, in short: nutrition, breathing, exercise, sleep, temperature, affection, love, security, safety, beneficial experiences, reason, understanding, satisfactory understanding, social activity, creative activity, reflection, self-control, internalization, meditation, experience of transcendence, and organism-appropriate rhythm of life (ibid., 39-41).

3. The Psycho-dynamic – The psychical energy

Definition, clarification of terms and aspects

Psychodynamics is a term that expresses something that you can observe, recognize, and experience. Psychodynamics is expressed in the whole variety of human actions. It is based on PSYCHICAL ENERGY. This term has a long and varied usage tradition:

Freud calls this power "libido". Reich called it "orgone energy". Fromm speaks in this context of "life instinct". In vitalism, the term "vital force" is used. Jung also calls this power "psychic energy"; but also speaks of "libido". Driesch specifies this energy as a "life factor" and refers to Aristotle (entelechy). Also, concepts such as death instinct and life instinct or instinct energy revolve around this force. This energy is then interpreted as a sexual drive or power drive (eagle). Parapsychology speaks here of "para-psychic energy", occasionally of "cosmic energy", "psychotrone energy", and "PSI energy". In Spanish circles of parapsychology and naturopathy, the term "bioenergy" is naturalized. The term "Urtrieb" (of man) is also used. Eros (Plato, Freud, Fromm) is, in a way, this life instinct.

The esoteric teaches a "cosmic universal energy", the "emanation", and the "aura energy". Magnetopathy (Mesmerism) taught a "magnetic energy", speaks of "fluidum", and "mediumistic energy".

Spiritual healing and various parapsychic healing techniques also imply an energy concept that is interpreted as "spiritual energy". Finally, mention should be made of the "prana" from the Far East, as well as the "mana kundalini" or "kundalini" (Eliade 1961, 132, 182, Campbell 1978, 249, Harish Johari 1977, Assagioli 1992).

We quote some experts, who deal with the psychic energy. The variety of aspects should clarify that psychic energy is a life phenomenon that cannot be discussed without any positivist science. Countless parapsychological research, with many hypotheses, lead to the core problem: (It is) to look for an unknown energetic factor (Bender 1972, 38). Meek assumes that "consciousness encompasses one or more new types of energy, with field properties" (1980, 330). Reich states, "The atmosphere contains an energy of which I have not heard of before: there is orgone energy everywhere" (1976, 113).

Russian researcher Vasilyev said, "The discovery of the energy - associated with psychic processes - will be as significant, if not much more, than the discovery of nuclear energy." (Quote from: Keller 1979, 330). This energy is called "bio-plasmic energy".

"Prana" is another word for "psychic energy, life force that reveals itself in outer space, but whose seat is in the heart of man ... sometimes compared to fluidum, ether or od ideas and magnetizers as pranic healers. " (Bonin 1976, 406).

Doucet speaks of the "energy field of a universal super consciousness" and assumes that this is the so-called "collective unconscious" of C.G. Jung (1975, 23). In transmission, in clairvoyance and telepathy, in mass suggestion, and in all kinds of PSI phenomena, an energy manifests, which Doucet refers to as a "psychic energy" present in all humans (ibid, 22). The author goes on to say, "awareness and the unconscious are one unit, they are a unitary PSI field." (ibid., 32). Thought experiments can be used to generate PSI fields in space, as Doucet describes (ibid., 52-54). The conclusion of parapsychic research is that everyone has PSI energy and can use it.

The ASW researcher Ritzl (1976) says that PSI energy is the basis for telepathy and clairvoyance, and the energy of the sixth sense (ibid., 36-38). Extra-sensory perception is a fact that countless people can confirm. ASW can even give us an unconscious, gentle guidance in life, and help us make the right decision- at the right moment- when it is most beneficial to our needs (ibid, 48). Positive thinking and prayer activate positive PSI energy, says Ritzl (ibid., 106-110).

The idea of an energy field and an energy body goes back to antiquity and is as well known in Christianity as in Far Eastern philosophers (Stelter 1973, 84 ff.). In parapsychological research, it is assumed that "the real place of our sensation is not the body - with the brain and the nervous system - but the energy body superordinate to the physical body" (ibid., 93-94). This energy body is "the superordinate and organizing part of man (ibid., 98).

Biologist and philosopher Driesch (1867-1941), dealt in detail with para-psychic phenomena (1975). To explain telepathy, the transmission of thoughts and clairvoyance, he assumes an energetic "field of souls" (ibid., 111). "The supreme basis is always the doctrine that body and soul are two beings, and that basic doctrine remains that souls (of paranormal reciprocal transmissions of knowledge) are capable in the field of souls" (ibid., 139).

The author has been doing research on psychic energy for 15 years and has developed several techniques to make this energy tangible and change its state (see: Schellhammer 1986, 1987). From this background we determine hypothetically: All these different concepts ultimately mean the same thing: THERE IS A PSYCHIC ENERGY IN HUMAN. Furthermore, some of the energy concepts contain the theory that there is also generally the same energy around the human or in the living space. We can only confirm that, but do not go any further, as it does not belong to the topic in the narrower sense. We then speak of COSMIC ENERGY.

Our first thesis is that there is an energy in man that is not biological. We call it PSYCHICAL ENERGY.

We imagine that this energy is a multi-dimensional fine net that also radiates outwards. This energetic body ("aura") has different centers or a tendency to condense or dilute in different places in the body. The "streams of vitality" according to the teachings of Yoga probably want to express this (Johari 1979).

This energy is malleable and gets a specific shaped quality through the individual psychic subsystems. Their intensity is different. All people know this energy.

It is experienced as tension, pressure on the chest or in the head, as a diffuse "knot" in the abdomen, or as a specific cramp. Whoever speaks of a "confused head" usually means that the energy in the head is simply confused.

The energy charge in emotions is nothing but "psychical energy". Humans can also experience this energy in a positive way, for example after a deep relaxation or in moments of special contemplative.

Kundalini is also an "aspect of the highest consciousness" (Johari 1979, 29). Yoga as a method of relaxation, inner collection, and general immobilization of psychic powers (consciousness) undoubtedly leads to a harmonious balanced energy state. The effect is the same as in autogenic training, in empty hypnosis and in some exercises of the imagination (Thomae 1976). But with techniques of relaxation, neither "bliss" nor "enlightenment" can be achieved. We advise against "sitting under a tree for three days" and waiting for the great "meeting of God". However, if God also means "psychic life", and thus the psychic organism (perhaps as a living image), then meditating will advance in personality development or mental-spiritual evolution.

The second hypothesis is that the psychic energy in man is formed by thinking, experiencing, feeling, and through all mental subsystems.

The inventory in the unconscious, thoughts, and even perception, can form the psychic energy through the experience: bring into vibration.

The third hypothesis is that the psychic energy is indirectly and directly influenced by the elements and people in the habitat.

Other people emit psychic energy. This can be transferred to other people in their condition. So, one can take up moods of others or give one's own energy unintentionally to other people. The happenings and the symbolic meaning of the built and undeveloped environment are known to affect our feelings, our thinking, our unconscious life, and in general all our psychic systems. This detour influences the energy of the human being from the outside.

In parapsychology, there is a theory that states that things also contain a "psycho-energetic impregnation", which can affect humans. We can only confirm this based on our research, but we do not want to go into that here (Driesch 1975, Bender 1973).

We formulate our fourth hypothesis: Psychic energy can make you mentally ill, in the form of disturbances of the mental functions and behavior.

As everyday mental disorders we know: nervousness, anxiety, depression, shortness of breath, indefinite grief, listlessness, concentration disorder, indefinite aggressive tension, oppressive constriction, the urge for overeating, smoking and excessive alcohol consumption, and more.

Psychical energy is, so to speak, the "stuff" of psychodynamics. Thus, we can provisionally record the connection between psychodynamics and mental or physical functions as follows:

Psychic energy influences the mental functions. In the positive state, the psychic energy is characterized by soft, flowing, calm, harmonious, centered, whole, bright, light, balanced, soothing, dynamic, and strong. This energy state has a corresponding effect on the mental functions. It can provide purposeful concentration, directed attention, relieved activity, calm thoughts, balanced and calm feelings, clear perception, inner collection, conscious rest, and intensified inner experience. If the psychic energy is hard, chaotic, unbalanced, torn, weak, aggressive, and dark, then this has a corresponding effect on the mental functions (See: Schellhammer 1987, 1987).

The fifth hypothesis is: Physical states shape or influence the psychic energy.

Those who have flu experience their energy as weak, diffuse, confused, and disturbed. Physical pain, especially over a longer period of time, determines the psycho-energetic state decisively. During our professional practice, we were able to learn that, for example, cancer patients have an enormously stinging, chaotic, and even "burning" psychic energy. The energy feels like the cancer itself in the microscopic sight: decomposing, angry, wild, and aggressive.

For example, by using autogenic training, with formulaic intent, we influence bodily functions. At the same time, the psychic energy always relaxes. The entire psychodynamic comes to rest and to a balance.

The exercises of autogenic training (Schultz 1970) effect:

Heavy:	Muscles: Tension reduction.
Heat:	Dilatation of the vessels in the extremities, Blood pressure regulation.
Heart:	Natural rhythm, circulation, adjustment to the heart activity.
Breathing:	Breathing normalization.
Abdomen:	Blood circulation of the internal organs, harmonization of the controlled gastrointestinal and muscle movements.
Forehead:	Reduction of head circulation,

Eyes and brain tension reduction.

The state of bodily functions influences the psychodynamics. By bodily functions, we mean in particular: muscles, cardiovascular system, respiration, digestion, nervous system, sensory organs, and skin. Since the "substance" of psychodynamics is the psychic energy, we can also say that the bodily functions influence the state of the psychic energy.

The sixth hypothesis is: Psychic energy can make you physically ill.
Psycho-somatic disorders caused by this energy are, above all: stress reactions of all kinds, e.g. Insomnia, migraine, headache, neck tension pain, vegetative dystonia, potency disorders, etc. Above all, the Reich and its successors have undertaken a great deal of research into bioenergy and its effects on the body (Reich 1976). In America, Siegel (1990) made known the influence of emotions on the body. We suspect that various forms of cancer are also due to a disturbed psychic energy. The psycho-physical context is formulated in the literature as follows: "Emotional factors cause physical reactions".

It must therefore be assumed that the quality state of this energy has a positive or negative or disturbing to pathogenic effect. How can one "prove" this? We must first identify the positive and negative states in their expressions. Then we must prove that by changing this condition one can also achieve a change of the psychic functions, or a suffering from the self-healing power of the body can be cured. The research on autogenic training and on the graded active hypnosis (Langen 1972) have provided various evidence. We also believe that it is possible to directly demonstrate the connection between (disturbed) psychic energy, emotional factors, and psychosomatic ailments. Such a project cannot be discussed here. It goes beyond the scope of our objectives. There are various ways to access the effects of psychic energy on the body (Hume 1979, Vester 1978, 47, 66, 82).

The well-known stress researcher - Hans Selye - does not define 'stress' negatively in principle (1982, 38). He states, "Stress is the non-specific response - of the body - to any request made of it." (ibid., 38). Therefore, "Stress is not just nervous tension, not always the nonspecific result of injury, and not something that needs to be avoided." (ibid., 40-41) "Stress is the spice of life" (ibid. 82). "Stress" thus means "burden", while "distress" has a negative effect on disharmony and dissonance (ibid. 13-14). Vester differentiates between "stress" and "conflict stress" (1978, 184); In his analyzes, however, the word use predominates: stress = distress. Stress is the body's answer - and with it the psyche - to all kinds of stress.

Stress research has shown in many ways that unresolved life problems can cause illness. The risk of disease depends on the extent of the "critical life events" and the ability to handle it constructively, and to overcome them (Filips 1979, Becker 1982, Pervin 1993). The key emotional factors are fear, helplessness, meaninglessness, guilt, anger, and aggression.

In stress syndrome, we can identify environmental factors, psychological personality factors, physical factors, and factors of action. Stress is always situation, stimulus, experience, and reaction. While the biological stress mechanism used to be vital (Vester 1976), today it has become a pathological event. "The stress makes me completely finished" (Weber 1987) is an everyday language statement that certainly makes it essential. Likewise, the director's statement at the dinner with the family, "I'm completely burned out", illustrates certain biological, psychological (Burisch 1989), and psycho-energetic facts.

Stress research and relaxation research have discussed a plethora of options for action at various levels. These include: psycho-energetic and physical relaxation, clarifying relationships, relaxing leisure activities (listening to music, hiking), a clearer separation of work and leisure, clarifying the workplace situation, looking for suppressed desires and interests, unconscious repressed instinctual aspects, search for life fulfillment (meaning finding), activation of desire to act (hobbies, circle of friends, reading, etc.) and, of course, the targeted analysis and direct elimination of the stressors.

Here we clearly see how andragogy is more than psychology or adult education didactics. Andragogy is actual human education. We also recognize that a reduced or narrowed andragogic psychology in life practice must fail. In particular, the depth-psychology and transcendental-spiritual forces such as the unconscious, the dreams, the imagination or contemplation and the power of love are indisputable parts of andragogic psychology. Because only they reach all human (intrapsychic) realities.

Emotional factors are:

Anger	Jealousy	Perfectionism
Aggression	Hostilities	Embarrassments
Fears	Receivables	Rivalries
Rejections	Fear	Sexual abuse
Dependencies	Remorse	Penalties
Adjustments	Helplessness	Dispute
Possessiveness	Hatred	Guilt
Desires	Conflicts	Longing

☐ Threats	☐ Complex	☐ Mourning
☐ Humiliations	☐ Sorrow	☐ Submission
☐ Scams	☐ Distrust	☐ Refusal
☐ Depression	☐ Inferiority	☐ Despair
☐ Disappointments	☐ Envy	☐ Anger
☐ Ambition	☐ Obligations	☐ Constraints

Becker-Carus (1981, 195) speaks of "stressors" and presents a list, which includes: death of spouse, divorce, separation, death in the family, injury, illness, job loss, sexual difficulties and more. The core thesis is: Cognitive evaluation leads to emotions and physiological reactions (Becker-Carus 1981, 178-179). The electro-physical changes, caused by emotions, we find in facial muscles, muscles in general, the brain, cardiovascular, respiratory, and autonomic system (Izhard 1981, 26, 35). Virtually all neurophysiological systems and subsystems are involved in emotions.

Our thesis says: Emotional factors cause physical reactions. They are, among other things: eating and appetite disorders, anorexia, nervous vomiting, obesity, disorders of swallowing tract, stomach neurosis, heartburn, chronic diarrhea or constipation, asthma, stuttering, bronchial, palpitations, anxiety, headaches, migraines, eczema, impotence , frigidity, menstrual disorders, sleep disorders, and cancer. We emphasize this connection made here should not be concluded that all forms of such physical reactions can be traced back over and only on emotional factors. The same physical reactions may well have non-emotional or non-psychological causes.

Dimensions of expression of the psycho-dynamics

Our interest here focuses on the psychodynamics in the individual. The individual dimensions are all based on this basic force, called psychic energy. They are expressive aspects of psychic energy. In principle, every human being has his or her own freedom in dynamics. The pathogenic or disturbing effect only arises after a certain intensity level of the negative quality.

Expressive dimensions of psychodynamics are:
1) Tension - Relaxation
2) Extraversion - Introversion
3) Psycho-physical reactions
4) Basic-Being
5) Stability - Lability
6) Sensitivity - Rigidity
7) Strength and intensity (or weakness)
8) Constructive - Destructive quality

1) Tension - Relaxation:
This dimension is relatively easy to capture because everyone knows the phenomenon of tension-relaxation. The autogenic training of Schultz (1970) has created in different circles a differentiated awareness of the importance of relaxation in daily life. Leuner and others have widely developed the methods of hypnosis and imagination for the purpose of relaxation (1975, 1980). We also find states of tension in Cattel's personality dimensions, in Bradburn's "Affect Balance Scale", and in the factor "nervousness" in FPI (Becker 1982).

Relaxation is described as: relaxed, calm, harmonious, comfortable. Tension is circumscribed with: tense, restless, disharmonious, and the like.

2) Extraversion – Introversion:
We do not understand this dimension as a positive-negative spectrum. Both sides have a meaningful effect in the normal expression. There are negative aspects for both sides if they are lived exclusively and for a long period of time. This often happens when there are people who know how to direct all their energy to the outside world and to discharge it outside ("exploding"). On the other hand, total introversion leads to "implosion". Eysenk, Cattell, and Guilford have captured this dimension by factor analysis, but emphasize more substantive and non-energetic aspects. Similarly, Jung (1972) described in his typology this dimension as a personality factor of the ego-environmental relationship. Spranger and Kretschmer also integrated this aspect.

In contrast to other models, we do not want to construct ideal types here, but to understand both extremes as poles with many intermediate gradations (see Hempel, in: Topitsch 1970, 87).

To 3) Psycho-Physical reactions:
The psycho-somatic reactions are largely determined by emotional factors (Cremerius 1978, Groddeck 1990, Boss 1978, Petzold / Reindell 1980, Alexander 1985). According to our theory, emotional factors activate psychic energy and shape it into action forces, according to the emotion. We have presented the list of the main emotional factors. Many clinical pictures and the entire catalog of psychodiagnostics could be listed here.

The psychological and psycho-somatic susceptibility depends on the degree of responsiveness of the psycho-physical response.

To 4) Basic conditions:
Basic physical condition - or basic mood - can be operationalized in various ways. It can be characterized with contentment, with emotional tone or with zest for life, as a basic attitude towards life (cheerfulness) or with well-being. The manifestations appear in various classical factor-analytical investigations (Pawlik 1971, Becker 1982). The basic condition is expressed in behavior. Kretschmer also a place within the scope of the temperament theory.

A positive basic condition is characterized by being cheerful, balanced, and lively. A negative basic condition is circumscribed with words like melancholic, gloomy, torn, unbalanced, heavy, dull, etc.

To 5) Stability - Lability:
This dimension is merely intended to express the constancy and variability of the overall dynamics. Cattel captures the factor as "Strength / Weakness". With Guilford, this aspect can be found in the temperament factor.

Stability is characterized by being stable and steady, whereas, lability is described as unstable, unsteady, and the like.

To 6) Sensitivity - Rigidity
There are people who can hardly be moved out of their movement by "banging beats", while others react sensitively to a quiet sound. The same applies to life topics of all kinds. While some have a very differentiated sensitivity, others react even to the hardest realities, without emotion. The psycho-energetic reaction is missing. The energetic system is rigid; we can also say: rigid.

These aspects too can be found in the classical factor analysis models. Likewise, this dimension finds a place in Kretschmer's Typology. The dimension "progression regression" of Jung (1971) is reduced here to the expression "fluently-rigid". Jung analyzes here the libido in the context of the psychological adaptation process.

Sensitivity is described as: sensitive, soft, easy to address, and flowing. Rigidity circumscribes itself as rigid, hard, difficult to address, and insensitive.

To 7) Power / Intensity - weakness:
This dimension can be experienced, felt, and perceived. It manifests itself in action through power and intensity. In Cattel's factor analysis, we find this dimension under "Strength / Weakness". Sniper assigns vitality, activity, and strength to the "I" (1976, 37).

Power and intensity are characterized by being strong, intense, vital, centered, and goal directed. While weakness is described as being weak, powerless, lame, chaotic, aimless, and so on.

8) Constructive quality - Destructive quality:
We talk about quality when the effects inside and / or outside have a certain effect. Psychodynamics can be aggressive or peaceful. It can be destructive or constructive. It can make you sick or promote health. It can cause imbalance or create harmony.

It can be disturbing, contagious or stimulating. It can build bridges or create abysses. It can hold freedom and independence with others or make it dependent and binding. It can be life-affirming or life-diverting. We may also interpret this quality in the sense of Fromm (1979) as biophilia and necrophilia. Freud describes this as the instinct for life and death (see Eissler 1980). We separate from the factual relation (topic of energy) and limit the aspect of psychic energy.

Constructive quality is described as: constructive, stimulating, life-oriented, liberating, and peaceful; and destructive quality is described as destructive, affective, life-diverting, binding, aggressive, acid, and the like.

We regard the diversity of individual differences and possible combinations as "normal" expressive possibilities of the human being. Every human being has his own dynamic pattern, which remains relatively constant throughout many situations or actions. The extreme forms reflect neurosis, psychopathy, and psychosomatics. In the intermediate field, stress is the expression of an overloaded psychodynamic. We do not want to distinguish theoretically between "Eustress" and "Distress" (Selye 1982, 50).

In the vernacular and in the general diagnostic understanding, one understands under stress an overload, a pressure, a long-lasting tension, an overstraining of the psychic forces, and if necessary, a discrepancy between the ability to assimilate and intensity of the "stressors". The causes can be outside and / or inside. Whatever the nature of stress, their basic energy is always the psychic energy, and is formed as a psychodynamic system (Pervin 1993, 493-501). Even in a very relaxed state, every person has their individual psychodynamic characteristics.

We do not understand the sexual energy (libido) as the basic vital force, but as elemental in all manifestations of the formed psychic energy. It should be emphasized that we do not mean chemical and bio-electrical conditions. Our term is psychological, not biological. Of course, sexuality itself, is a subjective body-bound psycho-energetic experience. (see "genital urge" in: Balint 1981, 84). The suppression of sexual relaxation is the source of many mental and psychosomatic disorders (Reich 1976, Lowen 1976, Freud 1961).

Psychoanalysis (of all coinages) has also demonstrated in many ways that some social problems (aggressive behavior, violence, oppression, war) have to do with the suppression of sexuality. 15 years of specific work experience have shown the author enough to say that the suppression of sexuality, and the suppression of sexual relaxation, are serious and causes mental disorders, suffering, and social conflict. However, the energy itself can - to a certain extent - be neutralized genitally and implemented as altruistic behavior. Whether this succeeds, as is often claimed, and whether it is also healthy for humans, is another question. There is the sexual (psychic) energy, the thought energy, the feeling energy, the complex energy, and so on. All these forms of psychic energy, and the appropriate manners of doing so, are vital for the development of personality - in the sense of individuation.

On the sidelines, there is the scientific question of whether these eight dimensions can also be crystallized out of research methodology (for example, factor analysis). The problem starts here when creating the individual items. With the test, the result of the mathematical analysis is already anticipated or limited.

We have created the eight dimensions casually based on our experiences. As a single dimension, they are informative. But the overall picture is fruitful for action measures. Only in the unity of the whole can we create a differentiated picture of a person's psychodynamics. If we interpret stress as the expression of a multi-dimensionally disturbed or burdened psychic energy, then we also have the basis for a differentiated package of measures. Autogenic training, and relaxation hypnosis, only cover aspects of psychodynamics. These eight dimensions are part of practical personality formation.

An example: stress analysis

We characterize stress, based on the previous statements, with the eight dimensions of psychodynamics:

1) High tension
2) Extreme value in extra / introversion
3) Significant psycho-physical vulnerability
4) Unbalanced basic condition
5) High lability
6) Excessive sensitivity or rigidity
7) Disturbed Mass of Force
8) Destructive energy characteristic

It follows that there can be different types of stress, depending on the intrapsychic situation, and the circumstances in the field of life. It is also conceivable that only a single dimension makes the stress and determines the psychodynamics. Every possible situation pattern can lead to other connections. For the detection of stress reactions, we refer to Klupp (1992, 140-142); "Stressors" lectures. (Selye, 1988).

Two possible images of stress are:

a) Example A of a type of stress:

Relaxation - Tension: extremely tense
Extraversion - Introversion: balanced
Psycho-physical reaction: slightly susceptible to failure, and mental powers
Basic condition: tends to be positive, slightly pressed
Lability - Stability: in balanced
Sensitivity - rigidity: sensitive
Power: strong, temporarily inexplicably weakened
Energy quality: predominantly constructive

b) Example B of a type of stress:

Relaxation - Tension: nervous
Extraversion - Introversion: very introverted
Psycho-physical reaction: very susceptible to interference
Basic conditions: dark, heavy
Lability - Stability: unstable
Sensitivity - Rigidity: hypersensitive
Power: weak
Energy quality: aggressive

From these examples, it can be seen that the quality of a stressed psychodynamics can be vastly different. Example A can hardly be an expression of inner psychological stress, while example B must undoubtedly focus on explaining the unconscious and the "state" of the love power, in the depth-psychological vision. How to recognize this?

If the unconscious is reasonably well-adjusted, high lability, at most, is likely under extreme external loads. A gloomy basic condition with simultaneous weak strength, lability, and psycho-physical health, which is very susceptible to interference (effective disturbances) and aggressive energy quality must also have enormous burdens on the inside.

Example A can be kept reasonably balanced, with regular relaxations, while example B alone with autogenic training is not solvable. However, it can be safely improved with personality development.

The ability to manage tension is defined as a criterion for mental health (Becker 1982, 2-13). These include various aspects, all of which have already been widely incorporated into human education or the doctrines of bliss in Greek antiquity. This consider: destruction of repressed emotions, intellectual control (volitional effort) of pleasure impulses, action competences in life situations (in "critical life events"), factual abilities - "to accomplish tasks and roles" - as well as simply to practice inner peace and relaxation. Personality education, in this sense, integrates these aspects.

Effects of tension and relaxation

According to our experiences, with systematic relaxation training, we formulate the following thesis: When the psychic energy is relaxed, all other dimensions are relieved and tend to "normalize".

The basic dynamics of the other seven dimensions must, however, be formed with the formation of the entire personality. The conscious control of one's own behavior, one's own psychic powers, and external influencing factors cannot be replaced by autogenic training. Of course, this also applies to all other methods of relaxation (yoga, progressive muscle relaxation, etc.). There are different levels of psychodynamic care.

Care of psychodynamics is done by:

1) relaxation techniques.

2) Formation of personality in the sense of individuation.

3) Control of daily actions.

4) Control of external factors, as far as possible.

Relaxation techniques, in the sense of formulaic intent formation (autogenic training, suggestion, hypnosis), cause a psycho-physical process that changes the mental energy state, but never the inner psychic systems. Relaxation is a cerebral switching process (Schultz 1973, Rosa 1977, Thomas 1976). Cerebral switching can also be created with imagination.

Autogenic training includes the following relaxation process:
The exercise begins with verbal suggestions (formulas), some of which contain a vague mental idea. This "idea" is internalized concentratively. This requires an inner commitment and consent. The person must accept this "idea". This is followed by an automatic switch according to the suggestion. The next step is a generalization and intensification of the "idea". By training, a conditioning is to be achieved.

A comparison between general relaxation, in terms of autogenic training and hypnosis, shows crucial differences in mental and psycho-physical response. The following table gives an overview, compiled from the literature (Langen 1972, Leuner 1975, Erickson 1978, Chertok 1973, Schultz 1976) as well as from own work protocols
State of the parameter "Relaxation" and "Hypnosis" – Comparison of the individual differences:

Psycho-physical	Deep relaxation	Hypnose

Reactions		level
Time warp	easily	yes
Reduced	wakefulness	easily yes
Narrowing field of consciousness	yes	yes
Of consciousness	no	yes
Fatigue	easily	yes
Partial sleep	no	yes
Somnolence (calm)	yes	yes
Somnambulism	no	yes
Emotional responsiveness	yes	yes
Heat experience	yes	yes
Changed voice quality	no	yes
Retardation of reflexes	easily	yes
Changed body feeling	yes	yes
Heavy arms, legs	yes	yes
Loss of body feeling	no	yes
Musculature immobilization	no	yes *
Delayed psych motility	no	yes
Catalepsy of the musculature	no	yes *
Concealed hearing	yes	yes
Reduced function of the senses	no	yes
Lowered sensitivity	easily	yes
Vegetative balance	yes	yes
Normalized heart activity	yes	yes
Lowered blood pressure	yes	yes
Slowed breathing	yes	yes
Illusion v. Body distortion	no	yes *
Feeling out of things	no	yes *
Reduced exercise reminder	no	yes *
Hypermnesia to prenatal time	yes	yes
Regression behavior	no	yes *
Reinforced dream-like consciousness	no	yes
Increased suggestibility (psycho-physical)	yes	yes
Rapport bond (willingness to sacrifice)	easily	yes
Reduced self-constriction	no	yes
Reduced ego control in introspection	no	yes

* = yes with increasing hypnotic depth

The difference between a deep relaxation and a hypnosis is produced by specific suggestions, during and after the relaxation phase. Andragogy has no specific constitutive interest in hypnosis for personality development. For the possible interventions, in the condition of medium to deep hypnosis, relate primarily to therapeutic objectives (Schultz 1976, Langen 1972). Self-knowledge and individuation, including the catharsis of the unconscious, do not require hypnosis. A deep relaxation is sufficient for all depths of the personal unconscious, including returns until prenatal. The main goal of general psycho-physical relaxation is the immobilization and harmonization of psychodynamics.

Next, the state of relaxation is the prerequisite for so-called mental training, i. the suggestive practice of formulaic intentions for reinforcement and training in learning processes. Mental training is learning based on one's own psychic powers with optimal focus of a content in consciousness.

The mental training accomplishes:

☐ Increase concentration and attention
☐ An increase of the memory
☐ Reinforcing concentrated willpower
☐ Mobilization of positive self-amplifiers
☐ Imprint of new adjustment patterns
☐ Conditioning (reconditioning) of reflexes
☐ Psycho-hygiene (daily events in the evening "adopt")
☐ Increasing the flexibility of consciousness (letting go of content)
☐ Activation of new impulses for creative solutions
☐ Reinforcement of specific thought-forces

Hypnosis is important for research on parapsychic powers, such as clairvoyance and telepathy - in andragogy. Hypnosis is also a prerequisite for so-called body exits and out of body experiences. However, these are forms of experience that are associated with considerable (often underestimated) dangers. Basically, we can ask from our own experimental experiences whether one should enter foreign realities if one does not have the authority from there, but this cannot define a clear goal (action task) and one cannot concentrate in it and control it in a self-responsible way? We will not go into that here.

In this context, the psycho-strategies of NLP (Neuro-Linguistic Programming) for reflection, are briefly presented here (see: Bandler / MacDonald 1991, Grinder / Bandler 1991).

Firstly, NLP technology is based on the fact that the ego does not want to see reality as it really is. The reality presented must, therefore, stand out clearly. It must be simple, intense, soft, warm, and lovingly designed. Movements should be simple, harmonious, and purposeful. This also applies to words. Repetitions, in variations reinforce.

Second, there are some perceptual psychological laws about what automatically enters the consciousness, even if it is not wanted by the ego. "Eye-catching" is clear bright or soft colors, slightly enlarged dimensions of the focused objects, pleasant and soothing beautiful naive pictures, a rather calm focused action, emphasized proportions, and of course a clear frame. At the same time, simple melodies penetrate the ear.

Third, the dynamics of the unconscious has a central function. There are the repressed needs (deficits), the secret longings, the urgent wishes, and the ideals about life. Anyone who can address and activate them, with catchy, simple, and lovingly warm images, will make people feel. Feelings are known to activate psychic energy.

Fourth, the NLP strategy also requires the techniques of suggestion and hypnosis: what one wants to enter must be brought to light, be soft, calm, warm-hearted, and connecting. There are many proven language patterns. The aim of the strategy is to create trust through emotional attention (rapport), to awaken hope through positive vision, to stimulate the self through positive amplifiers, and to consolidate the "rapport" - through a structured communication situation. Autogenic training is an example of the psycho-physical response. A suggestion ("arms very warm") causes a physical reaction (dilation of the blood vessels and thus the heat experience).

The fifth principle, which, together with Pavlov's stimulus-response reflex, has a significant functional meaning: what was at first, only a picture with a simple message, receives a physical reaction at the target of the manipulation process.

This brain-physiological and then often organic (or muscular) reaction then acts as a real impulse for action: the presented product is bought! The desired television channel is set, and the ego goes where the stimulus sets the direction.

The most important facts about relaxation techniques:
1. Relaxation techniques aim to relax the psychic energy. Relaxation always affects all dimensions of psychodynamics. Relaxation affects the entire psycho-energetic system: balancing, building, strengthening, and stabilizing.

2. Relaxation techniques are not psychoanalytic procedures. This means that neither complexes in the unconscious, nor "wrong" thought patterns (attitudes), nor behavioral habits, nor the personality as a unit are analyzed.

3. Relaxation techniques are not psychotherapeutic treatments. They heal neither neuroses nor disorders, nor psychopathic personality structures. However, they can reduce such a burden or compensate for something.

4. Relaxation techniques are means to balance the entire psychodynamic. Thus, favorable conditions can be created for: learning processes, self-reflection, psychiatrists, unfolding, growth of the inner life, balance of life, building inner stability, strengthening the will and the ego, positive self-experiences, and building self-confidence.

5. Relaxation techniques indirectly have a healing significance. They bring about a stabilization of the physical organism and increase the psycho-energetic load limit, whereby self-healing powers become more effective.

6. Relaxation techniques are not intended to create transcendental experiences. They have nothing to do with religion. Relaxation is, however, a prerequisite for contemplative - and therefore also transcendental - experiences.

7. Relaxation techniques are part of an andragogic life practice. Their philosophy includes a vision of life, where relaxation or the "hygiene" of psychodynamics belongs to the quality of life.

8. Relaxation techniques are not hypnosis and not self-hypnosis. However, the induction of a hypnotic state always begins with relaxation and the hypnotic state is always a state of relaxation.

9. Relaxation techniques are part of psychotherapeutic interventions, e.g. suggestions, returning to childhood, and psycho-catharsis. Relaxation techniques may also support andragogic counseling, e.g. in crises and conflicts.

10. Relaxation techniques are andragogic practices, built into holistic personality development.

4. The I (me, ego) and the control mechanisms

The subsystem of the supportive functions

What is the "me"? We use this word daily in all sorts of situations and contexts, such as: "I think", "I feel", "I am", "I want", "I do", "I know", "I love", and "I hope". Obviously, we mean, first our psycho-physical wholeness, even if it is not included in the sentence. "I am myself" means that the ego is aware of itself, thinking, wishing, and acting (Scharfetter 1976, 36). Because if someone says, "I think", of course, not the whole person thinks. For example, the word "I" initially means nothing other than something that could be described as the "center of consciousness", the "conscious highest authority" of this psycho-physical entity.

In a spoken picture, the ego is the captain of the ship (this wholeness). We want to consider the self as a controlling instance. Following Jaspers, we can distinguish three aspects of the ego: the activity, the unity, and the continuity of identity (Barz 1977, 24). Another aspect (according to Neumann 1955) is that "the ego is the center of consciousness". The ego is the central instance of a primary subsystem containing the so-called auxiliary functions. These auxiliary functions are the actual control mechanisms on which the use of all other subsystems is based. Of course, the other subsystems are also at the service of the ego.

Scharfetter (1976, 36) sees the ego as follows: "The ego makes the waking, conscious, and clear-sighted person, who knows about himself, who is correct, judges, perceiving, wishing, needy, driven, demanding, feeling, thinking, acting in the world, and has continuity of his life story."

In psychoanalytic ego-psychology, there are various theoretical constructs. We quote some fragments of Freud from his work "Psychology of the Unconscious" (1923): "The ego can also be unconscious ... An individual is now for us a psychic id, unrecognized and unconscious, and the ego sits superficially on it. The ego represents what one can call reason and prudence. In contrast, the id contains the passions ... The ego, in relation to the id, resembles the rider- who is supposed to restrain the superior power of the horse ... The ego is to differentiate between self-ideal and superego .... We summarize the core as: The task of the ego is to establish a relationship with the outside world, to the id, and to the super-ego, to mediate claims and dangers. "The ego (is) the real field to which our (psychoanalytic) observation must constantly be directed" (Anna Freud 1973, 9).

Sándor Ferenczi (1978, 223-224) describes the ego ideal as "the model that is set up in its interior to measure all its actions and qualities". "This ego ideal takes on the most important functions of reality testing, moral conscience, introspection, and censorship of the mind. It is also the power that is at work in creating the 'unconscious repressed' so important to neurosis." The "identification" contributes to this: "In this process, objects of the world and of AES, are imaginarily 'incorporated' or, as we would say, introjected, that is, their properties are annexed and attributed to their own ego."

Jung writes about the development of the ego. He suggests, "Intellectually, the self is nothing but a psychological concept and a construction, which is supposed to express an entity. This, we do not recognize it as something we can grasp ... It could just as well be called 'the god in us'! Humanity has not progressed... The overcoming of the Law falls only to those who understand it. The one who completes individuation feels as the object of an unknown and superior subject (ie, God; Author) "(1971, 134-138).

And finally, to the extended view, philosophers describe the ego as follows: "The ego is the pole on which all states of consciousness are oriented" (Husserl). "So that I can become, you are necessary a condition" (Buber). "The extinction of the ego is the highest" achievement (Schopenhauer). "The ego is a unitary reference point, last carrier, and active source of reason" (Lotz).

This subsystem of helper functions contains:

☐ The consciousness
☐ The self-confidence
☐ The defense functions
☐ The integration forces

☐ The will / willing
☐ The controller

In the practical formation of personality, the individual auxiliary functions can be taken as orientation for a first "inventory" in general questions. With an extended question the first subjectively experienced educational needs can be directly inquired. The questions require the knowledge of the individual topics.

Questions about self-knowledge are:

1. a) How do you experience yourself?
   b) How would you like to experience yourself?
2. a) How do you experience other people?
   b) How would you like to experience other people?
3. a) How do you experience goods and things?
   b) How would you like to experience the goods and things?
4. a) How do you experience the world?
   b) How would you like to experience the world?
5. a) How do you experience the spiritual?
   b) How would you like to experience something spiritual?
6. a) How do you experience your willpower?
   b) How would you like to experience your willpower?
7. a) How do you experience your defense functions?
   b) How would you like to experience your defensive functions?
8. a) How do you experience your integration dynamics?
   b) How would you like to experience your integration dynamics?
9. a) How do you experience your control?
   b) How would you like to experience your control?

Consciousness and Reality

How consciousness comes about cannot be said to date by physiological psychology (Becker-Carus 1981, 119). We can thus mean "the totality of our ego experiences" (Leibnitz) or, in the sense of Herbart, the "sum of all real and simultaneously present ideas." Jaspers spoke of the "stage on which psychic phenomena occur and go." We choose that largely familiar picture "screen." In this screen we find all kinds of realities.

The reality that people perceive on a daily basis contains some significant outstanding characteristics. These are:

- The personal living space
- The moment, the hour, the day
- Especially external appearances
- Tendencies of gross overall impressions
- Predominantly your own everyday reality
- Ostensible psychic life
- Pleasure-related values
- The erupting emotional experience
- The vague surface

These realities "fill" the entire consciousness. If we think of consciousness as a "screen" then it means that this screen always stays the same size and the perceived reality always fills the whole field of consciousness. The formal characteristics are: narrowness and breadth, selective attention, and concentrated attention.

The image, which shows itself in the consciousness as the reality, experience the humans as the reality. But reality, which man has excluded from his perception, is also his reality. The ego has no access to this part of the excluded reality. The ego orients itself for its action at the perceived content and at the experience of this consciousness.

We expand the context: consciousness - unconsciousness - knowledge – ignorance.

What man does not know, he is not aware of! There are many realities that people do not want to see. He does not want any knowledge about that. We call this state "not knowing" or "being ignorant". Man can know something and "push" that knowledge out of his consciousness and displace into the unconscious. There are many realities that man sees and displaces immediately or later. "Living unconsciously" means everyday language does not get into the consciousness, and, to a certain extent live without being aware of the realities and consequences. For example, do not feel, not see, or not hear.

The terms "ignorant" and "unconscious" must be clearly separated. We see the following distinction as helpful. "Ignorant" means that he individual does not have the knowledge. "Unconsciously" means that the ego acts without reference to a possible consciousness, so to speak, outside of the consciousness. The term "unconscious" also has its central significance in connection with the unconscious.

Censorship mechanisms control what is received into the consciousness and what needs to be discarded from the consciousness. Again, this term has its specific meaning, especially in connection with the unconscious. We understand these mechanisms of censorship as the controlling authority that allows or disregards events in the consciousness or the acceptance or rejection of facts, thoughts, feelings, and emotions of any kind.

Theses on coping with realities

Thesis 1: There are inner and outer realities.

Thesis 2: Many people neglect the inner realities and "see" the external reality very subjectively.

Thesis 3: There are many realities for every person but hardly anyone wants to see them. They are not conscious.

Thesis 4: There are so many, and so precise, realities for humans, as they absorb and process realities.

Thesis 5: Rarely, people realize that many internal factors influence the reception and processing of realities. Only what is in the consciousness, they consider real.

Thesis 6: There are many words about every inner and outer reality. But words are only labels with - not infrequently - different meanings.

Thesis 7: When people talk to each other, they seldom realize that:
☐ Every person in consciousness has his own reality.
☐ Each person has his own vocabulary.
☐ Every person experiences many words in their own way.
☐ Everyone thinks in their own way.

Thesis 8: Man generally has little awareness of his performance and the performance errors of his own psychic functions.

Thesis 9: The psycho-spiritual realities of man make man human. And these varied realities do not see people only as inadequate.

Thesis 10: Coping with life can never have more quality than the individual psychic powers are consciously formed.

We distinguish three levels for personality development:

1. Man does not have the knowledge of the psychic powers. He has not learned what important things there are to know about living from the psychic systems.

2. Man does not want to take the work of the ego into consciousness. Again, there is a problem of knowledge first. Man needs knowledge to arrive at this distinction.

3. Man does not want to allow much of what he knows (or knew) into his consciousness. The knowledge is repressed into the unconscious. Again, there is a knowledge problem: Man does not know how the material can be retrieved from the unconscious. By itself, much of it does not return to consciousness, even when the ego's strong desire is present.

Self-confidence and self-expression

What does the ego know about itself and its entirety? What does the ego have for an "awareness of existence" (Jaspers 1956, 110) about itself? In general, people do not know 90 to 95 percent of their psychic powers. Most people do not have a differentiated awareness of their inner-psychic reality. This has different causes:

The school does not provide any knowledge or inner experience about the psychic reality. Even in the home, most people learn little or nothing about it. People are educated - as toddlers - not to notice this inner world and not to take it seriously. Everyone learns to suppress the forces of inner life. To let those forces, pass over them, and to make life without them, with the exception, are simple thinking operations. Religion and politics do not teach this inner reality either. Every day, life is geared to outward values and facts. It is always important to first see what is outside. The human in our society should not have any problems. Those who are in difficulties, with themselves, often cause a distancing from their fellow human beings. The zeitgeist, and the general norms in society, urge people to adapt to this "problem-free" self-image.

Further causes for the lack of internal perception include: no one likes to see himself with his fears, with his unhappiness, with his failure, with his inability, and with his crises. Consumer goods, careers, and lust for life, attract and cover what man is essentially. This being a creature that can only do what it has learned and as a personality is what education has shaped through life. What man perceives about himself in this conditional field of force is only a small part of his actual reality.

We explicitly do not develop any theory of the "self." "Self" has a reflective meaning here. From the context it becomes apparent what "self" refers to. The self is not a psychic function, as is often claimed in psychology, unless one calls the content of the consciousness - that the individual has over himself - as such a psychic function. A realistic and comprehensive self-image is not self-evident. This requires versatile activities and, above all, learning processes.

The realistic self-image is based on:

- The want to expand self-image
- An acquired knowledge
- Consciously recognizing feelings
- Keeping social adjustment flexible
- Viewing and edit the defrauded
- Making the suppressed conscious
- "Fate" (life) to answer for
- Taking mental life seriously
- Willingness to learn
- Readiness for self-education
- Openness to self-critical perception
- Learning inner orientation as a method
- Wanting development and growth

To see, you must want to see. If you do not want to see, you do not see what is there. Above all, this includes looking behind the "facades" and "masks". Most people see predominantly this elevated reality and not the underlying. Here is the question of "who / what am I actually?". This central question of self-knowledge must always first threaten the ego in the state of ignorance and unconsciousness. Developing a realistic and comprehensive self-image requires courage, too.

According to Kohut (1973), the "self" is the sum of the contents of ego, id and superego. Hartmann (1972) equates "self" with "person". Others (such as Jung) understand the "self" as the sum of psychic phenomena in humans. Battegay interprets the "self" as the "central representation in ego, id, and superego that represents self-worth experience." (1979, 30) None of the definitions makes it clear whether it is conscious content or the totality of all mental functions that can be conscious.

If one extends the (obsolete) psychoanalytic model of Freud (ego, id, superego) to our total psychic system, then the "self" would be identical to the term "personality". However, we find it more practicable for the scientific discussion to understand the "self" as the sum of those parts that an individual consciously refers to as himself, whereby the set of parts cannot always be clearly delimited. This paraphrase of the term "self" does not imply a theoretical construction but is a classification.

"Self-consciousness", in fact, does not mean the "size" or "strength" of the ego, but in substance. All that man knows about himself is self-esteem. "Self" has a reflective meaning here. The ego of the human being has free access and a free disposition of the psychic powers as far as the realities of the ego are concerned, and that I have knowledge about.

When we say "the ego acts unconsciously", this generally means that the ego acts without knowledge of the individual psychic powers, and at the same time, does not want to have this reference back to the knowledge about it or is not aware of the possibility of knowing. This also applies to the living space. With regards to facts in the living environment, man can act unconsciously, as he does not (or does not want to) have certain relevant knowledge, but in most cases could easily have it.

The essence of the idea is that the ego has its own momentum, which urges us not to have differentiated consciousness, because this consciousness means duty, responsibility, and challenge. And vice versa because the unconscious lifestyle works superficially easier. The ego reacts here decisively, due to the constructed self-esteem. This value forms from prenatal time (see Balint 1981, 232-245). We know that consciousness always threatens self-worth because it is always "guilty" towards the ego. The ego of the self-experience concerns the ego existentially, so to speak, at the roots of existence (Scharfetter 1976, 36-39).

The self-living varies every day, often every hour, and is always an approximation to or a part of the whole. You can never fully experience yourself in one moment. Consciousness always has a focal point. The daily routine, the external conditions, and the psychically activated life determine this focal point and the content of self-experience. Self-living can be recorded qualitatively and quantitatively:

The I-experience has different qualities and modes of action. The experience of the ego is usually not very conscious as it has little language and little reflection. Nevertheless, the ego-consciousness is characterized by it. The ego experience can be divided into four aspects:

1. I experience myself: "I am here." This includes:

☐ My existence is unique, lively, good, useful, and challenging.

☐ My existence is myself and world design possibility.
☐ My physical existence offers many opportunities.

2. I experience myself: "That's me". This includes:

☐ I am individual, unmistakable, and unique.
☐ I have a great richness inside and out.
☐ I am my life opportunity, with my wholeness.

3. I experience myself: "I am separated from you and the world". This means:

☐ I am me; the other is the other; the world is the world.
☐ I can take my place in the world and live like everyone else.
☐ I can make the world a living space, just like any human being.

4. I experience myself: "I am meaning and value"; that means:

☐ I am meaningful, valuable, good, and interesting.
☐ I myself am my highest sense of being.
☐ I myself am my highest life value.

Self-living recreates the first basic attitude:

☐ Interest and disinterest
☐ More and little
☐ Integration and defense
☐ Objectivity and impropriety
☐ Care and neglect
☐ Truthfulness and lies
☐ Action and idleness
☐ Attention and avoidance
☐ Relationship and unrelatedness
☐ Responsibility and irresponsibility
☐ Seriousness and indifference
☐ Openness and closeness
☐ Competence and incompetence
☐ Respect and recklessness
☐ Consideration and neglect
☐ Growth / unfolding and blocking
☐ Constructivity and destructiveness

Ways of defense and patterns of reaction

The relationship between consciousness and defense mechanisms can be characterized as follows (see Freud Anna 1936, Battegay 1973, 99-149): Consciousness is like a screen. The contents of consciousness are the images and the language. The screen is always the same size and is always filled, with much or little content. The content is the subjective reality. Anything that is unpleasant to the ego, for whatever reason, is repressed into the unconscious. Much of what a person perceives, with their senses, does not appear clearly in the screen of consciousness, but is directly deported into the unconscious. The less the human being absorbs the existing reality as it is, the more the content of consciousness is distorted in meaning, in scope and in value. Some things seem too big in the consciousness and others too small. The unconscious preserves what the ego does not "like" and has therefore been removed from consciousness.

In psychoanalysis the following classic defense mechanisms are discussed:

a) Regression: self-punishment, self-devaluation, withdrawal, reduction, neglect, isolation, and intolerance.

b) Displacement: projection, identification, compensation, inversion, acting, undoing, decomposing, and symptom formation.

c) Defense: averting, denying (ignoring), rejecting, disfiguring, moving away, superimposing, forgetting, discarding, and rationalizing.

Man lives in constant psychic dynamics between pleasure and aversion. What he does not "like" always means pain. The inner and outer realities often cause discomfort, resulting in tension. This would create an imbalance that the ego seeks to avoid. Hardly, does anyone, learn to overcome this balance disorder in school or at home. Due to the lack of learning processes, man regulates this balance with the mechanisms of defense, regression, and displacement. With this, man creates distance to his inner world and to the real world outside. But that is never a solution. Misconduct, but also frustration and guilt are the consequences. These effects must then be kept away with defense. The cycle becomes destructive and difficult to reverse.

The persistence of the ego in relative unconsciousness has a special andragogic meaning. One can say that there is no evolution, without degradation of the unconscious (Neumann 1971). At the same time, this perseverance, in the unconscious, always has destructive or regressive consequences. Projection is the natural mechanism that always ensures that the repressed and self-contained (which is kept away from the consciousness) always opposes the ego outside in the world, in objects, in people, or in another form (Jung 1971) , 1973). Projection is the mechanism that "forces" man to face the repressed or defended the thing outside. This can be in mythology, in religion, or simply in everyday life with another person or object. Projection does not actually mean defense but forced attachment to the defensive in the outside world.

The consequence is that the stronger, and the more frequently the human being lives in projections, the lower his psychic-spiritual developmental stage. Projection means one's own mental feature or psychic reality in a person This means it is: unconsciously transmitted to a person, perceived as a characteristic (property) of this person, and the projection process can also be done on something.

In very general terms, "other people's psychic powers are interpreted as a function of their own tendencies" (Meili / Steingrüber 1978, 44).

There are three variants of the projection:

Variant 1: The characteristic transmitted by person A is objectively not in person B or thing B. Man B or thing B are projection fields on which something of their own is perceived.

Variant 2: Person B or substance B arouses the impression of containing the characteristic that displaces person A, due to special peculiarities through an associative link.

Variant 3: The element transferred from A to B is also present at B objectively.

Projection is not simply a classical defense mechanism, as psychoanalysis teaches. Rather, in this psychic function, we see a force that works according to nature. This is in direct proportion to the force we call "integration". For reasons of scientific tradition, and because the projection is related to the defense mechanisms, we have this function in the field of defense mechanisms.

The defense mechanisms are intrapsychic functions. They are also the "putting on of masks". The presentation of facades and the creation of scenes (with furniture, clothes, and goods of all kinds) contain defense function. In many forms of communication, defense is reflected. The purpose does not always have to be in the organization of one's own content of consciousness. The "play of the masks" has an enormous meaning in the social handling. Here we are in the middle of the topic "lie". Freud called psychoanalysis a work against the lie (self-lie).

Defense mechanisms, and such forms of lies, complicate life and cause enormous damage. They force people to live against the power of love and against the spirit. This is evolution regression, and not progression. Comprehensive personal development means, among other things, removing the masks and learning to live consciously.

We have referred to the functions of defense, repression, and projection on the background of traditional psychoanalytic theories. It remains to be mentioned that perception research opens new aspects of observation for this purpose. The human brain stores the millions of information recorded by the perception in patterns and blurry pictures. If one looks at an already stored image, an interaction arises between the newly perceived information and the patterns present in the brain cells (Vester 1991, 144-147). Knowledge does not arise here through analytical thinking, but through holistic perception.

One question concerns the interplay of perception and the function of defense, repression, and projection. Another problem arises for human education: How to organize analytical and / or holistic cognitive processes? Or in other words, how can the analytic process of knowing psychic life be extended with holistic working methods? "Psychoanalysis" as a term, and working method, has to be developed in the context of the scientific findings on cybernetic perception and cybernetic learning.

Andragogy will have to focus on new, scientifically sound methodology for the targeting of education and the organization of learning processes.

The defense mechanisms are treated in depth psychology as an intrapsychic process, and in classical psychoanalysis as "censorship mechanisms". If we consider the action of man, then we can recognize the entire variety of defense mechanisms in behavior or in the relationship between behavior and conscious ego-leadership. Quite descriptive, and without judging, we recognize in human behavior many forms of disfiguring, lying, acting, dodging, mixing, "pushing" (in the sense of projection), regressing, undoing, reversing to the opposite, and so on. People put on masks and make facades to play.

Apparently, defense mechanisms not only have the function to regulate the content in the consciousness, but also to manipulate the inner and especially the outer reality purposefully. To our knowledge, this teleological function has not worked up psychoanalysis. The theme was philosophically reflected by Macchiavelli (1469-1527) and later by Lenin (1870-1924). This situation, that is, the disfiguring handling of reality, is not only psychologically relevant to any theory of action, but also, in particular, to philosophical anthropology, and thus of fundamental importance to Andragogy.

Integration: Forms of coping with reality

The elimination of repression, projection, and rejection of consciousness is done by turning to reality. It is also through the integration of the actual inner and outer reality. Integration means to cultivate, to affirm, to have an interest, to exercise patience, to mediate, to cope, to establish a relationship, to turn, to consider, and so on. We will discuss that ultimately only the power of love can develop the capacity for integration. The psychoanalytic term "introjection" primarily means what we call "integration." Integration means life-giving. This is the opposite of what the defense mechanisms do. The outer and inner reality is integrated. Integration captures the past, the present and the prospective future.

Suitable forms of perception of reality and coping with reality are:

- Apply
- Look
- To become conscious
- Accept
- Give the appropriate value
- To perceive comprehensively
- Be tolerant and understanding
- Reconcile yourself with reality
- Accept yourself
- Maintain
- Protect
- Unfold
- Act objectively competent
- Be realistic and real
- Consciously self-directed
- Take responsibility
- Consider
- Process

The more the human being supports the activities of integration, the more they diminish: life lies, defense mechanisms, resistances of all kinds, habits, compensation, conversion, projection, alienation, aggression, frustration, fears, guilt, illusions, manipulations, as well as dogmatic and fundamentalist thinking.

The valuable individual and collective consequences are clear. The mental and psychosomatic illnesses decrease. Aggression of all kinds, especially violence is reduced. The accident rates are lower. Wars are almost impossible. At the same time, individual happiness increases. People live authenticity and truthfully. Psychic life becomes the central reality, which needs to be nurtured and developed.

In general, the psychic life becomes as important as the external life. With the appropriate skills, a balanced approach, and through comprehensive integration, people can learn to resolve and solve their problems and difficulties at the right pace. Integration of the realities of life is fundamental work of personality development. That's part of our vision.

A simple systematic compilation of forces into a system model, shows that the ego is overwhelmed when the individual has not learned how to coordinate and balance all these forces. The philosophy and pedagogy of earlier decades and centuries see the solution in the term "morality" and "conscience education". Christian human education still speaks of "conscience education". Religions have delivered their dogmas and politics an ideology with the human image of the "responsible citizen". This was, and still is, trying to solve the dilemma of the ego - from the outside with education, threats, and coercion. But this is at the expense of consciousness and self-reflection. The solution, from the point of view of personality formation, as we present it here, requires the formation of psychic powers through conscious grasping and understanding, and through integration and life with responsibility.

Will and habits

The use of life presupposes conscious decision of the will. The will, and thus the willing, is another auxiliary function of the ego. Psychology speaks of "wanting" because it cannot identify the will as a psychic force (Barz 1976, 167).

We understand will and willing as one unit of meaning. Modern psychology understands willing as a driving force, whereas in the past the will was interpreted as being close to moral formation. Will, on the one hand, is seen as an instinctual life; on the other can, it also contains mental content. We define will as a construct in the context of ego control (Düker 1975). To this end, some theses are formulated:

Thesis 1: The ability to will (want to) is vitally important in life.

Thesis 2: The more man, unconsciously, lives in a drive-oriented manner, the less able he is to perceive and use his capacity for will.

Thesis 3: The will (or willing) can be learned and trained.

Thesis 4: The life that is not integrated into the consciousness is usually stronger than the will power.

Thesis 5: The freedom of man is never greater than his will.

Thesis 6: Habits are often stronger than the will.

Habits include: schemes, inflexible mechanisms, time fixations, and ground patterns. Habits often replace the conscious act of will. They therefore harbor various dangers in themselves, including:

- [ ] Habits hinder inner consciously lived freedom.
- [ ] Habits slow impulses to learn new things, and to change existing ones.
- [ ] Habits reduce responsibility and conscious self-control.
- [ ] Habits promote stagnation, rigidity, inertia, and passivity.
- [ ] Habits tighten creativity and intuition.

Düker (1983) experimentally investigated volition, based on the theory of Wilhelm Wundt and others, who say that highly practiced daily activities are originally dependent on the will, and as a result of frequent repetition they are later transformed into reflexes and thus run independently of the will. Düker defines: "Want is the ability to purposefully coordinate, activate, and control all processes necessary to achieve a goal.

The psychological processes upon which willing is based are self-interest, striving (desire), decision-making (decision-making), and activating. Also necessary for wanting is a concrete goal (1983, p. 13). The distinguishing criterion for volition and reflexes is the ability to be influenced by other actions occurring at the same time (1983, 17).

Wishing is in experienced actions a "subliminal psychic process", which is no longer clearly perceptible due to lower intensity. The result of the investigation is clear: "Action does not transform actions into reflexive movements; meaning, the (still today) prevailing conception of the reflex character, of high-performance activities, of daily life is untenable (1983, 101, 104). Düker assumes that every action, even the seeming will-free action, is subliminally controlled by volition, for example, facial movements, finger movements, vegetative reactions, and perception.

Will understood as "realizing intentions" implies various mental activities and processes (phases). Gollwitzer describes four phases: motivation, fractional volition, actional volition and post genetic motivation (evaluation) (see in: Heckhausen 1989, 212). Monitoring and overcoming obstacles are partial aspects of the will, such as the actual "fiat", which is the initiation of the action of the execution.

Such research results are of considerable importance for human education. Formation of will therefore implies: clear goal-setting, high interest, clear desire, determination, and activation energy. The central disturbing factor is the distraction by another simultaneous action. Formation of the willpower, therefore, happens indirectly through concentrated formation of these individual psychic powers. Change of unsuitable patterns of action thus requires: identification of the subliminal goals, the hidden interest, the unconscious desire, the original determination, and activation energy. Then comes the confrontation with desirable alternatives, and finally the deliberate concentrated practice of new ways of acting. The analysis of "critical event situations" offers the starting point. The formation of will in the context of the action analysis is elementary in the formation of personality.

I-Control (self-control)

The self - as a steering authority - has to fulfill different tasks. These include: to establish a relationship to the living space, to manage life, to direct one's own wholeness, and to tune and control all the forces of action on the ego. In a sense, the ego stands as a mediating and controlling authority between the psychic inner world and the outer world. The less awareness man has about these two worlds, the more he must navigate through habitual patterns.

The decisive step, that the ego almost naturally wants to avoid, is self-responsibility in the ego control. But this is essential for a progressive and constructive life. No matter how human live, it always has consequences. Man creates his living conditions in which he then must live. He is born into living conditions and can increasingly participate in shaping them. If he does not take responsibility, then he can only "explain" and endure the consequences with "fate", "God's will", or with some fatalistic patterns of thinking. But this in turn promotes the defense against reality, with which he seeks to evade responsibility even more.

The ego control not only contains opportunities but enables a truly creative and exciting life. Man can be captain of his own ship. He determines his itinerary. He arranges his life ship in such a way that love can also grow. Self-control begins daily with the awakening. Throughout the day, man holds his rudder in his hand. In the evening, perhaps tired from work, he still has the wheel to hold in his hand. Man always keeps his life safely in his hands with his conscious ego control. This includes: watching television or reading a newspaper, eating and talking, driving or recovering, relaxing with others and at parties or at the regular's table in the restaurant.

What more could man want for freedom than to hold his life's tax firmly in his hands? This means that attention is required in all sub-steps and areas, including, concentration, reduction of disturbances, and environment control (Meili / Steingrüber 1978, 128).

5. The Functions of Intelligence

The main four functions

Life without the functions of intelligence is not possible. Everything starts with perception. Every reality is expressed by the human being. Thought processes the perceived reality and stores it in memory. Every human being has his own way of judging reality and the result of thought. The underlying values and value orientations are very versatile. Cognitive learning processes result from the use of intelligence functions. What man takes into his consciousness also depends on how he uses his intelligence functions. The intelligence functions are not a contrast and no alternative to the functions of the mind, the feelings, the love, and the unconscious. All psychic subsystems complement each other, and can only be constructive, if this interaction is constructively possible. If man uses his intelligence functions a little, then his coping with the world is less constructive. How a person lives, and sees himself, depends essentially on the performance of intelligence.

Considering the andragogic interests, we group the main functions of intelligence, bearing in mind that there are a variety of different models of intelligence (Meili / Steingrüber 1978).

- Perception and experience
- Language (in thinking and in communication)
- Thinking and judgments (values)
- Cognitive learning (through the language and thought processes)

We want to work on the main functions of intelligence step by step. But it cannot be the goal to scientifically unroll all aspects of intelligence, including speech patterns and memory. Our orientation is the practical formation of personality. We want to leave it open to whether this division into four areas will do justice to all aspects of intelligent assets. The classification has a practical purpose in the first place.

Perception, experience, and their subjective factors

Perception includes the various perceptual functions. Perception is a complex physiological and psychological process (Lück 1986, 88-113, Barz 1977, 40-49, Scharfetter 119-123, Becker-Carus 1981). We are dealing with the psychological process of perception. For every person, it is the reality that they experience, because of their perception. Gestalt psychology deals with perception. Central insight is that perception forms so-called "templates", that not individual stimulus fragments are consciously perceived and stored in memory, but a wholeness. Perception is stimulus processing. It differentiates and structures the stimuli. Memory enables classification, comparison, and weighting. According to Barz (1977) "sensations" are "unconscious perceptions". According to Dorsch (1987) the "simple experience of a life is stimulation on a sense organ". Memory and engram formation are discussed in connection with the unconscious.

In general, sensory functions are: seeing, hearing, smelling, tasting, feeling, balance, and sensing movement. We should also mention the inner perception (James). Bandler and MacDonald (1971, 64-68) describe the sub modalities and distinguish between auditory, visual, and kinesthetic perception. Perception is at the same time an interpretive experience. For example, "phenomenal causality," is where a succession of movements is interpretatively causally perceived (Merleau-Ponty, 1974).

Seeing: the fact is that man does not simply see what comes to his attention. At the moment of seeing, the censorship mechanism can discard those elements of reality that should not be included in consciousness. Seeing can also happen "unconsciously", meaning, what you see does not remain in your consciousness. Seeing is also dependent on hearing, feeling, smelling, tasting, thinking, and remembering. Thus, the individual can also see superficially, intense, and pale. Man sees things differently, depending on whether he is open or closed, positive or negative. One can also see, in a sense, as an observer or as a participant.

Listening: The qualities of hearing are many. The scale ranges from loud to soft, melodic or unvoiced, fast or slow, rhythmic or monotone. Each sound can, for example, be recorded harmonic or disharmonious. What is heard is usually a message that is often connected to the situation experience and what is stored.

Feeling: This kind of perception has different qualities and depends on different factors. Feeling is internally and externally oriented. It can be intense or weak, continuous or unsteady, selective or unfiltered.

Feeling, is bound to the body: this means an experience. This includes smelling and tasting. The feelings of feelings, we call bodily perception, because with very many feelings, the whole body is in "vibration" or a feeling just in the body (in the stomach, in the chest) is experienced.

Kinesthetic perception: Motion perception has different qualities. We have described these in part in the experience of relaxation and autogenic training. The quality can be strong or weak, short lived or longer lasting. The corresponding physical sensation can be pleasant or unpleasant. Psycho-physical reactions and the experience of movement are also holistically stored situationally. Kinesthetic perception is not understood in psychology as a physiological functional sense such as seeing and hearing. Various sensory elements are components of kinesthetic perception. As a muscular sensation, and a feeling of movement, this perception could also be classified in the category of "Feeling".

Inner perception: The individual can see, hear, smell, taste and feel inward. The quality is also very variable: light-dark, loud-quiet, warm-cold, good-bad, pleasant-unpleasant, differentiated-inaccurate, and superficial-deep. Imagination and dream experience, as well as daydreams, are inner perceptions.

Perception of all kinds is the beginning of all mental functioning. As soon as this perception comes to consciousness, intelligence has the first function of the assignment of language and mental processing. Perception is a complex process, especially because this process involves many components and sets different forces in motion. We note some aspects of this.

Characteristic aspects of perception:

☐ Is a prerequisite for knowledge
☐ Is limited by perceptual grid
☐ Activates emotions
☐ Is influenced by the current emotional state
☐ Is limited by the known
☐ Always captures only aspects of reality
☐ Is predominantly subject to projection
☐ Is co-controlled by defense mechanisms

- Depends on knowledge and previous experience
- Is influenced by expectations
- Is subject to the dynamics of habit
- Captures the focused and surrounding elements
- Depends on the language skills
- Is influenced by thinking skills
- Is always value and meaningful life

There are realities that human beings can understand only through empathic understanding. This includes, first and foremost, the psychic life. The reality of human values and meaning requires a certain amount of ethical sensibility to be perceived at all. Self-perception tends to be situational. In the perception of others, on the other hand, personality characteristics are first formally perceived.

We conclude from the previous explanations a thesis of considerable importance is anthropological and andragogic: Perception is always a subjective process. The perceived reality is therefore first a subjective reality. The more complex the reality, the more different it is perceived by different people.

The visual perception in the first place, but also the other forms of perception, can be judged under different modalities. A general list shows the diversity of the perception process and the quality of perception.

The complexity and quality of perception can be described as follows:

vague, diffuse, foggy	clear, precise, alert
undifferentiated	differentiated
superficial	profound
one-sided, partial	versatile, comprehensive
in a mess	in clear order
coarse mesh, flat rate	finely divided
rigid, fixed	flexible,
short-sighted	farsighted
emotional	factual
thoughtlessly	considered
in predetermined patterns	open, object related
without reference to the past	with reference to the past
without a future perspective	with a future perspective
without value and meaning life	with value and meaning life
without extended horizon	with extended horizon

indifferent	responsibly
in the narrow ego area	in the extended area of expertise
concealing, obscuring	open radically
defensive, repressive	absorbing, integrating
with presumptions	with expertise
with fragmentary interest	with a holistic interest
with prejudice	without prejudice
mixing, twisting	disassembling, clarifying
with taboos	free of taboos
habitual	intentionally
aimless	purposeful

Language and communication

Writing about the relationship between perception, language, and reality, requires going deep into the history of philosophy to its origins. Wittgenstein (1918 and 1973), Schleichert (1975) and Kamlah / Lorenzen (1967) searched for the basic building blocks and their relationships. Whorf (1963) comprehensively analyzes the enormously complex relationship between perception, language, and reality.

In all the attempts to create a new beginning in language development, and to define knowledge based on it, the language of the people remains a jumble. No grammar can change the problem of ambiguity. Billions of people have their thousand languages and dialect forms, however peculiar and spongy every meaning assignment may be. Here we focus on the life-practical and psychological aspect of language and communication as a form of coping with reality.

We formulate some theses for discussion:

Thesis 1: The everyday language is essentially vague, ambiguous, inaccurate, and indefinite.

Thesis 2: The term uses have mostly different scope, without exactly clarified framework.

Thesis 3: The concrete content of many words is imprecise.

Thesis 4: Some conceptual uses are factual, emotional, and judgmental at the same time.

Thesis 5: Many people speak in the same words and still mean something quite different.

Thesis 6: The same words can evoke different feelings and valuations.

Thesis 7: A small part of language refers to the concrete, empirical reality. A much larger part of the language captures an experience, a value, or an individual meaning.

Thesis 8: Behind one word stands a complex reality, biographical relationships, different, and often subjective "theories".

Thesis 9: A statement contains different levels of: factual information, value judgment, sharing of an experience, a subjective theory (prejudice), interpretation, factual (logical) deduction, explanation, reason, opinion, hypothesis, desire, expectation, instruction, command, threat, prognosis, proposed solution, and action suggestion.

Conclusion: Many people are predominantly responsive to slogans, emotional expressions, prejudices, clichés, simplified conceptual units, and undifferentiated labels. Thus, the reality is easier and clearer. But from such a perception of reality arise in everyday life unsuitable solutions.

Those who think and / or talk about themselves and / or others use many words with many-sided, often subjective meanings:

A list of many words with variable meanings:

intelligent	intellectually	secular
vital	deliberately	mentally
imaginative	defensive	strict
live facing	suppressing	creative
honestly	introvert	talkative
industrious	dominant	extrovert
open	superstitious	strong-willed
disciplined	correctly	awake
strongly	unconsciously	relationship capable
cheerfully	learning open	live out
successfully	educated	rough
in time	integer	rigid
established	impressive	arrogant
proud	modest	lazy
wise	active	fanatical
confident	moderation	tolerant
angry	well	positive
negative	defiant	unstable
ripe	smart	hostile
pedantic	moody	sensitive
neurotic	broody	facade way
greedy	dear	loaded
conscientious	hollow	stupid
authoritarian	naive	kind
sophisticated	independently	religious
locked	accessible	curious
persevering	warm-hearted	secular

We conclude that if two people use the same words, that does not mean that they mean the same thing. In many cases, people have only vague ideas about simple words.

Relationships are the central reality of life for all people. Relationship design always contains communication. Man cannot be non-communicating (Watzlawick 1971, 53). The interactions of communication processes are many. Communication is a feedback process. But even in soliloquy we can recognize a kind of control loop when the ego speaks to itself. In interpersonal relationships, communication tends toward a degree of homeostasis. The same applies to self-reflection. As people speak, so do they think; and vice versa: as they think, so they talk. At the same time, communication tends to be more human-related than object-related. Everybody knows, because he experiences it every day: Facial expressions, gestures, mood, and attitude, are also communicative.

We have described that perception is a subjective process. Furthermore, we have stated that the verbal processing of the perceived is also a subjective process. Now there are the human aspects that make communication even more subjective.

Human aspects in communication are:

- Personal language code
- Fear of punishment (rejection)
- Prejudice
- Frustrations
- Fear of life
- Projection dynamics
- Guilt
- Defenses
- Emotional reference to words
- Need for power
- Fatigue
- Concealed advantage search
- Need for protection
- Feelings of inferiority
- Need for appreciation
- Egocentricity
- Role expectations
- Sympathy / antipathy

Talking without words can also be informative. For this purpose, some examples are presented. Speeches without words: look into one another's eyes, wide-open eyes, frowning, scratching while talking, smiling, smirking, piercing-stern look, looking away, distorting facial features, moving arms and legs, tapping with fingers, sighing and coughing, Blushing, adjusting clothes, looking at the clock, and so on

Many ways of speaking make the communicated reality again, subject to a subjective process. We have many kinds of talking (and thinking): friendly, aggressive, happy, approving, disapproving, punitive, threatening, interested, empathic, distant, bored, humiliating, respectful, ideology-fixated, dedicated, appreciative, pejorative, hostile , deceptive, moody, spiteful, helpless, hurtful, faith-fixated, role-determined and so on

Many actions in daily life are "critical" in the context of talking. The close connection between perception and the assignment of words creates a subjectivity that is conflictual. We consider it a particularly important task of personality development to train people in this complexity and subjectivity.
This requires a considerable degree of readiness for self-reflection, openness, and empathy with other people.

Exciting group exercises: Individual participants note their own meaning and their associations, to a list of words, from the everyday psychological everyday language. Role exercises (topic-centered interaction) are also a form of communication training. Personality development can be practiced in a playful and creative way with clear goals.

Thinking and Judging: Factors of influences and performance

Here we limit ourselves to a few elementary facts of thought based on Bruner (1971), Guilford (1964), Meili (1971), Oerter (1972) and Rosemann (1979). Our interest lies in the level of self-reflection. Thinking is always work, or we say: processing of information (cybernetic cognitive research). Thinking is a conscious process, even if many thought processes are automatic. The quality of thinking can be very different. Thinking is subject to learning processes. Thinking is difficult to define. We want to introduce some elementary components of thinking.

Thinking as a work process includes:

☐ Forming concepts, find words
☐ Capturing meanings, understanding meaning,
☐ Assigning values, set values, taking a moral judgment
☐ Capturing linguistic relationships
☐ Dealing with creative language, also varying playfully
☐ Create categories, organize them systematically, classify
☐ Assign to the memory material
☐ Classification in existing knowledge
☐ Flexible handling with different elements
☐ Establish and associate analogies and similarities
☐ Disassemble into parts and reassemble
☐ Weigh, combine, compare, recognize differences
☐ Save in memory, remember
☐ Capturing cause and functional relationships
☐ Thinking through future possibilities
☐ Targeted processing
☐ Abstracting space and time, the concrete "case"
☐ Identifying emotional experiences
☐ Activation and use of existing knowledge
☐ Logical and mathematical reasoning, practical reasoning
☐ Restore the reality relation of the thought result
☐ Define intentions to act, decide life-time
☐ Identify the concrete implementation of the thinking power

Intelligence is cognitive performance (Meili 1971, Rosemann 1979). Cognitive abilities consist of many functions that work together as a bundle of functions. What intelligence is, researchers define with their tests. Here is a summary of the individual achievements of the intelligentsia (Compare Oerter / Montada 1987, 205-214, Meili / Steingrüber 1978, 50-141).

The central cognitive abilities are:

☐ Perceptiveness (organization of sensory impressions)
☐ Ability to judge the perceived (reflection)
☐ Reasoning, logical operations, ordering, selection
☐ Restructuring, decomposing, analyzing, giving new forms
☐ Memory performance (retrieve knowledge)
☐ Classify perceived
☐ Linguistic skills (vocabulary, sentence structure, speeches, understanding)
☐ Assimilating ability (internalization)
☐ Accommodation (internal forming), transform thinking mode
☐ Empathy
☐ Cross taboos and question
☐ Ingenuity (creativity), use imagination
☐ Can evaluate psychological experiences
☐ Problem-solving ability
☐ Ethical feeling and judgments
☐ I-you-demarcation
☐ Change attitudes and keep them flexible
☐ Can apply what you have learned in new situations

In thinking, prejudices are often decisive. They replace the differentiated thinking. The list of people's prejudices is very extensive. Prejudices characterize daily behavior, linguistic processing, and thought processes in general. Let us introduce some examples from life: "I value simple solutions, I have my established knowledge, my conscience is clear, the world is alright, conventions are to be preserved, one should not question everything, politicians have world problems already under control, people are fundamentally evil, man is basically good "... etc

One aspect of thinking is creativity. We understand creativity as a rational function that does not work with the logic of thinking (Preiser 1976, Ulmann 1973, Mühle 1970). Creativity means expressing the inner forces in all processes of thought and action. On the one hand, there are the spontaneous ideas, the random ideas, the intuitions, and impulses from the unconscious. On the other hand, creativity is an expression of openness, flexibility, spontaneity, and playful handling of elements. This includes a certain curiosity, the desire for playfulness, risk-taking, and unconventionality. Without experiencing, the dynamics of creativity are considerably limited. It should also be mentioned that fixed moralizing attitudes, regulations, emotional blockages, and rigid patterns of thought (prejudices) hinder - and even make impossible - for the flow and development of creativity.

Creativity is valuable, in thinking and acting. Creativity leads to new ways and enables solutions where logical rigorous thinking can no longer find a way out. Creativity also means self-expression, because the inner forces from the other subsystems "have a say" in what the ego is trying to master in a constructive way. Creativity makes life exciting and interesting. A certain lust for life and thus a corresponding satisfaction promotes the positive self-living and coping with one's own life in general. Creativity not only promotes thought but is also an aspect of intelligent life.

Characteristics of creativity are:

- Flexible and comprehensive thinking
- Determination for unfamiliar tasks
- Interest in new problems
- Free from dogmatic ideological thinking
- Free from "white-black" thinking
- Sense of humor and novel design
- Little conventional living and flexible in traditions
- Open to irrationality from the unconscious and from dreams
- Willingness to make mistakes
- Free from the idea that everything has to be controllable
- Little interest in always wanting to master the circumstances
- Inner freedom and flexibility
- Realistic view and acceptance of the "imperfect"
- Regardless of foreign reviews

Judgment has to do with values, with morality, and with ethics. Judgment is a cognitive ability, and a thinking process. Is that already the "conscience", such as the "inner voice" in the sense of Socrates, or the "superego" in the sense of Freud? There are countless definitions of conscience (see Oser 1976, 115-119, Blum et al 1958). We cannot analyze this topic analytically here, but merely highlight some aspects that can certainly be counted as the moral formation of man.

For the purpose of the discussion, we propose the following thesis: Conscience, on the one hand, comprises the contents of the superego and the attitudes / beliefs that we have in the inventory of the unconscious- where saved life experiences can found. Furthermore, the experience of meaning and value, as we discuss it in connection with feelings, has an active function in connection with the mode of action of conscience. The power of love also has a constructive (reconciling, transcendental) impact on the experience and the setting of values. We recognize, in the working of the mind, in dreams, and meditations moral directives, which we also interpret as part of the conscience. Moral judgment is another part that is constitutive of conscience. We want to make it clear that the "conscience" cannot be equated with the "superego" without reservations.

We are guided by the extensive study by Oser / Althof (1994) and pick out some elements in connection with moral judgments. In terms of developmental psychology, Kohlberg's six levels are referred to in brief keywords:

1st stage: Orientation towards punishment and obedience; adults as a source of morality.
2nd stage: Morality has to do with interactions; reciprocity becomes the guideline for the morally correct.
3rd stage: Consideration of the needs and attitudes of others, especially their own family and their own circle of friends.
4th stage: Inclusion of the social perspective, and of the whole interpersonal space.
5th stage: Beginning of the principles-led moral thinking, e.g. justice, charity, dignity of man, and so on.
6. Sixth stage: is the level of universal ethical principles (Oser / Althof 1994, 53-68).

Only a minority of adults reach the fifth stage according to Oser / Althof or Kohlberg; Most people move to levels 3 and 4. Moral judgment depends - on the one hand - on the ability to think. On the other hand, it depends on life experiences and the processing of them. The development of stages depends crucially on the examination of social experiences and social institutions (Oser / Althof 1994, 71-75). Ibid also discusses other factors that enable the performance or level transformations: perceived contradictions, stable emotional affection, open confrontation, communication, participation in decisions, and responsibility.

Moral judgment does not guarantee moral action. The "willful reaffirmation", the meeting of a choice, the experience of responsibility, the self-living, but also habits and practiced roles, all play a decisive role in the bridge from judgment to action.

We would like to add a little extra to this topic...

More is lied about in daily life than man can drink water. Those who do not wash, pact, intrigue, or act, are economically, socially, and power-related, are mostly on the losing side. Economic and social survival comes before morality. And finally, the overburdened unconscious is always stronger than the moral judgment and the will. In other words, the stronger the external pressure to act and the stronger the irrational action of the unconscious, the less likely it is that a moral judgment is followed by a corresponding moral act.

For human education, we can conclude that working on one's own biography, and the processing of life experiences, promotes the capacity for self-determined moral judgments. We can adopt the transformation model of Oser / Althof (1994, 105):
1) uncertainty / borderline experience
2) recognizing new elements
3) dissolving the old structures
4) installation of new elements
5) Assembly and application of the new structure.

It should, however, be pointed out that, in our opinion, this should be considered as a rule in human education:

One should not take off supports before new supports are constructed, otherwise the structure collapses. As supports, we refer to the formation of a positive strong ego, the formation of practical life skills, recognition and seriousness of the basic needs, thinking training, development of the ability to love, the contemplative reflection of values - such as justice (and fairness, tolerance, dignity, etc.), as well as philosophical thinking about human images and meaning of life. This, in turn, we call individuation according to our model of human education.

Cognitive learning: Capacities of learning and life management

Here we rely on classical theories of learning (Hilgard / Bower 1971, Haseloff / Jorswieck 1970) and discuss those aspects which are relevant to the development of personality and the like.

Aspects that influence learning are:

- ☐ Reward or punishment/threat of punishment influences learning processes.
- ☐ A climate of security and reserve promotes learning.
- ☐ Social pressure influences learning.
- ☐ Observation promotes learning activities.
- ☐ Learning by doing promotes interest in learning.
- ☐ Life experiences can keep learning processes active.
- ☐ Acclimation is a way to learn.
- ☐ Imitation is a form of learning.
- ☐ Associate, link; structuring initiates learning processes.
- ☐ Hypno-suggestive framework conditions promote learning processes.

Good learning conditions promote learning processes. Learning processes are the basics of behavior or human action. With the activity, the human being designs his life and his habitat. This in turn is regarded as the framework and basis of all new learning processes. Life and learning are thus in a mutually conditional cycle. Bad learning conditions cause bad action and thus bad conditions for all subsequent learning processes.

Conclusion: Learning again and again for a lifetime is a life's demand.

For learning, there are some prerequisites for the individual who are themselves subject to learning processes. The individual functions and conditions are summarized in the section Intelligence. Basically, learning requires an interest. If the human being does not want to learn anything in his psychic-spiritual life, then the cycle of learning processes in this area is regressive. In the long term, this not only hampers learning processes in all external lifestyles, but also forces learning in a direction that runs counter to life. This then becomes a regressive control loop. Personality building - in andragogy - must therefore be geared towards creating the favorable dispositions for lifelong learning. From the previous considerations, there are some aspects that we want to list below.

Cheap learning dispositions are:

☐ Being open to learning, and having a basic willingness to learn.
☐ Ability to organize and design learning situations.
☐ Interest in knowledge and creativity, in the field of psychology.
☐ Stamina, perseverance and ability to concentrate.
☐ Clear perception, mental presence and far-sighted thinking.
☐ Positive acceptance of life problems and challenges.
☐ Willingness to recognize and understand psychic reality.
☐ Interest in a differentiated development and personal growth.
☐ Devotion to values such as truthfulness and love.

Many critical / problematic situations must be meticulously dissected by humans to achieve change and renewal. This is because many problems have to do with the whole person and his whole life story.

Many renewal attempts fail in advance, despite all good will, because the intra-psycho-sexual interdependencies are too little systematically and too little deeply recorded and clarified. Anyone who tries to master his life, only with thinking, and disrespects feelings or needs will ultimately fail. Any attempt to "positively" manage life, excluding one of the psychic subsystems, is ultimately regressive and thus against life. During one's life, there are always critical / problematic situations of considerable significance, for every human being. A great deal of time, attention, and patience for learning processes, is essential if you want to develop and grow holistically.

For Piaget, the inevitability of imbalances is considered the "motor of cognitive learning processes". This corresponds to our definition of the valence parameter (see chapter on needs). On the one hand, thinking structures are constructed in conflict with the environment; therefore, they are not exclusively innate. The formation of moral judgments (Piaget 1973) also occurs in this system interconnectedness. Components of the personality structure, and the structures of the norms (including the objects), are woven into a network. Consequently, everyone constructs their world through the cognitive process of internalization (accommodation). External content changes cognitive schemes. However, reality is often recorded in such a way that existing schemes are preserved. The internalized reality is then the outer world assimilated to existing cognitive structures (assimilation).

This has an important meaning: Man changes the contents of the environment through his peculiar way of thinking. Personal ties, emotions and motivations also play a significant role in these learning processes. We have seen that action can also be analyzed or dissected into structures.

Structures are an explanatory hypothetical construct and a generalization of real situations, actions, and objects. Learning processes can thus be understood as an attempt to dissolve contradictions and conflicts between inner (cognitive), personality-specific, and habitat-related structures. The dissolution happens through the restructuring and rebuilding of the cognitive and normative structures (equilibration). This provides the basis for a system-theoretical conception of personality formation (Schneider 1981). Any kind of problem solving and restructuring of the psychic subsystems is dependent on the cognitive structures or their person-dependent possibilities for innovation.

Let us state: "Language is the most comprehensive, most differentiated, and most succinct expression of mental and spiritual being" (Pfniss 1988, 41). The subjective factors of condition (Fuchs 1985, 436) - we recall - from perception to thinking, from understanding to action - urge anthropologically to form a thorough humanity.

6. The Emotions

Criteria of patterns and components of emotions

Feelings are not definable, say different authors and experts (Jaspers 1965, 90). The question is, however, what does "defining" mean? We want to try an approximation. First, we clarify the term: "Emotion". We synonymous with "feeling", even if here and there the emotion has a special quality of depth and duration. Second, is the term: "Affect". This, in itself, emphasizes that it is a feeling that suddenly and very intensively breaks out (Barz 1977, 128).

There are basic emotions that are in phylogenetic continuity; These are: interest, joy, displeasure / mourning, surprise, fear, anger, disgust, and shame (Heckhausen 1989, 71-76). This means that emotions cannot simply be put into opposition to cognition (thought). Vital basic situations (threat, suspension, etc.) have an innate pattern or congenital emotion triggers. Emotions would, therefore, be a kind of "flash communiqué" about the given situation. Becker-Carus (1981, 193) confirms this brain physiological theory and others. in the aggression. It must therefore be assumed that the human brain has also pre-structured such basic emotions. It is also undisputed that emotions trigger or accompany many physiological reactions (Vester 1991, 148-152, Heckhausen 1989, 113, 377, Becker-Carus 1981, 213, 306). Here we put the physiological aspects, of the emotions, in the background and want to concentrate on the psychological aspects.

A feeling can be viewed from different angles. It can be established that there are no feelings without a content or an object. Even if the individual is unaware of why certain feeling are present, there is a theme in every feeling. The topic can also mean the current existence. A feeling is always triggered by something, be it from the outside world or be it from the inner world (the mental subsystems or a psychic individual force). We call this subject the "object" (Barz 1979, 122).

Furthermore, we can see that the ego, and the feeling, are always two separate things. The ego is, to a certain extent, the subject. You always say, "I feel". Thus, as a third element, the specific experience is identified. Here, we can speak of emotional character, by which we mean the specificity of the corresponding feeling (joy, fear, desire, hope, etc.).

After all, we know that this experience is different in intensity and duration. Everyone experiences – somehow - positive or negative feelings. The ego is receptive or negative to this specific experience. To that we say: The ego gives the experience a certain value (Jung 1972). The (theoretical) possibility of polarizing a feeling always gives it an opposite character.

The individual does not always respond in the same way to an object. A melody or a sunrise does not always cause the same experience. There are also individual differences between people: what person A experiences as pleasant does not necessarily have the same feeling for person B. Man can, to varying degrees, control, suppress, or increase his feelings. In the chapter on psychodynamics we have shown that a feeling acts energetically on bodily functions: contains a certain energy, which we have called "psychic energy". Thus, we can define a feeling with the following components:

A feeling consists of:
- Subject
- Object (inside / outside)
- Quality of experience (body feeling)
- Feeling character (type of value)
- Intensity / duration
- Controllability
- Responsiveness
- Psychical energy

You can categorize the many different emotions according to different points of view. Jung (1921) describes feeling as one of the four basic functions. This type of theory must be considered obsolete. It is also wrong if one considers the fullness of the psychic subsystems. What can be considered a "basic function" depends on a tiered or layered model at best.

This type of model typology has mainly disadvantages compared to the system model, as we have shown (see Roth 1969). However, there is no satisfactory universal classification anyway (Barz 1977, 125). But, what does "satisfying" mean? After all, it is already "satisfying" to be able to recognize some aspects of a view, and to classify feelings according, to this point of view. We can define the following aspects, based on the different models (Dorsch 1991, Jaspers 1973, Jung 1921 [1977], Barz 1977, Scharfetter 1976):

Division criteria of feelings (character or value of feelings):

- positive - negative
- pleasant - unpleasant

- sensual (physically) - mentally
- worldly / world-related - spiritual / transcendental-related
- subject-related (I / you) - object-related (habitat / things)
- hostile / averted - peaceful / forgiving
- progressive - regressive
- constructive - destructive

Feelings can also be captured in a model of tension and put into a developmental psychological context of the individual (Sroufe in Foppa / Groner 1981, 14-33). This is a feeling of dependence, on either earlier or similar feelings, on the specific content of this event and on the subjective meaning (meaning / value) for the individual. This results in a broad variability of the expression of a feeling. The stress parameter for this model corresponds to our "valence parameter" as we develop and define it in the Needs chapter.

For the subdivision into pleasant and unpleasant feelings, we orient ourselves to their diversity. The fact that the pleasure life can also be perverted (pleasure in the plagues and the humble), we ignore here. A pleasant feeling does not necessarily have to be a "positive" feeling. For example, one can experience nostalgic longing as pleasurable and ignore the pain contained in it or not recognize it subjectively. The other classification criteria offer some considerable interpretation difficulties. The same feelings can occur subject-related and object-related, sensually and psychologically, objectively and mentally. Then there are feelings that are neither hostile nor peaceful; at most, they may be felt painful by the individual (for example, grief).

The following two lists are therefore based on the criterion of subjectively pleasant and unpleasant experiences. This classification coincides largely with the criterion of hostile-peaceful. If one assumes healthy lustful life, and unpleasure life, then this fifth criterion is a meaning-based interpretation. It can also be in the sense of life-giving and avoidance of life (Fromm 1979). The evaluative component is content related and no longer only experience related. Life and emotional character can always be described in the context of the opposite. Finally, we can subdivide the feelings into: sentimental, instinctual (vital, social), and personality-related feelings (Rohracher 1971, 453-458).

Emotions emerge and form through:

- Perceptions of all kinds
- Empathize
- Thoughts

☐ Inner ideas, fantasies
☐ Imagination
☐ Dreams
☐ Psychic energy of other people
☐ Psychic "atmosphere" in the living space
☐ Needs and drives
☐ Body functions
☐ Images in the subconscious
☐ Love power
☐ Existential experience

A pleasant and unpleasant experience has different qualities: a) The pleasant experience is described as: well, elated, fresh, releasing, liberating, attractive, warm, invigorating, stimulating, calm, harmonious. b) The unpleasant experience is described as: unwell, lethargic, tired, weak, cramped, cramping, blocking, cold, repulsive, depressing, exhausting, restless, tearing, and so on.

It should also be pointed out that a feeling can be experienced in a particular way or comprehensively. The emotional expression can be more introverted or more extraverted. It is also particularly important that the individual can have multiple feelings, at the same time. A certain basic feeling can be superimposed by another feeling. Suddenly breaking in new feelings can overshadow the existing emotional disposition for a moment or for a while.

The expression of a feeling contains strength (vitality, depth, intensity) and is denoted by the words: intense, strong, enhanced, fresh, poignant. Duration and tempo can be described as follows: long, persistent, far-swinging, sustainable; and polar: short, unsteady, mercurial, occasional, etc.

Pleasant, positive feelings are:

☐ Love	☐ Encouragement
☐Tenderness	☐ Sympathetic joy
☐Satisfaction	☐ Justice
☐ Protected	☐ Surprise
☐ Appreciation	☐ Warning
☐ Interest	☐ Duty
☐Grant	☐ Silence
☐ admiration	☐ Security
☐Respect	☐ Warmth
☐ Trust	☐ Peace
☐ Worship	☐ Beauty

☐ Cheerfulness	☐ Affection
☐ Approval	☐ Harmony
☐ Compassion	☐ Sympathy

Unpleasant, negatively experienced feelings are:

☐ Hatred	☐ Envy
☐ Loveless	☐ Displeasure
☐ Ridicule	☐ Fainting
☐ Disgust	☐ Emptiness
☐ Arrogance	☐ Revenge
☐ Mistrust	☐ Contempt
☐ Offense	☐ Resentment
☐ Aggression	☐ Rejection
☐ Jealousy	☐ Hopelessness
☐ Contempt	☐ Boredom
☐ Ingratitude	☐ Insult
☐ Outrage	☐ Conflict
☐ Futility	☐ Inferiority
☐ Alienation	☐ Anger

Causes and release button of emotions

An important question is, which "objects" have external and internal facts, and what do feelings do? One problem is that people react to the same facts with different feelings. In addition, some feelings are transformed. Furthermore, feelings can also "infect" and are therefore to be determined as emotional triggers. Here it makes sense to divide the living space into people, objects, and living conditions. So, we formulate:

1) Through their actions and feelings, others cause others:

a) Unpleasant feelings that trigger actions such as: hurt, humiliate, harm, punish, mock, scold, smile, abuse, cheat, steal, attack, disturb, ignore, deceive, discriminate, exploit, lie, torture, be violent, act intriguing, outrageously treating, constricting, penalizing, rejecting, annoying, not taking seriously, suppressing, weakening, deceiving, mistrusting, envy, hate, etc

b) Pleasant feelings that trigger actions such as: appreciating, praising, cooperating, taking seriously, accepting, understanding (trying), protecting, caring, trusting, affirming, helping, supporting, giving attention, strengthening, loving, honestly speaking to show sympathy, to give pleasure, to participate, to listen, to be free, to be benevolent, to support, to turn, etc.

2) objects cause in humans:

a) Unpleasant feelings from: dirt, bad air, noise, anonymous big buildings, urbanization, threatening objects, and so on.

b) Pleasant feelings from: pleasure producing products, beautiful houses, plants, loads of decreasing products, clothes, food, and so on.

3) Living conditions in humans:

a) The cause of unpleasant feelings come from: unemployment, lack of money, lack of primary living conditions, disorder, unresolved conflicts, being alone, worries, and so on.

b) Things that create pleasant feelings are: work, enough money, good housing and living conditions, order, clarified conflicts, security, relationships, and so on.

4) Solving personal events:

a) Unpleasant feelings come from: illness, suffering, death of a person, failure, loss event, etc.

b) Pleasant feelings come from: health, relationship experience, success, birth and so on

5) Inner-psychic situations can occur in the individual:

a) The cause of unpleasant feelings include: severe superego, unprocessed past, negative thoughts, suppressed anger, limiting attitudes to life, suppression of sexual desire, undeveloped mental powers, blocked inner growth, misunderstood dreams, weak will, weak self-confidence, low self-esteem, being at a loss to be able to update feelings, no meaning in life, to be inwardly unfree, to be dominated by needs, blocked life forces, beset by unconscious forces, bound by dogmas and ideologies, fanaticism, refusal of responsibility, emotional deficits, suppression of one's own possibilities be of one 's own projection dynamics, an experience of alienation, etc

b) Things that creating pleasant feelings include: balanced over-ego, life-oriented attitudes, positive thoughts, willpower, healthy self-esteem, measured self-esteem, inner growth, integration of pleasure, competent experience of the dream messages, processed past, controllability of the feelings, sense in to update one's own life, inner freedom, developed psychic powers, can be flexible in the needs, vital active life forces, be free from unconscious forces, be anchored in the inner mind, can think freely, live responsibility, balanced needs, updating your own possibilities, being free from projections, participation, and so on.

6) Solve social national and international situations:

a) Unpleasant feelings from: Crime, violence, wars, hardship, poverty, fanaticism, fundamentalism, racism, recession, etc.

b) Pleasant feelings from: peace, security, prosperity, pluralism, healthy economic life, freedom, and so on.

The variety of forces that cause emotions pushes people to different solutions: some can be touched; others can compensate for their feelings; many suppress their feelings; quite a few get sick under the pressure of opposing emotions. Once we ignore the small pleasant and unpleasant feelings, in everyday life, we can see that the stronger and longer lasting feelings are entangled in a complex web.

It must be concluded that many feelings are not easily changeable. They always come back. Sustainable and lasting pleasant basic feelings can only be created through complex, internal, and external measures. Therefore, you cannot just tell a person to "Think positively," or "See the world from the good side," or "Just enjoy the good things." It can hardly be the goal of personality development to lead people to the fact that they only have positive feelings. This is not a realistic life show. Realistic, however, is to educate people to deal with their feelings, to identify their causative powers and, wherever possible, to take responsibility for their emotional state.

The human in the consumer society seeks to cope with his unpleasant feelings with goods. Nobody wants to see that he creates in the background or in the depth of his unconscious life only new unpleasant feelings. Humanistic psychology misunderstands the variety of the forces, which are acting and covers the complexity of the unconscious and the social conditions, through the use of communication and emotional interaction.

Psychology has its limits where the existence pushes for meaning and for a transcendental rooting. Education does relatively little to empower young people and to help them understand and control their emotions. Philosophy does not take this reality very seriously and seeks to understand life in other dimensions. But there is no life without feelings. Emotions are an experiential expression of the updated life, and therefore, belong to a comprehensive personality formation.

Two aspects should be emphasized for human education. On the one hand, "Happiness and satisfaction reflect not only a combination of short-term, medium-term, and long-term processes, at the individual level, but also an interaction between cultural and individual influences" (Inglehart 1989, 309). However, on the other hand, "The real quality of life is marked by mass, race against the clock, loneliness, stress, disturbances, constraints, planning, dependency, devastated landscape, and reality" (Opaschowski 1994, 243).

Data reports on the environment and society make it questionable whether 60% or 70% or even 80% of the German (Swiss and Austrian) population are happy and satisfied (as sociological studies report). Postmodern lifestyle and adventure society act rather as a black cloth, which should cover all deeper emotional layers. Obviously, it is theoretically and practically in-depth to practice self-reflection. The researcher and scientist becomes a collaborator of the mechanisms of repression and lies of life, if he does not work out the complexity of the feelings and their origins to the roots psychologically as well as educational theory and educational practice (for the adult education). Feelings are one of the most central aspects of being.

We have found no specialist literature in Andragogy, where this anthropologically important condition (we mean the whole range of emotional diversity), is extensively and thoroughly researched for a concrete education. We suspect that there are clear reasons for this. Whoever lifts the lid of the feelings of the collective and looks into it, feels the horror: immense fear of life, massive sexual suppression, screaming sadomasochistic pain, miserable despair, crying yearning for God, insatiable desire for love, and heavy burdens. Where are the professors, the researchers, and the practitioners of Andragogy, who have the courage and the competence to educate people in these depths?

The feelings together with the unconscious and implicitly with the defense mechanisms belong to the "hottest" educational material of adult education. Since feelings always bind psychic energy, they have a tremendous subliminal contagion effect. The concatenation and potential escalation of emotions, as well as their interconnection with the other psychic subsystems, make this humane reality a fascinating core theme of personality development. This has consequences in the understanding of everyday situations (biography research), as well as in the concrete educational work.

Interrelations of emotions

Many unpleasant feelings have an aggressive content, as a cause or effect. The literature on aggression is extensive (see, e.g., Freud, Lorenzen, Dollard and Miller, Bandura). Without wishing to develop its own theory of aggression here, some aspects of this basic dynamic are considered a little closer to dynamically understand how feelings work.

Aggression always has a direct or indirect harmful effect. There is little constructive effect, from the characteristic of the aggressive feeling and action. By "aggression" we mean: hurting, suppressing, torturing, killing, destroying, plaguing, exploiting, abusing, stealing, cheating, lying, inflicting mental pain, practicing violence, and waging wars. All such actions damage and hinder growth, and the psycho-spiritual life. Aggression, in this sense, means a denial of life, having an aversion to life, and a lie in life (Fromm 1979). Aggression is the opposite of life's respect. Hatred is an extremely aggressive sentimental attitude. Love is its antipode.

It has been scientifically proven that frustration usually causes aggression, and that aggression usually causes frustration. It is, indeed, an interesting phenomenon of the aggressive dynamics of a human being: the dynamics want to infect. In the extreme form, the "evil" wants to force the "good" by constant aggression, even to become the "evil". Anyone who has been repeatedly cheated will also cheat. Those who have experienced hatred, hate themselves. He who has been humiliated again and again, humbles him. Anyone who has been injured can, depending on the depth of the pain, develop so much hatred that for a lifetime he has only one single life content, namely, to hurt others. Whoever cannot go through the internal processing, as a solution, due to his superego not allowing him to, will gets sick. Psycho-somatic suffering is always the expression of experienced aggression.

There is only one way out is love. "Love your enemy" does not mean that you should subjugate him. Rather, love demands that one cannot be captivated by the aggressive dynamics. To turn away and reconcile inwardly, is the actual "act of love".
Another psychodynamic contains oppression. Many people live with the basic feeling of being oppressed, without being psychologically ill in the sense of psychopathology. It is significant that a solution cannot be found in the pleasurable consumption-oriented life-giving. Also encouraging words, as often proposed by coaching, or with prayer and courage, cannot change such a basic feeling. Man, in the feeling of being oppressed, is bound in feelings of aggression to his inner psychological complexity and to habitat conditions. The path to liberation ultimately only leads to love. And love in turn can only grow as far as man grows in individuation.

Characteristics of being oppressed are:

☐ dull heaviness	☐ basic mood of hopeless
☐ diffuse detuning	☐ meaningless: everything is meaningless
☐ lack of ideas and imagination	☐ every activity needs a lot of strength
☐ being used up	☐ indefinite grief
☐ internally blocked ego strength	☐ paralyzed in will, decision
☐ little power to self-assertion	☐ turning thoughts
☐ minimal self-esteem	☐ boring self-doubt
☐ response inhibited	☐ generalized displeasure
☐ everything is against me	☐ without sexual desire, "turned off"
☐ emotional contact inhibited	☐ sleep
☐ being unable to…	☐ discouraged
☐ high level of self-accusation	☐ ignoring, to let go
☐ no satisfaction	☐ anxious
☐ blocked in drive	☐ addictive behavior

As a third example, we briefly discuss guilt. Guilty feelings, like aggression, are entangled in a complex chain. The chain of feelings can be described exemplarily in seven sequences:

1. Charge: "I cannot like you …"; "Because of you, I have so much …"
2. Feeling guilty: "I am to blame for that …"; "Because of me …"
3. Anxiety: "I am afraid of punishment (before my loved one, etc.) …"
4. Inferiority: "I am worth nothing …"; "The other one is better …"
5. Loneliness: "I am alone …"; "Nobody understands me …"
6. Despair: "I see no way out …"; "There is no solution …"
7. Adaptation: "I must be like the others …"

It can be seen here that man owes his life to himself. He measures himself by others, not by his potential for growth. He gives the other a higher value than his humanity. He does not love himself and expects the love of others. Here, too, the solution is to manage emotions, which means to grow holistically in the sense of comprehensive personality development, love, and individuation.

Many people are relatively free of such chains of feeling. They have overwhelmingly pleasant feelings and master variations in their possibilities quite differentiated. They are educated, little neurotic and genuinely able to love. They are ready to have confidence in other people. They are basically open, transparent, and helpful. They can transmit real feelings of affection to their fellow human beings. They can show joy, they are true, and they love life. They can be genuinely tender and bring constructive dynamism to groups. These are people who are ready to shape a people-centered life in terms of personality development.

In contrast, we present another type of human being. Life teaches us that there is that too: people who know how to use the above type of human with a "client-centered" approach; People who ruthlessly deceive others lie and exploit wherever they can; People who, with friendly faces and soft voices, seek only one thing at every opportunity, namely to gain a material advantage; People who, despite their deep feelings about inner experiences about truth and love, again deny these experiences; People who are no longer capable of solidarity with psycho-spiritual values, when it comes to money; People who know all the ways and means to acquire power and even more possessions; People who scoff at every feeling except their own sense of triumph; People who have a lot and do nothing that could bring even a drop of love and hope in the world.

So much is certain: In these people, the love power and individuation fails as a solution. Talking about feelings is futile for these people. In these people, personality education is not in demand. But with great capital and power, such people decisively determine the course of history, of the world and of humanity. They alone have the opportunity to give billions of people a chance to build "pleasant feelings". However, they cannot have them because the conditions of life are not given, because they are prisoners of their unconscious, because they have not consciously formed their psychic powers, and because they do not know individuation. They must fight daily for the material survival, and not for psychic-spiritual development, let alone reasonably life-oriented feelings.

Introspection to explore one's own emotions

Introspection is a direct way to identify, understand and transform one's own feelings. We are guided by psychoanalytic reflections on this method, and some reflections that can help familiarize with introspection.

Introspection is: "looking inside or in other people or things", "to see through and contemplate", "attentive, mindful observation of all processes in themselves in the physical and psychological realm" (Scharfetter, in Wagner-Simon / Benedetti, 1982, 48). Benedetti: "Psychoanalysis means first and foremost systematic introspection, strict will for truth, self-discipline, with years of trying to achieve a comprehensive self-knowledge" (ibid., 16). The aim of introspection: "the uncovering of the unconscious" (ibid., 17). It is to be discovered introspectively: the defense mechanisms, the ideals, the suffering, the potentials, the impulses, the conflicts, the superego, and the 'neurotic elements' (ibid., 17-25). Introspection makes it possible to deal thoroughly with one's own past and unconscious present.

"Self-analysis was the form of introspection (by Sigmund Freud)" (Hunziker-Fromm, in Wagner-Simon / Benedetti, 1982, 106). "... he had driven his need for truth inexorably to analytical self-inquiry" (ibid., 108). "As a prerequisite of self-exploration, one must, according to Erich Fromm, initially be physically and mentally quiet, relaxed, and collected" (ibid., 117). According to Fromm, introspection is "feeling, feeling, and feeling the inner state" (ibid., 117). "As a way of introspection, self-analysis is a way to cleanse oneself, to prepare the inner space, to let it free, where other things can happen ..." (ibid., 119).

"Introspection as a self-questioning, self-reflection, self-knowledge, and self-assessment is an everyday human behavior to us. We do not look into an inner abstract cavity, but we consider a concrete present action. We think about what we have done, or introspection is self-reassurance about how it stood around us, enabling us to consciously lead our lives "(Saner, in: Wagner-Simon / Benedetti, 1982, 238). "Introspection (is) not just thinking, but acting and reacting to the self in the breadth of its possibilities: grief, regret, disappointment about loss and failure, happiness in the present success, fear and hope in the face of the still open" (ibid., 238) ... "Introspection isa return of the subject to its being and doing" (ibid., 238).

Another point of view: "introspection is straight, yes even exclusively in prayer." He refers to the historical development of the Delphic "Know thyself" as "Reflection of the spirit on itself, i.e. self-knowledge, and reflection on its origin from the divine, i.e. knowledge of God" (Balthasar, in: Wagner-Simon / Benedetti, 1982, 73). We take over a quotation from Augustinus: "Do not lose yourself, go back inside yourself. In the inner man, the truth lives. And when you discover that your being is changeable, then you exceed yourself; but, keep in mind that you surpass a spirit-thinking soul, so go where the light of spirit-mind originally appears "(ibid., 74).

7. The Needs

The basic needs and their direction

Every human being has needs. Nobody will doubt that. But which needs are vital? Which are essential to man? What are needs that contribute to human happiness and its evolution and could be abolished without harm or constriction? The question can certainly be asked, because in industrial society many needs are artificially generated and induced from the outside. Gradually, we take this subject of needs and lean on studies by Lewin (1963, Hull 1952, Bühler Charlotte 1959, Maslow 1973, Allport 1949, Gehlen 1974). The term "motive" is clarified in order to examine to what extent motives have a connection with needs.

Need first means experiencing a defect and a need for life. This condition creates tension and activates a force that pushes for achievement of the goal. The defect, or the too low, or too high state of stress, must be eliminated. Lewin speaks of tension, force, valence (i.e., prompting character of the situation), vector field (i.e., the targeted forces), and locomotion (change from state A to state B in the habitat) (1963, 62). Characteristic is that needs have a driving force, a so-called "drive" (Murray 1963). This driving force is also called "urge" and "desire". Need always means a lack of experience - and thus the elimination of this condition (Lück 1986, 159). Gehlen speaks of an urge to expand: man always insists on expanding his scope of action. He endeavors to expand his space of disposing (1964, 75).

A need thus not only wants to remedy a defect, but also create an extension of the possibilities of life. In this sense, e.g. the needs "growth" and "transcendental experience" of Maslow (1973, 52-72) are interpreted. Once the goal (locomotion) has been reached, the need (at least for the moment) is satisfied.

"Need satisfaction" is a basic tendency of life, according to Bühler Charlotte (1959, in: Bühler / Eckstein 1973, 374). The fulfillment means "stress reduction" or stress compensation (Haseloff / Jorswieck 1970, 49). The need is an element in a homeostatic system (Maslow 1973, 44). Lewin defines need in a "dynamic field". From this we define the "basic need," which is synonymous with "primary needs," "originary needs" (Allport 1959,, 137) and "drive needs" (Hehlmann 1974, 46) Basic needs are needs that are not dependent on other needs can be traced back, which are neither "artificially" induced, nor have pure replacement function.

"Drive experience" is a term from psychoanalysis and is physiologically based (anal, oral, phallic, urethral). Schultz-Hencke gives the drive experience the following characteristics: intentional, adaptive (oral), retentive (anal), aggressive (valid), urethral (ambitious, let go). The components of a drive are: perception, imagination, emotion, excitement, motor skills, fear (1950, 20 ff. And 123). Today, this conception may largely be regarded as obsolete, has been extended and / or restructured by a few hundred learning psychological theories and "mini-theories" (Heckhausen 1980). Nevertheless, we maintain that needs and drive experiences are closely related to each other. We want to understand this drive more psycho-energetically than physiologically. But that is just the decision to a viewing aspect. Every psychic experience is linked to physiological reactions (Becker-Carus 1981, 15).

Characteristics of the basic needs are:

- Vital necessities for conservation and health
- Natural desire of the realization of existence
- Condition as lack or need for expansion
- Goal in the sense of fulfillment / saturation
- Psychic energy charge (tension, power)
- Validity for humanity in general

The formal definition of this is: a need is an experience. The individual experiences a state of deficiency that urges for satisfaction. In the experience of this state is an "urge" for a changed state. The urge is the need tension, also called "valence". The individual has an idea about the goal state. If a need is saturated, then the urge disappears, until the same need reaffirms itself as deficient urge. According to Lewin (1963), a need contains the following components: initial state, valence, tension, locomotion (state change), and target state.

Physiological needs come first in the range of basic needs: hunger and thirst. Adjacent to these needs are the instinctual needs (sexuality). We identify the urge for physical activity and the exercise of physical functions (sport) as a category of basic needs. Cultural history teaches that man experiences not only an urge, but also a necessity to create his or her habitat and to produce products for coping with life. Goods production is a vital need. If a person experiences a need for action in a situation, be it anticipating a goal state or wanting to lead a situation into a new situation, he experiences an urge to do so. We call this the "need for action".

Since immemorial time, people play. We assume that humans have a basic need for play that does not have to do with the need for group affiliation or group performance. Next are social needs. These include: having relationships, belonging to a group, communication, and so on. Separately, we call the needs for a man-woman relationship. Man has a basic desire for mental, physical and social security, and stability. It can also be seen that the human seeks an activity, a performance opportunity, a work, as well as cultural and artistic expression.

In this context, the skills are to be mentioned as a need: they urge to be used or to be expressed. What man discovers and creates (produces), he wants to absorb into his habitat. We call this urge "taking possession" and emphasize that having - in contrast to Fromm (1982), not polar to "life" means, but also "having for life" means.

The intellectual needs are another group. Man can think and wants to use his thinking. He wants insights. Further one can call the needs like love, luck, truth, and wisdom. Close to these needs is the quest for transcendental anchorage. After all, man has a need to develop himself, to grow and become all that is life-oriented in him.

The need for freedom, autonomy and self-determination is also to be understood as a basic need. In some textbooks, the need for God goes unnoticed; however, "God" is defined. It seems that this need only gains access to basic needs theory, when it is a personal need of the scientist. If God does not exist for him - however defined - there is no such basic need for God.

From Maslow (1973, 91-93) we take new perspectives of the needs and their fulfillment. To the question of meaning in the light of the values of being - we quote by choice: "In any case, the antithesis to our ordinary knowledge and reaction is very harsh." Usually we proceed under the aegis of mean values, that is, usefulness, desirability, badness, goodness, or expediency.

We evaluate, control, judge, condemn, or endorse ... We respond to the experience in a personal way and make the world nothing more than a means for our purpose. This is the opposite of being detached from the world, which in turn means that we do not really perceive them, but ourselves in them or they in ourselves. So, we then perceive in a deficit-motivated manner and therefore can only recognize deficit values. This is different from the perception of the whole world, or that part of it we accept in the borderline experience as surrogate of the world. Then, and only then, can we perceive their values, more than our own. These values I call the values of being ... ", these are:

(1) Wholeness: unity, integration, tendency to uniqueness, simplicity, organization, order, structure ...
(2) Perfection: necessity, straightforwardness, inevitability, appropriateness, justice ...
(3) Perfection: termination, finitude, fulfillment, destiny, skill ...
(4) Justice: fairness, orderliness, legality ...
(5) Aliveness: process, spontaneity, self-regulation, full functioning ...
(6) Richness: differentiation, complexity...
(7) Simplicity: honesty, nudity, materiality, and abstract structure
(8) Beauty: correctness, form, vitality, simplicity, wealth, and uniqueness.
(9) Goodness: correctness, desirability, justice, benevolence, honesty.
(10) Uniqueness: individuality, incomparability, novelty.
(11) Ease: lack of effort or pursuit, grace.
(12) Playfulness: fun, joy, entertainment, happiness, humor ...
(13) Truth: honesty, nakedness, simplicity, beauty, authenticity ...
(14) Self-sufficiency: autonomy, independence, separateness ...

We can thus first categorize and leave open whether the basic needs of Maslow (1971) should and can be formulated into a hierarchy. Our category list serves as a discussion contribution. We have put them together from the wealth of suggestions in the literature at our own discretion and considering our own professional experience.

It is difficult to prove that a particular category of need is no longer traceable, as a dynamic entity. This is also a semantic problem. Construct terms include implicit theory and judgmental elements, such as growth, love, self-updating, power and community need, meaning, God, and transcendence. Our list can be expanded, reassembled, conceptually labeled differently, and interpreted interpretatively as self-reflection:

The basic needs of man are:

- ☐ Physiological needs
- ☐ Need for sexual satisfaction
- ☐ Need for exercise
- ☐ Need for Action (Creation of Life Situations)
- ☐ Need for habitat design and production
- ☐ Need for relationships and group affiliation
- ☐ Need for a man-woman relationship
- ☐ Need for own children
- ☐ Need for safety and stability
- ☐ Need for work and performance
- ☐ Need for culture (experience and design)
- ☐ Need for play
- ☐ Need for autonomy and self-assertion
- ☐ Need for truth and truthfulness
- ☐ Need for well-being, happiness and joy
- ☐ Need for mental-physical health
- ☐ Need for ownership
- ☐ Need for knowledge and thinking
- ☐ Need for love, purpose and value
- ☐ Need for growth and development
- ☐ Need for self-updating
- ☐ Need for God (transcendence)

Fromm (1980) mentions various "basic needs": need for identity, need for "being socialized" (like others), need for self-preservation, need for transcendence, need for natural life, need for material growth, need for more satisfying work, need for connection, and the need for orientation and dedication.

Rogers (1972) mentions various needs in connection with his 19 theses on the self, as well as his exposition on the process of self-realization (1973; 1977), some of which we wish to emphasize here: growth, differentiation, independence, social identification, self-updating, respect, trust, appreciation, emotional warmth.

Maslow (1973, 1977) divides his hierarchy of needs into: physiological needs, need for security, need for social affiliation and love, need for self-esteem, need for self-realization.

Jourard (1974, cited in: Becker 1982) lists 11 basic needs: affirmation of life, physical needs, love and affection, recognition and approval of the reference group, need to move freely and express freely, need to be challenged, meditation (Detachment), cognitive clarity, answer to question of meaning, stimulus variations, and close connection to the body - including the natural environment.

Murray mentions 20 needs (referenced in: Bishop 1983, I, 119-120): humiliation, achievement, affiliation, aggression, autonomy, resistance, defense, deference, domination, display, avoidance of injury, avoidance of humiliation, tenderness, order, play, rejection, sensation, sexuality, assistance, and understanding. Jung speaks of "organic needs" and "cultural needs".

Murphy (cited in: Bishop 1983, II, 110) gives a classification of four needs: visceral needs (physiological needs), activity needs, sensory needs, and self-preservation needs.

And from a different point of view, as it were negatively considered, let us mention the ten neurotic needs of Horney (quoted in: Bischof 1983, I, 264): inclination and recognition, dominating partner in life, narrow boundaries of life, power , exploitation of others, prestige, personal admiration, ambition for personal success, self-sufficiency and independence, perfection and unassailability. These in turn are "values" ("dispositional dispositions") and thus "motives" (see Heckhausen 1989, 79).

Von Cube points out that man is not only a spirit with "psyche and spirit" in the sense of educational tradition or a technically oriented being, but fundamentally and primarily a nature being. Every human being has "preprogrammed behavioral dispositions", such as, primarily non-learned patterns, e.g. Sex drive, instinct for curiosity, instinct for aggression, tool instinct, herd instinct, competing behavior, and functional desire (v Cube, in: Roth 1991, 125, 127, 129, 130). We can determine these instinctual patterns as body-related or bodily-oriented basic needs.

Since man always strives for pleasure, without effort, there is a mismatch between stimuli and natural behavior in industrial society. Excessive irritation leads to a reduction and disfigurement of the instinctive behavior. This in turn has destructive consequences, partly related directly to the environment and partly to humans.

From this cube postulates education as a central educational topic for those who want "educated people" (von Cube, in: Roth 1991, 279-280). By "education" of Cube means above all "reflection", which is to combine in a masterful manner, gain an overview, draw consequences, and arrange. This directly includes, self-knowledge and self-conscious, whereby the instinctual life is integrated and controlled freely by superego and morality or traditional norms. This type of education means after cube "effort". The core question asked by Cube is: "Which type of human being is capable of surviving in the future?"; and his answer: Only the human being, who is reflecting in a larger evolutionary context (von Cube, in: Roth 1991, 131).

Psychoanalysis tries to explain human behavior in the first five years of life, from the point of view of instincts and instinctual experience (especially in education). Motives such as the pursuit of power and possessions, performance motivation and aggression, money and work, as well as much more, should be explained from the drives and drive elements. Today, motivational research presents much more comprehensive explanatory models that decisively expand and correct the psychoanalytic vision. Socialization, conflict theory, cognition, and self-concept are just a few examples (Heckhausen 1989).

The general difficulty in identifying basic needs in the relevant specialist literature is that a researcher theoretically constitutes one thing as a basic need, while another scientist interprets basic needs as part of human nature (instinct, drive). Thus, to take an example, one can describe Spranger's ways of life as basic strivings and reinterpret them as basic needs: the theoretical, economic, aesthetic, social, political, and religious basic needs.

Furthermore, as is customary in antiquity, one can certainly determine the pleasure-aversion principle as the main criterion of all basic needs.

Secondary is the path to this balance: in one case directly, in others under short-term renunciation in favor of long-term pleasure satisfaction, and again in others above reason or reality principles (according to Freud). Lewin (1963) solved the 'theoretical' problem by formally defining the need with "any longing for achieving a set aim".

Finally, we can basically ask whether the satisfaction of all or as many basic needs as the main criterion of happiness, of happiness and sense of life par excellence, can be called. We cannot share views that philosophically (or physiologically) understand such a happiness experience as the core goal of human existence. There may be moments of rejuvenation, although basic needs (for example, sexual gratification, work, material growth, autonomy) are not satisfied. The experience of the central transformation processes of individuation means a deeper happiness experience than the physiological satisfaction of pleasure.

The term "basic need" also gives the impression that it contains a claim to be fulfilled or satisfied. The need for "hunger", for example, contains the vital need to be satisfied. The need for sexual gratification or the expression of feelings (as part of self-expression) can make the vital claim that failure leads to illness, misconduct, and destructiveness. Finally, as a criterion for the validity of a basic need, its enrichment in human being and life (psyche, mind, and body) could be determined.

One difficulty in identifying basic needs is the fact that people in industrial societies are not given any vital necessities by the media and the diversity of consumer goods. Imagine, on the following day, someone buys everything that TV advertisements say is clever and necessary for a pleasant life, neatly hypno-suggestive to the viewer, with all the rules of brainwashing (Fromm 1982). That would not only force such a person into a crazy buying urge, but make him somehow "crazy". He does not need most of the products, and what he wants to fulfill in terms of mental and spiritual needs, because it is a basic need, he achieves without this abundance of products.

Man is drilled daily through and through, worse than some sects, that these and those products and activities are absolutely necessary to freedom, love, affection, security, sexual desire, contentment, a good relationship, appreciation, strength, originality, and to achieve much more. Man is so "deformed" that one can no longer ask him what his basic needs are.

You cannot ask the other half of humanity, which has too little of all this, what they have for basic needs. "The Arrogance of the Sated" (Galbraith 1982) cannot be a measure and poverty has its own arrogance, which only distracts from what is present in man in terms of actual physiological, material, and above all mental-spiritual basic needs.

There are needs about an individual's life possibilities that cannot be met without material dimensions. It should also be pointed out that Christianity creates psychological dispositions through dogmatic doctrines and alienated rituals that distort the real basic needs to the point of being unrecognizable.

On the other hand, there are needs that are developmentally psychological and change during a lifetime. Many are also culture dependent. Children do not have the same basic needs as adults. The basic needs and the "quasi-needs" are subject to change and a variety of possibilities of design (Lewin 1963, 312, 317). Although we assume that the human brain contains a "pleasure center" with the experience of "pleasant and unpleasant" (Becker-Carus 1981, 165-167), we cannot simply reduce any kind of need to this category of experience.

We can identify four orientations about the inner relation of basic needs:
1) related to themselves
2) related to other people
3) related to the goods and the living space (world)
4) related to transcendence

We refrain from developing a theoretical construction, but believe that these four orientations, as a whole, constitute a "bundle" of basic needs that are mutually dependent and need to be balanced, in order to balance the balance of the entire subsystem. The basic needs are focused on: oneself, other people, the world and goods and transcendence.

The "Quasi-Needs" and their characteristics

A "secondary need" is a need that builds upon, or is constitutively part of, a primary need. Lewin speaks here of "quasi-needs" - in contrast to "objective needs" - (Lewin 1963, 148, Lewin in Thomae 1969, 145). Socio-critical here is often the talk of "luxury needs" or "consumer need".

Without a doubt, the term "quasi-need" is not very suitable for everyday language. Therefore, we consistently use the term "artificial needs" in our works. We speak of "substitute needs", if we want to emphasize the function of substitution. "Quasi-need" does not sound very realistic. Nevertheless, we accept it as a concept of theoretical construction.

Characteristics for "quasi-needs" are:

- ☐ Trained
- ☐ Induced by society (environment)
- ☐ Artificially stimulated from the outside
- ☐ Not necessary for life and development
- ☐ Physiologically and psychologically not by nature
- ☐ Significant individual differences
- ☐ Compensation function
- ☐ Perversion function
- ☐ Exaggeration in the measure
- ☐ Not relevant to mental and physical health

"Quasi needs" cannot be meaningfully categorized. In contrast to the basic needs, they are characterized above all by their exaggeration and substitute function. The individual thus does not create a necessary and activating space for mental-spiritual growth or the realization of existence.

The value and goal orientations of the "quasi-needs" lie in the following areas:

- ☐ Products, goods, property, capital
- ☐ Experience opportunities
- ☐ Mobility margin
- ☐ Power and strength
- ☐ Experience intensity
- ☐ Employment abundance
- ☐ Record-breaking death risks

Lewin and others consider an organization of hierarchical needs to be possible (1963, 305). Creating a hierarchy, however, means assuming one needs must be met for other needs to be up to date and fulfilled. This certainly applies to the primary physiological need. The fact is that man can hardly realize himself, without money. His self-actualization then lies at the level of creating his primary living conditions. Injection displacement converts to other needs, which, as psychoanalysis has proved, never has a constructive effect (Freud 1961, Fromm 1979, Adler 1966, Reich 1976).

It is therefore sensible to set the observance of the instinctual needs before the search for God - or rather parallel to it. But this is rather a work-practical problem, which belongs in a concept of the versatile balanced personality formation considering the comprehensive satisfaction of needs.

Now there are a whole range of other needs, such as the need for cleanliness, order, job satisfaction, free mobility, justice, rest, peace, entertainment, dominance, tranquility, and success. Such needs should be placed interpretatively in the categories mentioned above. It should also be emphasized that the needs can vary during a lifetime, sometimes receive a different form of expression (than in childhood), and sometimes no longer have the same "drive" as in younger adulthood. In addition, there are basic needs that can (and must) be given a variety of forms through education, socialization, and enculturation.

Many forces hinder proper handling of basic needs. If the "quasi-needs" are always an exaggeration (and distortion) of a basic need - which, of course, each contains a subjective interpretation - then even the basic needs never exist "pure" and "clear". They have an individual character and an action characteristic, which stands in the personal living space and is thus subjective to understand. This requires keeping an eye on influencing factors.

Factors that influence the satisfaction of (quasi) needs are:

☐ Uncertainty	☐ Lack of knowledge
☐ Inhibitions	☐ Habits
☐ Stress	☐ Settings
☐ Feelings of inferiority	☐ Models
☐ Relations	☐ Learning opportunities
☐ Prejudice	☐ Application aids
☐ Insufficient thinking	☐ Overworked
☐ Disorientation	☐ No role models
☐ Penalties	☐ Wrong suggestions
☐ Lack of courage	☐ Personal living space

☐ Little creativity	☐ Money
☐ Strict superego	☐ Extended environment
☐ Inertia	☐ Labor market
☐ Convenience	☐ Political situation
☐ Indifference	☐ Knowledge / Education

The fulfillment of the basic needs is usually an exhausting and difficult matter. Such needs are usually not immediate and cannot be satisfied directly. What many really feel about needs requires a painstaking learning process until fulfillment, for example: freedom, truth, wisdom, love, happiness, artistic activity, relationship happiness, transcendence experiences, insights (eg on man and life), self-determination, growth, and self-updating. Our study also aims to show just the viable and safe ways to realistically meet such basic needs.

The way to meet "quasi-needs" is easier, and above all, shorter. It is precisely the characteristic that such needs lead away from being human and provide a direct aid to the outside world: "Do this, it is very easy"; "Take this, this makes life more beautiful"; "Come to us, you will experience fun and joy"; "Buy this product, you will feel good"; "Take this variant, it makes everything easy". And again and again are associatively linked to: freedom, love, tenderness, fatherly love, harmony, maternal love, success, praise, recognition, to be understood, the unique (life), chance, desire, enjoyment, great experience, ego strength, competence, family happiness, relieves, and similar things more.

The associative links in advertising (television) clearly show the characteristic of "quasi-needs". With a few exceptions, they make life essential, which is not vital at all, and give the impression of a positive realization of life, where everything remains superficial. They link to basic needs, where the offer has nothing to do with it. They address the person where he is helpless and can be totally manipulated, with NLP practices.

In shops, one should work with the needs of customers. Music in the background creates atmosphere in the "consumption habitat". The client-centered communication, modeled on humanistic psychology, should also encourage buying behavior. Every good seller knows this today. Even the waiters in some restaurants have trained this method: "How are you? ... Where are you from? ... Nice weather today ... not true ... But you also have dear children ... May I help you? ... I suspect that you will like this ... Immediately ... We are there for you ... I understand ... ". The customer should not be surprised if he gets a strange feeling. Because personally, such words are not meant. That has nothing to do with people-centered manners. This is usually nothing more than stimulating the customer to even more consumption.

Adequate satisfaction of the basic needs is actually a challenging life. One seems to demand more than the "quasi-needs". But, in fact, this is not true. Stronger and more expensive are the "quasi-needs". They produce their own momentum, with increasing costs and finally a dependency from whose "glue threads" the customer tries to free himself. For somehow, the ego senses and everything in the psychic inner life becomes more and more distorted, more and more chaotic, more and more difficult to guide, more and more complicated to live, more and more harmful in the interpersonal, and then bigger and bigger the hole of inner emptiness comes. Where first a pleasant satisfaction of the "quasi-needs" was, later stands a juggernaut, who opens his mouth and never gets full.

Definition of "Motive": critical use of scientific terms

Psychology looks for "motives" that explain every behavior. However, many actions cannot be explained by the concept of the need tension. But what else is there for "motives", "Motifs" outside the list of needs? What is the place of the term "motive" in the entire psychic system and in the subsystem of "needs"?

To anticipate the result of our following conceptual analysis, we have defined the term "motive" as something that is not a specific psychic basic force and is not an independent force in addition to the psychic subsystems. "Motive" cannot be meaningfully defined or used as a psychological construct concept. "Motive" is the classic and correct term for a psychological question: "What is the motive?" The answers are always localized in a psychic subsystem: a feeling, a drive, a thought, a need, an attitude, a dream and so on. We never ask for the "motive", for example, if the TV suddenly has a fault, or an engine damage occurs on the car.

"Motive is a concept that is supposed to explain something" (Heckhausen 1989, 9). This explanation is a "hypothetical construct". The problem is hardly solvable with this definition: "How many motives one should distinguish as distinguishable content classes in the barely overlookable amount of human action goals is still controversial" (Heckhausen 1989, 10).

Motives are also described as "dispositional dispositions", which in turn are defined as abstractly as possible: on the one hand with "momentary directionality to an action goal" (that is the definition of the term "motivation"), and on the other hand operationally in the networking with action and situation. "Only the connection between disposition-indicating indicators (measurement of the" motive ") and subsequent characteristics of behavior under defined situational conditions, as proven within the framework of a nomological network, justifies understanding motive as a hypothetical construct" (Heckhausen 1989, 10).

Motive Psychology offers many theoretical approaches to explaining an action. Confusing in the scientific literature is that often "motive" is equated with "need", "interests", "drive", "pleasure-aversion", "action goals", "instinct", "incentive variable", and "innate impulses" (Allport, Lewin, Freud, Thomae, Lersch, Maslow, Rogers, Hull, Heckhausen). Close to these concepts are always emotion, affect, urge, purpose, will, and purposefulness (Roth 1971, 69).

In some definitions, the objective aspect is part of the definition of the concept "motive": the anticipation of a goal state is the "motive" (Lewin). Athematic models (Allport, Thomae) are next to polythematic models (Freud, Maslow). As with Needs, it attempts to construct a division into "primary" and "secondary" motives.

Further efforts have been made to reduce the motives to a single basic force: libido, power, deficit, psychic energy, self-realization. All motives are, according to behaviorism, traceable to the primary, physiological, and emotional states of tension of the instincts (Begins 1960, 493). An attempt has been made to clarify this dynamic with the model "stimulus reaction" and with "habits" (Haseloff / Jorswieck 1970).

Next to them are models that take on different basic motifs, such as: needs, values, delights, feelings, insecurity, meaning, curiosity, achievement, expectation, affective disorder, aggression, sex, fear, power, etc....

Scientists generally try to reduce the motives to a single basic force. Others claim that "motive is everything that sets behavior in motion". This makes a systematization impossible, and a definition diverse (Roth 1969, 76).

The term "motive" is actually a misleading construct (Kelley, in: Thomae 1969/5, 498 f.), and incompatible between the many theoretical approaches, including: psychological theories, instinct theory, personality theory, motivational psychology, cognitive psychology, association theory, psychology of activation, psychology learning etc. (see: Heckhausen 1989, 19-54).

Science has constructed an unsolvable scientific problem, with the concept of motive and the many definitions and abstract constructions. We want to clarify this scientifically complicated topic, examine the term "motive" more closely, and establish the connections to the "needs". We neither seek a single driving force to explain each action, nor do we create a polythematic theory. Likewise, we do not intend to create a concept that immediately captures the functioning of the entire personality. We also do not hypostatize a kind of "dark drive box" that could explain human behavior.

"Motivational" questions are, for example: "Why did you help him in the garden? What moved you to speak like that to me? What is your reason for humiliating me? Why are you screaming? Why are you feel so depressed? Why did you marry this man? Why is he going to a prostitute every week? Why is he perverted? Why is she oppressing her Man? Why is he so aggressive? Why did he kill him? Why do these people exert so much violence? " Such questions seek the motive.

The key question is "WHY?". Obviously, it is about the explanation and justification of an action. Formally, the answer to the "why?" question is the "cause", with psychology using the formal term "motive" for a particular type of cause. "Motive" means the "moving", and / or the "reason" of an action. The reason sought is the "psychic power" that leads man to action. We can do different considerations.

In general, it is not common sense to use the word motive in the context of events, so we do not say, for example: "What is the reason that the tire has burst?". In natural science, this is called causality. Habitat factors that cause an action in a situation are generally not interpreted as "motivational forces".

One does not say for example: "The red light, was at that moment, the motive for Mr. L. to not cross the street at the zebra crossing". Thus, we have a first term limitation: "Motives" are part of the psychic powers of humans and not the forces in the habitat. The acting factors from the habitat cannot meaningfully be called "motives". In addition, the ego often has no free space available. Here we are talking about causes, factors, or determinants. Not "motive".

Who after the "why?" asks, for what reason an individual in a certain situation, at a certain time, acted so and not differently. This usually implies a certain act of will in the acting individual. But the conscious act of will is a dazzling thing in many concrete action situations.

Furthermore, the "motive" question usually contains the assumption that the actor has an awareness of the motive. The individual knows what moved him to a certain action. This is often not the case. The motivations in everyday life are rarely clear in consciousness. A "motive" can also be causal or final (teleological). We interpret the problems of will, of consciousness, and of the nature of the cause (causality / finality) from the term "motive". These should be separate questions or considerations.

There are many types of actions in very different life systems where it does not make sense to talk about "motivational power" or "need". Forces from the unconscious (a complex or a superego) can trigger action. An idea can cause a certain action. Likewise, a feeling, a certain self-experience, a dream, a need, and the love can lead to a behavior. There are obviously "motives" that can work from all subsystems.

We can recognize from this: The term motive is formally to be grasped further than the term need. "Motive" captures the entire psychic system with its many individual variables and single force. The term "motive" means, in this psychological orientation, either a need or "quasi-need". This then belongs in the subsystem under the same concepts; or he means a motive that cannot be located within this psychic subsystem. Then you must choose terms from other subsystems. If the motive is a feeling, the result of an act, a thought, a pattern of life in the unconscious, a dream, or the power of love, then we speak in the terms of this corresponding subsystem and not of a specific "motivational force" delimited from it.

Many people often think little, wrongly, or one-sidedly in their actions. Many behaviors happen form out of habit (automated mechanisms), rather than from reflected motives. Some behavior also happens because of a lack of learning processes. Sometimes the individual has no choice at all between different possibilities of action, either because of external determinants, or because the individual has learned no other pattern. The "ability" that brings about the new state (goal of an action) determines with its quality how the result will be. You do what you can, often without asking if there are more appropriate behaviors. The result of an action can obviously be traced back to many diverging psychological relationships and framework conditions (as determinants). It does not make sense to talk about "motive" in this variety of causes.

The implications of these considerations are: In all cases, the term "motive" is not a specific psychic function. Every functional unit, in every psychic subsystem, has a specific concept. The term "motive" does not belong to the actual personality theory, but to the questioning consideration of human action and its psychic powers of action. The term motif belongs in the language of the external view and always means the moving forces in the human being. All psychic individuals can be considered "motives."

Valenz-parameter of all psychical forces (functions)

We have hereby decomposed the term "motive" into its parts and thus made superfluous as a term for a specific psychological force. What remains are the individual psychic subsystems, or their individual variables, referred to as "psychic individual forces". There remains a residual problem. In some concepts of psychology - on the subject of motive - clearly comes a force expression, in a sense, the "energy" of the psychic individual functions that makes the urge to act possible. Its terms are in psychology: libido, plastically, expansive life energy, vital energy, impulse, stimulus tension, impulsive force, orgone energy and "drive".

Suppose first of all, that we are dealing with the un-specific psychic energy, in general. This can be "loaded" topic specific. This gives a psychic, individual force, an urge: a psycho-energetic topic-specific tension. Examples include: a thought is a simultaneously formed psychic energy, a feeling theme becomes a formed psychic energy, a particular need receives a certain shaped psychic energy, physical pain generates psychic energy, sexual (organic) sensation activates psychic energy, a content of consciousness can activate psychic energy.

One can say here, "A psychic individual force (variable) - we also include the perceptions and sensations - binds and forms psychic energy through a topic (content), whereby we use subject or content to describe the state of a subjectively experienced value or meaning (a specific quality)". We assume that people react differently psycho-energetically to the same "topics". For the experience, above all has subjective (personal) value and meaning.

The question is, are there different topic-specific "energy centers" active in each psychic subsystem, as an organic entity, perhaps as "subunits"? In concrete terms, this implies - in theory - that there is an energy organization in thoughts, feelings, unconsciousness, love, needs, mind, consciousness, sensations, and so on. We expand this hypothesis: there is also a psychic energy field in the whole body, which is also formed by the body functions (regardless of the consciousness) or constantly activated.

The energy field is a complex organized psycho-energetic space. There are many experiences that confirm such a complex psycho-energetic hypothesis. We have already explained this in the chapter on psychodynamics. Reich, Lowen, and others in the field of "Orgone Theory", have done basic and meaningful research. Hypothetically, we can look at two other aspects, how, in general, does psycho-energetic dynamics work? Is it automatically? And further, how, as organic wholeness, do these energy centers work together?

Activated psychic energy urges always come after action. It is, to a certain extent, the action "thrust" (Lewin). Through action, the tension breaks down again. If the topic is then up to date, this in turn this generates a new "charge". If this voltage cannot be removed, it will be automatically moved. Even an "undervoltage" can generate an urge to act. Blocked tension works in a neighboring psychic system (displacement): it transfers to bodily functions (conversion). Or it disturbs, because it is not channeled by the ego, or the general / particular behavior.

As you know, you can relax with energy relaxation techniques and "revitalize" an undervoltage. However, autogenic training, empty hypnosis (for relaxation), and yoga exercises, can only momentarily balance the energy space, but never "redeem" the topic. The topics generate, if they are still current, again and again the previous state of tension.

There are complex systems of ideas, whose goal is to never (or as little as possible) translate this shaped energy into action. But what is this? This is a denial of life, and ultimately, a hatred of life. It is a unique opportunity to implement the different forms of energy in life. Unfortunately, people do it wrong. They live out any kind of aggression in any way. They allow themselves to be pushed by the tensions, according to the motto, "As fast as possible discharge".

Personality development, in this sense, wants to use this psycho-energetic diversity to build life and to form the human being. If the psychic functions are life-building, then there is a harmoniously functioning psycho-energetic space. But, if the psychic functions are not formed, or are wrong or chaotic, then this can lead to considerably divergent living forces structures. The social reality reflects this.

If a person cannot reduce tensions, either because he does not know relaxation techniques, or because he does not convert them into actions, this always results in mental disorders or psycho-somatic suffering.

The blocked sexual energy in the lower abdomen, the tense thought energy in the head, an aggressive emotional issue in the chest with simultaneously activated unconscious complex (usually experienced in the abdomen), together, cause in the best case complex muscle tension throughout the body. The more this energy space becomes tense, and the longer this state of tension lasts, the greater the susceptibility to mental disorders and (or) psycho-somatic diseases.

The andragogical possibilities of psycho-energetic relaxation techniques are enormous. Particularly in the field of all kinds of addictive behavior, there are thus still largely insufficient opportunities for research. For example, if every four hours, the organic addiction deficit puts the psycho-energetic state to peak tension, then a 'deep relaxation', every four hours, is the most effective support that anyone in this workspace can possibly desire. Similar hopeful perspectives exist in the area of all psycho-somatic diseases, including many forms of cancer.

In an athematic sense, we can generally understand this energy as a space in which it works homeo-statically, from undervoltage to overvoltage. In theory, we assume that this energy has the tendency to rebalance a strong over or undervoltage (like the blood pressure with diastole and systole). According to Lewin, this energy contains a "valence". This is defined, by him, as the "strength of impression" and the "prompting character" of an intrapsychic or external situation. You can also describe this as an "action urge". The urge to act is always a basic need from the nature of the thing itself.

Therefore, we define an athematic force outside the basic needs and "quasi-needs". We call this force "valence parameter". Specifically, several valence parameters can be activated simultaneously. This variable magnitude, of the urge to demand, pushes itself out into a homeostatic equilibrium, and thus into action, as soon as an increased tension is created intra psychically, or between inside and outside, or the tension becomes too low.

We can call this force "drive" or "driving force". Every psychic function, in the psychic system or in a psychic subsystem, can to some extent, provide this "valence parameter", with a psycho-energetic charge. All human life contains this basic force. It is generally called "psychic energy". This energy was discussed in the chapter on psychodynamics. The psychic energy (with the valence parameter) is accepted in the personality theory. We call the conversion of a valence parameter an elementary basic need of human life (see Oerter / Montada 1987, 87 f., And 637 f.).

We summarize the result of our analysis:

A motive may be a need, but it does not have to be. Moving reasons for human action lie in the psychic system and in the habitat. The nature of a motive can be some psychic function. The collection of learned action essentially decides how a person acts in a situation. Each action can also be explained dynamically, in terms of past, present, and future. A motive can be conscious or unconscious.

The act of will is a separate consideration. A subject does not have to be vital and can be irrelevant to health. From this, we conclude that the term "motive", as psychic power and function, is unsuitable for personality psychology. The term cannot be meaningfully used as a theoretical construct.

The only universally recognized characteristic of "motive" is a dynamic force, which we call "valence parameters of psychic energy." Only as a question construction can the term "motif" be usefully used. But then the question is focused on intrapsychic forces and never on determinants of the living space. Moreover, there is still a consensus as to whether the "motive" implies an act of will and awareness of the moving psychic force, or whether it is irrelevant to the questioning consideration.

On the instinctual psychology approach of theorizing, we highlight some considerations:

The question of the number of "impulses" - that are peculiar to man - has already led Schultz-Hencke to make an action-oriented limitation: "The number of drive types is still undetermined." With a certainty, one can speak of an infinite variety ... "(Schultz-Hencke 1985, 21).

His psychoanalytic theory of neuroses, therefore, limits those types of impulses that are neuroses-psychologically significant. We do not want to continue that here. In the context here, of importance are at most the "driving components". These being: perceptual, presentation, emotional, excitation-like, motoric, and fearsome. We can reduce these parts to valence and energy on the one hand, and perceptual psychological and reactive (action), on the other hand. That is near the model of Lewin, which contains the following components: the "theme of the imagination" or the actual need and the locomotion (change in the psychological place, and the force or the valence) (1963, 82-83, 305-306).

If we consider that certain basic feelings can also be understood as "drives", since these are based on brain-physiological patterns (Izard 1981, 23-24), then it becomes understandable if a drive concept becomes fundamentally problematic: "The fruitful days of the drive concept are almost over, "concludes Heckhausen (1989, 100) from this chapter.

It should be noted only marginally that the discussion about instinctual concepts contains a double value aspect, which seems rather problematic to us. First, when people talk about their "instincts" (or about those of others), that usually has a disrespectful tone, for example, in the sense of the "court of desires are low." And secondly, evaluative opinions are already mixed in the definition, for example, the term "Thanatos", which is the "instinct of death and destruction". The problem is grasped with two aspects of the question: Is the biological decomposition of the body "destructive"?

Is not there perhaps an underlying evolutionary principle and a transcendental principle at work? The other aspect of the question is, will not the drive, say the "urgent nature" of man, be "destructive", perhaps only through lacking or false human education?

Is it not perhaps a somewhat premature judgment of human nature to call the aggression and death instinct "evil"?

If andragogy has the education of the human being as the main task, then the needs represent a special challenge. First there stands the man, with all his instrumental and mental potentials. The science of education assumes that, from birth onwards, a human being brings with it a broad spectrum of positive possibilities psychologically by nature. Andragogy understands education as a correction or change and as a continuing process of unfolding these potentials.

Marcuse discusses needs in the context of pleasure and happiness (1968, 128-168). It clearly distinguishes the factor eudaemonism (pleasure for pleasure) from the possibility of living pleasure with reason. Thus, the satisfaction of needs becomes more than mere: "happiness through lust life". The true bliss, the fulfillment of the highest potentialities of the individual, cannot exist in what is commonly called happiness: it must be sought in the world of the soul and of the mind (1968, 130). The reality of happiness is the reality of freedom, as the self-determination of liberated humanity in its common struggle with nature (1968, 167).

For Andragogy it follows: The fulfillment of the basic needs takes place in the systemic connection with the power of love, the mind, the intelligence functions, and with the other psychic subsystems. According to Balint, the full satisfaction - the "Endlessness" (1981, 78-82) - in our context we would formulate here as the "fulfillment of bliss".

"Prelude fixation" (according to Balint) we understand the pleasure principle as the inability to create this happiness, and of unfolding and differentiation of all potentials.

This inability is characterized mainly by lack of learning, by lack of awareness about the mental life, and by blocking the growth tendencies. The theme of pleasure thus transcends the pregenital or genital dimension and transcends itself in the meaning and value of the liberation and realization of the possibilities of the psychical organism. Here, andragogy transcends what psychology captures. Andragogy takes the step of forming the whole personality.

A taxonomy of needs (for example, Murray had already proposed far before humanistic psychology in 1938, see: Bischof 1983, 118-120) would have go beyond the brain-physiological and lust-oriented model, and reach philosophical-anthropological dimensions. Frankl has tried this with his "sense therapy", Maslow with the "I-transcendence" (inner values and growth values), and Fromm with the "love". We place these aspects in the first chapter in the overarching framework of the individuation process.

Basic needs: Meaning and fulfillment of life

We place the fulfillment of need in the context of the question of the meaning in life. The psychoanalyst Frankl has made decisive contributions to this topic. We take some reflections from his works (A: Man before the Question of Meaning, 1985; B: Anthropological Foundations of Psychotherapy, 1975).

"The human being, in search of meaning, is only frustrated in the social conditions of today, and that is because the affluent society is able to satisfy practically all human needs. Only one need is left empty and that is the need for meaning, as this is the deepest need of man. For man needs to find meaning in his life, or better, in every situation in life, and to go and fulfill it! " (A, 46)

"And finally, it has been proven that man can find meaning, regardless of whether he is religious or not. Where we cannot change a situation, we have been required to change ourselves, that is, to mature, to grow, and to outgrow ourselves. " (A, 48) "No animal cares about the meaning of life." (A, 119)

"Sense not only has to be found, but can also be found, and in the search for it leads the conscience of the people. The conscience is a sense organ." It can be defined as the ability and unique sense and hidden in every situation." (A, 156).

"There is no situation in which life would cease to offer us meaning, and there is no one for whom life has not given a task, and the ability to make sense of it." (A, 157).

"In the fulfillment of meaning, man realizes himself. If we now fulfill the meaning of suffering, we realize the most human in man, we mature, we grow, and we grow beyond ourselves. Suffering has meaning if you yourself become another. " (A, 160-161) "We have to learn that it never really matters what we still expect from life, but rather what life expects of us." (A, 173)

"If we really wanted to see the whole meaning of life, in sheer lust, then life would ultimately have to make no sense. For what is lust after all? A state of affairs." The materialist (hedonism goes along with materialism) would even say, "Lust is nothing but some process in the ganglion cells of the brain, and for the sake of attaining such a process shall it be considered to live, to experience, to suffer, or to do anything? " (A, 223)

"Let us only ask ourselves what the real result would be, if a human being was able to fully satisfy all the needs that it may have in the temporal. What would be the result: the experience of fulfillment, or rather the opposite, that is to experience an abysmal boredom - a bottomless void - just the existential vacuum? " (A, 229)

"The purpose of life is ... not to ask, but to answer by answering for life, but it follows that the answer is not to be given in words, but in fact, through action. " (A, 234)

"The interpretation of meaning is not identical with meaning: the human being who tries to interpret the meaning of life seeks not to arbitrarily give any sense to being, but to 'the' meaning find." (B, 304)

"Attitude values are superior to creative values and experience values of moral height. But to realize values of attitude requires not only a creative ability, not only the ability to experience, but also the ability to suffer." The acquisition of the ability to suffer is an act of self-styling .The human being never decides only something, but also himself; and, self-decision is always self-organization ... "(B, 310-312).

8. The Unconscious

Definitions and a new conception

The unconscious is not only a difficult topic, but also a very controversial psychic construct. The positions are far apart from a strong rejection of the existence of a subconscious to the irrevocable clarification, "There is the unconscious". But that is not a scientific problem. This is a problem of those scientists who deny the existence of a subconscious. At most, one can speak of a language problem and ask for a discussion on which term best characterizes the phenomenon "unconscious". Another really serious problem is the exact definition of what is meant by the unconscious. There are different ideas about this. The history of the construction, of the unconscious, begins as early as the 19th century, with Charcot and Janet.

The use of the term "unconscious" contains scientifically different theoretical approaches. But even in everyday language, the unconscious, is often spoken about. "X acts unconsciously", or "X is pretty unconscious". This usually means that a person does not look, does not remember, does not think, is not 'awake', and generally acts in the 'twilight state'. A theory is rarely associated with it. Such statements are meant to be negative.

Depth psychologists usually use this word in the context of their practical activity or "cases", which then addresses elements of the "neurotic". In many cases, they also mean "not knowing". The theoretical context is consistently directed to the founders of the corresponding theory they represent. Freud (1975) understands everything suppressed and defended among the unconscious. These are the instincts or the instinctual desires and their affects or emotions. As far as the superego is unconscious, that part must be assigned to the unconscious. According to Freud, impulses are basically capable of consciousness, through dreams and thus through memory in connection with word ideas.

Let Sigmund Freud speak in more detail (1923): "The distinction between the psychic in the conscious and the unconscious is the basic prerequisite of psychoanalysis ... We have learned that there are strong mental processes or ideas, ... all the consequences for the soul life ... only they are not aware of themselves ... because a certain power opposes that, otherwise they can become aware ... So, we gain our concept of the unconscious from the doctrine of the repression We see, however, that we have two unconscious things, the latent, yet conscious, and the repressed, in itself and without further unconsciousness ... (From the ego) are also the repressions, through which certain mental strivings are to be excluded not only from the consciousness, but also from the other kinds of validity and activity ... But since this resistance sic emanating from his ego and belonging to it, we are faced with an unforeseen situation. In the self is something that behaves just like the repressed, that is, expressing strong effects without becoming aware of oneself ... "

This is contrasted with formulations by Carl Gustav Jung (1916-1936): "The personal unconscious contains lost memories, repressed (intentionally forgotten), embarrassing ideas, so-called subliminal perceptions (such as sensory perceptions) that we are not strong enough, and finally, content that is not yet ready for consciousness, corresponds to the figures of the shadow often appearing in the dreams. One is disappointed if one believes that the unconscious is something harmless. Of course, the unconscious is not dangerous under all circumstances, but as soon as a neurosis occurs, it is a sign that there is a special accumulation of energy in the unconscious, a kind of charge that can explode... In all ordinary cases, the unconscious is unfavorable or dangerous only because we disagree with it in contrast to this. ... Being unconnected with the unconscious means something like instinctual and rootlessness ... The unconscious mind is constantly active and creates combinations of its materials that serve to determine the future. "

Jung (1975) characterizes the unconscious primarily in terms of content, with the so-called "complexes". These are the emotional experiences that have been repressed and separated from consciousness. What is in the unconscious was once in consciousness. These can be thoughts, feelings, experiences, and events. These are also the instinctual impulses and wishes. This also includes the personality parts he calls "the shadow". The unconscious is the "non-remembered" and the "unconscious." According to Jung, the "collective unconscious" lies in a deeper layer of the unconscious. The "archetypes" are the contents of the collective unconscious. We will do some discussion at the end of this chapter and comment on the term "archetype" in the chapter on dreams. In the collective unconscious, the basic themes of being human are stored, in a sense inherited.

Schultz-Hencke (1951) speaks of "unconsciousness", meaning the "difficult-to-remember". In terms of content, he places different drives here. These include: sexual drive, striving for ambition, striving for love, and striving for possession. Adler (1966) rejects the unconscious but distinguishes between "conscious" and "unconscious". Boss (1953 and 1957) also rejects this term, speaking of "possibilities of life that escape perception", of "forgetting, concealing and not knowing", of "an unimportant reference" as well as of "possibilities of life that are overpowering are pressing for. "

Jaspers (1959) differentiates between different aspects. These are: that which is separated from consciousness, the unknown, the source of the creative, and the "absolute being" (as a metaphysical concept). The "familial unconscious" of Szondi (1965) contains the conception of the collective unconscious of Jung: the phylogenetic inheritance of humanity and, according to it, specifically "the totality of ancestral claims".

Striking is the tendency to negative characterization of the unconscious. We think this is fundamentally wrong. We want to demonstrate that the unconscious fulfills a positive function - as a psychic system - and can never be defined only from the psychopathological point of view. Maslow et el (1973, 24-26) pointed out the positive function of the unconscious, above all the superego (conscience). Jones (1978, 316) also describes the unconscious with positive aspects: the "source of inspiration". Discuss the individual aspects about the "unconscious".

The core aspects of the unconscious are psychological and philosophical (according to Dorsch 1987 and Laplanche / Pontalis 1994). These are:

- 1. The psychically real being in general (i.e. a transcendental dimension).
- 2. Lost material, not stored in the brain.
- 3. The material is repressed, suppressed, pushed away, and ignored ...
- 4. The not remembered, but rememberable.
- 5. The unrecognized and the unintentional.
- 6. A power within: source of creativity.
- 7. The never conscious, e.g. instinctual.
- 8. Especially infantile wishes and fantasies.
- 9. A part of the ego and the superego.
- 10.A reality that encompasses more than the sum of external experiences.

If we collect the building blocks from the psychoanalytic literature about the unconscious, we find salient parts, depending on the specific theory. We can also rewrite these 'parts', 'themes' and 'forces' as aspects of the subconscious mind; we list the most important ones:

- The unconscious inventory, i.e. 'normal' life experiences of all kinds.
- The so-called complexes, i.e. the painful, 'unredeemed' experiences.
- Specific life experiences, related to sexual drive.
- Difficult child-parent relationships, with rejection-binding ambivalence.
- Deficit experience of general basic needs.
- The foundation of conscience (superego), through the father relationship.
- The internalization of religious images and practices as the truth.
- Feelings of inferiority that tend to turn into power needs.
- Exaggerated affective, restricting attachment of a parent to the child.
- Voluptuous interest in oneself, in others, and in the world of life.
- Cramped unilateral pleasure bonds.
- I-ideal images of all kinds; in addition: one-sided positive misperceptions.
- Wishes in all directions (allowed, unauthorized, fulfilled, unfulfilled).
- Emotional bonds through fear of punishment and fear of life.
- Bonding through primary relationships of trust and love.
- Unsaved guilt, subjective and objective.
- Generally undesirable, but pleasant (interesting) sensory experiences.
- A 'secret' defense mechanism that keeps content out of the unconscious.
- Ego aspects that are unrecognized or averted (shadows, masks, etc.).
- Injured, offended self-esteem issues.
- Shifts / transformations (of a complex) into other topics.
- Indirect, difficult to recognize utterances: e.g. Somatization, constraints.
- A psychic energy that acts according to the inventory element.
- A strong imbalance between the unconscious and the consciousness.
- The distortion of the 'truth' into the opposite.

We first refer to the general conception of the unconscious from the psychoanalytic teachings and note that the unconscious is something like a "reservoir". Consciousness content enters this reservoir ("vessel"). Furthermore, we can generally say that the material in the unconscious consists of images and pictorial ideas. Furthermore, as a general theory that the image inventory comes mainly from the life experiences. This seems to be widely recognized. Everything that human beings experience emotionally and visually from the time of conception, can come into this reservoir. Already prenatally, the human being absorbs basic moods of the mother and the emotional atmosphere of the family (Verny 1981, 11-63).

The early childhood decisively shapes the unconscious. The young person absorbs many experiences in his unconscious. Through emotional experience, the outside world is internalized and stored. All these experiences remain in the unconscious for a lifetime. That is certainly very much and different material of life. It can be said, that in this sense, the entire life story of a human being is embedded in the unconscious. On the other hand, we mean pure arithmetic formulas, banal facts without emotional meaning, names, and facts of all kinds are not inventory of this vessel. Only signs, numbers, letters, formulas, and facts are inventories of linguistic memory.

Basically, it does not matter if these images are meaningful or meaningless, positive or negative, progressive or regressive, harmful or useful. Man experiences the realities often distorted and often illusory expanded. In dealing with the world, he forms his pictorial ideals and his ideas about the value and meaning of a thing or an action. Insofar as these experiential experiences are pictorial, they can be inventories of the unconscious.

We have defined the so-called "valence parameter". In other words, every unity of a psychic force is charged psycho-energetically by the experienced meaning (value). Specifically, this means that: thoughts bind psychic energy; emotions bind psychic energy; needs bind psychic energy, and experiences of all kinds bind psychic energy.

In the widest sense, all life experiences (self-experience, experience of man and world) bind psychic energy. This energy can be discharged, either through performance, through processing, or through the normal non-specific process of energy reduction. The higher the valence, the more activity is needed to discharge. Our experiences with returns until the prenatal period have repeatedly confirmed that both hardly emotionally afflicted images, as well as adjusted, are stored in this reservoir. This "vessel" is naturally localized in the brain. This is a conclusion that arises from the fact that the processes around the "unconscious" are closely related to brain physiological processes.

If the images, with the energetic charge, are deported into the unconscious (through repression, suppression), then the image stores itself with the active psychic energy in this reservoir. Over the years, the image is constantly recharged by similar experiences, while at the same time expanded into a complex entity. The energetic charge of the same or similar thoughts, feelings, experiences, and needs (and of course also sexual instinctual impulses) becomes more and more intense. So, the unconscious stores many images, with differently shaped energetic charge. We call these pictures "complexes".

The images in the unconscious generally tend to be realized outside. They attract or peel off. They serve as an inner orientation, even if they are energetically free. Based on our observations, we believe that the images outside the conscious ego control affect the various psychic subsystems. They are the inner space that represents the starting point of psychic functioning.

Energetically charged images push through different ways to be broken down, but recharge again and again, partly by external stimuli and partly automatically, as long as the picture is not "redeemed". Tension sometimes happens directly by repeating the original experience. In many cases, however, the discharge takes place symbolically in a shift, projection, inversion (to the contrary), compensation, or conversion (into somatic reactions).

It is known in psychoanalysis and psychosomatics that the psycho-energetic charged images (complexes) cause mental disorders, create physical illnesses, and often "force" people into criminal acts. However, symbolic discharge does not "relieve" a complex, so that the unconscious becomes increasingly destructive during life as it becomes increasingly repressed. The many individual painful realities of life, and the collective social reality, are images of the discharges of this strained unconscious of the people.

This means that the images in the unconscious are the "code program" of life. They bind life by fixing the scope for action of the ego. Thinking is constantly influenced by inner images. The feelings always receive inner resonance through the picture world in the unconscious and thus an amplification. The power of love can only develop in the context of the cleaned-up images. The need urge receives thrust and direction from the subconscious. And psychodynamics is always "colored" by the psychic energy of the unconscious image inventory.

The result is a clear positive function of the unconscious: if the inner images are life-affirming, differentiated, reconciled, realistic, growth-promoting, and balanced, they have a constructive effect on the other psychic functions and actions. We regard this aspect as elementary and constitutive. The images in the unconscious are the vital patterns without which the ego is never able to master life. The ego needs all mental subsystems for living.

The inventory in the subconscious is not rationally reachable. This has long been known in psychoanalysis. You cannot change images with will, with logical thinking, with "commands", and "persuasion". No matter how reasonable or unreasonable the pictures are, the I cannot dispose of it with the intelligence functions. The only access routes are dream interpretation, imagination, and contemplation as well as role play.

The professional experiences teach us, the more an image is energetically charged, then the higher the valence of an image, and the more difficult it is to return to consciousness and the transformation or cleansing. The psychology of border psychology, whether hypnosis, NLP technique, mental healing, or psycho-energetic rituals, cannot restructure in three to five or ten consultations, which has grown over many years. Probably, only in rare cases is a mental disorder or a psycho-somatic condition attributable to a single complex, which at the single point in time X has caused or caused the disorder in the past.

Step by step, the networks of images are to be recalled and processed. Thus, even the most difficult complexes can be disassembled and reassembled into a reconciled image, until this can then be "deposited" as a life experience.

Let us take a closer look at the valence parameter in this context. What is displacing the ego? Why does man displace life experiences, including his inner experience, be it about self-worth or needs? What man represses tells us why he is repressing this. We think that these are predominantly valences, such as emotional value and sense experience of the following kind.

Emotional sense and value experience of stressful life experiences include:

☐ Pain	☐ Offense	☐ Uncertainty
☐ Suffering	☐ Failure	☐ Seriousness
☐ Mourning	☐ Displeasure	☐ Aversion
☐ Unpleasant	☐ Duty	☐ Injuries
☐ Embarrassment	☐ Responsibility	☐ Efforts
☐ Shame	☐ Threat	☐ Calls
☐ Humiliation	☐ Punishment	☐ Hardship
☐ Debt	☐ Fear	☐ Hard reality

From our casuistic observations, we can further postulate the thesis that life experiences and inner experiences - with such valences - always form in addition a compensatory counterpart in the unconscious.

From the work of the unconscious we can record the following theses:

☐ The personality is always a lived past.
☐ The lived past shapes the present and with it the future.
☐ The bondage of man is rooted in the images in the subconscious.
☐ The pictorial material in the unconscious is the experience for life skills.
☐ No one can "escape" from his own unconscious.

We regard it as an elementary and decisive basic fact that man has a biography worth discovering in self-reflection. No human education and no psychotherapy come around this fact. Plus, no educational concept can transform these imprints with any kind of "art", with little work and effort.

The characteristics of the unconscious are:

- The experience
- The picture
- The reference to life
- The feeling
- The value neutrality
- The reality relativity
- The psycho-energetic charge
- The degree of awareness
- The steady effect in life
- The influence of mental functions
- The activation of the projection
- The urge to external reproduction
- The irrational autonomy
- The physical causative agent
- The mental disease cause
- The "thrust" to affective actions
- The constructive power to life
- The changeability of the content
- The expandability
- The building vitality

The functioning of the unconscious leads to the following thesis, which has a central meaning for Andragogy: No one comes around to being what the first years of his life have made him. If man wants to change his present, he changes the past in his unconscious; that means to understand, clarify, process, reconcile, arrange, and correct.

We assume that prenatal imprints, early childhood experiences, school experiences, emotional life conditions and particularly "critical event situations" into old age influence the various psychic forces and actions. Behind every facade and mask, behind many roles and pleasing manners, this unconscious "lurks", which is also different.

The less this "unconscious" is clarified and edited, the more entangled the human being in these shackles. Here is the actual "life lie" to determine.

192

We still must point out a special problem. Imagine: A person experiences a need for sexual relaxation or experience with a partner. For various reasons, this can be done neither in the hour nor after. The need is displaced. It is followed by a compensation, for example, with food, action, or power. Another example: a person clearly experiences that they should reconcile a dispute with the partner, represses this duty and, for example, plunges into cleaning.

Another example: A person clearly recognizes that a particular situation is complicated and emotionally moving. An exact mental occupation is required. The person displaces the first thoughts and turns to a change. We can extend the examples of this kind: A nightmare unsettles a person enormously. He displaces the experience in the day's events. Or, a person has been experiencing a state of tension for a long time, does nothing about it, but displaces the unpleasant experience through distraction. Our key question is, what happens to the repressed experience of this kind? Does this all fall into the unconscious? We mean, usually no, but partly. We want to explain this.

Freud's orthodox psychoanalytic model simply manages complexity, but theoretically does not solve it. We can certainly assign all impulses to the so-called "It". What is the theoretical gain? We suggest using the term "repression" or "repression" for all subsystems.

That is, we can say, a person displaces thoughts, feelings, needs, the power of love, the dreams, and the psychodynamics, or a function of the own ego-system (for example the ego-control). What is repressed here does not have to become part of the unconscious. The repressed remains part of one of these subsystems. However, if the repressed is an element of a situational and "critically experienced" event, with a certain valence, then we can assign this repressed experience to the unconscious. In this case, not the thinking, not the needs or the feelings are generally stored as repressed or suppressed, but rather the experience situation.

The theoretical gain is in all subsystems: the unconscious can be clearly limited. All subsystems can be "suppressed" or "repressed" as being what they are or contained in whole or in part, thus making the analytical work more differentiated, since a clear assignment is possible. In the other case, it is about how the suppressed forces of the corresponding subsystem can be integrated and lived by the ego.

In other words, what separates the ego from the consciousness, be it elements from the outside world or elements from the inner world, does not necessarily have to fall into the unconscious solely because the person has no time, no interest, or no possibility to either deal with it or to look closer at the moment. If these are powers from the psychic subsystems, then these are not in consciousness, but they are still there.

They are "unaware". They may be "repressed." But according to our observations, they only become part of the unconscious in a context of experience, with a certain charge of values. Judud assigns this to the "preconscious." We leave the individual forces where they are: in their system context.

Thus, not everything that pushes into consciousness from the inside is part of the unconscious, and thus of the "id" or the "superego". This inversion arises from our systemic model of the psychic organism. Furthermore, it follows from our model that the so-called unconscious cannot simply be equated with sexual desires, impulses, pleasurable ideas and Oedipus (Elektra) complex. We consider this old psychoanalytic theory as false.

Further, it follows from our constructions that the principle of "pleasure-aversion" does not determine the psychodynamics of the unconscious. The psycho-energetic effects of the unconscious depend on the type of image inventory. This means that the whole richness of values, of meaning and feelings, forms a complex and contradictory functioning of energy. This "energy ball" seeks a way to relax by discharging in one action. The discharge itself has nothing to do with "wish fulfillment" or "gratification of the pleasure apparatus." Also, one may not set the desire-unpleasure linearly in the parameter of tension-relaxation. Increasing pleasure can also be tense.

In retrospect, we can now briefly touch upon a few more aspects of the psychoanalytic theory, and some supplementary concepts. Freud sets a mental condition between the consciousness and the unconscious, which he calls the "preconscious". The inventory in the preconscious contains elements from the unconscious and from the outside world. The preconscious is "easily aware" because it is a linguistically conceptualized reality, while the unconscious contains "material occupations". We dissolve this separation and call all inventories of the unconscious fundamentally aware.

Next, Freud, as Jung later, quite well recognized that primal human processes ("archaic parts") are in dreams - and thus must be stored in the unconscious. Jung assigns these, as we will discuss, to the so-called "collective unconscious". We set the opposite to the thesis that the psyche as an organism by itself tends to unfold, to grow, and to function "optimally healthy". There is no reason to associate this momentum with the unconscious - or the collective unconscious - by the fact that this reality and its urge are in dreams, and because they have been part of mental functioning since time immemorial.

If we assign the archetypes to the system of the mind, then we can define the unconscious as a homogeneous subsystem just as we suggest here. We have expanded the drivers in the context of needs. What Freud means by "life drive" we can identify with "basic needs" and in addition, expand with all other subsystems. All the "contents" of the unconscious, the instincts, and the drives, as identified by Freud, Jung, Adler, Schultz-Hencke, and Boss, are thus vital forces that are part of the psychic organism, and not just "inventory," and certainly not "Basic drive", "motor" or "aspiration" of the subconscious.

Furthermore, Freud speaks of the "primary process" of the unconscious, meaning the dynamics of condensation, displacement, identification, and projection. This construction is to be revised. On the one hand, there is the image material in the unconscious, which is composed according to our own (we presume: associative and holistic) laws. On the other hand, we have the psychic energy of the valence parameter, which urges for "discharge."

We postulate the thesis that the dynamics of energy is the whole "variety" of displacement, compression, conversion, projection, uses, and not the image inventory directly. We did not find a fact that would entitle us to make the characteristics of pictorial compositions in dreams (the manifest material) identical with the characteristics of the inventory in the unconscious. The dreams contain many more realities than the inventory of the unconscious.

We have hereby reconstructed the psychoanalytic models by this extension or "displacement" of individual elements. This has consequences for the dream theory, in which we define a subsystem with "mind". If one understands the unconscious as a subsystem, together with other subsystems, then all theories of learning theory (for example, classical and operant conditioning, generalization, and imitation) can be adequately placed or integrated alongside the unconscious, with its own dynamics. Furthermore, the construct that Freud called "it" is unnecessary. Defense and censorship also receive a new place in the overall network of psychic subsystems.

This new construction is not simply a "new" psychoanalytic theory. Nor do we want to remotely disprove the often-confirmed findings of psychoanalytic practice. Rather, we have synthetically reassembled the various elements on a new construction plane. It should be noted that we do not build these theoretical constructions on the psychic material of "mentally ill", but on the whole variety of psychic experiences that we cannot call "pathological". Thus, our overarching psychoanalytic model is not primarily therapeutically oriented, but fundamentally educational in the sense of andragogy.

If psychoanalysis is defined as a "procedure for uncovering the unconscious with a therapeutic goal", we understand the guided process of becoming conscious and transforming the contents of the unconscious as an andragogical educational process, which is also embedded in a variety of educational processes in all mental areas subsystems. We are not aware of any substantive argument that might suggest that andragogy should not be concerned with these deep layers, or the "traces of the unconscious" in memory, as described e.g. Senzky (1986, 47).

Numerous different researches, on the prenatal period and the psychic life of the fetus, confirm what we have also been able to prove by means of returns to the prenatal period on the basis of various examples (Schellhammer 1987).

We summarize the most important research results of Verny (1981):

1) An emotional relationship develops between mother and child from the very first weeks of pregnancy. Also, between father and child develops a prenatal emotional bond. Attention and avoidance (refusal), moods and emotional behavior have a "stamping effect" on the fetus.

2) The emotional state of the mother affects the psychic life of the prenatal child: "Almost every emotion of the mother seems to communicate to the child": thoughts, grief, quarrels, fears, personal stress, bad marital relationship, threats, etc., but also love, affection, affirmation, serenity, feelings of happiness, and contentment. The physiological factors (such as nicotine, alcohol, drugs, etc.) we will not discuss here.

3) The child is prenatal from about 28-32 weeks, with a consciousness and a clear ego identity, and it has the basic prerequisites for learning. The child already reacts differentiated and organizes from the fifth week with a "complex repertoire". From about 10 weeks the child reacts to touch, taste, sounds (music). The child reacts increasingly from the 16th week to light. It even must be assumed that the child is dreaming from the 32nd week.

4) The first noticeable signs of brain activity begin from the 11th week (but has also been found from the 5th week). One assumes, "The first thin grooves of the memory traces break themselves sometime in the last third of pregnancy across the brain of the fetus". The unborn child evidently forms the first attitudes, the first self-esteem, and different basic feelings as engrams early in the prenatal period. Positive as well as negative imprints determine the life of this new becoming man, fatefully for a lifetime.

The psycho-physiological effects can be explained by the example of stress. Stress produces more hormones. There are biochemical processes in the womb, as well as in the body of the fetus. The hypothalamus as the "regulator of the body" is subject to the emotional or physiological effects of the mother. This increases the biological susceptibility of the prenatal child. Biological dysfunctions - and mental reactions - are already caused prenatally, or are based on engrams. The consequences are, for example: depression, anxiety, attachment problems, tantrums, disturbed sexual behavior and so on.

It must be concluded that the personality development begins prenatal. First traces are formed early in the prenatal phase. The reaction patterns on sensory stimuli are already starting from the fifth week.

The so-called "unconscious", i.e. the pictorial and emotionally (with valences) occupied engrams, also begins to form from this time. If this is true - we are convinced - then the various psychoanalytic teachings about the unconscious are wrong. They are subject to a total revision. Furthermore, the ego development and the drive theory of psychoanalysis are already wrong in the beginning and require fundamental correction.

The social-psychological concept of ego-identity and the self-concept of depth psychology, or humanistic psychology, must be broadened or conceptually revised through the findings of prenatal engram formation. The textbooks on educational psychology are to expand, with this vital part of mental life. The concepts of adult developmental psychology do not adequately capture psychic life, if the unconscious is not integrated into it.

We can also determine the so-called unconscious from the point of view of biopsychology or brain physiological trace formation (Becker-Carus 1981, 15). First, let us pick up on what we have discussed for perception and expand the aspect of sense perception to engram formation:

We know that we have five senses, when we think of the "inner senses", refraining from the visceral senses (blood pressure, venous pressure, lung strain, etc.). The five senses, also called "the sensory modalities", are: seeing, hearing, smelling, tasting, touching / feeling. Each of these senses has different receptors. They react to pressure, heat, noise, light, and chemical substances. Each receptor has its own specific form of energy. A receptor has a physiological stimulus-absorbing and stimulus-processing function. This means that the absorbed stimulus is converted into electrical currents ("information converter").

Each stimulus has an "electric generator potential": it can trigger complicated chemical and electrical processes (giving off nerve impulses). The stimulus intake is also related to the level of attention. In other words, if the stimulus is too weak, and if it does not have the necessary intensity and size, then it scarcely receives any attention, meaning it is not passed on, apart from the "subliminal" processes. If the stimulus is strong enough, a threshold is crossed and the "action potential" comes into effect: the converted information is forwarded to the brain, to the central nervous system (CNS). The forwarding takes place by means of impulses over the nerve paths. This is a biochemically complicated process that we will not go into here.

In the central nervous system (CNS) are receptive brain areas where the arrived impulses are stored. Brain areas are innate, physiological patterns, which are also divided into modalities. This is called "perception trigger pattern". In the brain are areas for: language, logic, reading, writing, mathematics, pictures and so on. The information arrived in the brain areas now interacts with the existing memory traces, and with previous stimulus recordings and stimulus stores (engrams). The storage is done by creating neural patterns. Each newly acquired stimulus activates the already formed neuronal patterns (Becker-Carus, 1981, 245). "One might think that in the neural mechanisms a whole coherent register of the past experiences is created, in which besides from the sensory impressions, also their emotional meaning is registered" (Becker-Carus 1981, 218).

Furthermore, we can assume that sensory perception is accompanied by a synthesizing perception. So it is not just the various information of the modalities stored in different places, but also the wholeness is marked as an engram.

In this holistic engram, elements such as space and time, meaning, quality of sense modality, self-evident aspects, and subjective interpretation (the experience) are included (Ebbinghaus 1971). The consolidation process is subject to certain factors, such as disturbances, repetition, degree of emotionality, annoyance, frustration and so on.

There is enormously rich and at times contradictory literature on electrophysiological correlates of learning (Becker-Carus 1981, 255). We can at least interpret: every change made to a trace is, in a sense, a learning outcome that goes hand in hand with chemical and electrical changes. New tracks are formed, and a new pattern of activity is created.

The recorded stimuli are apparently stored simultaneously from different points of view (aspects, levels): where the information comes from, side-effects, semantic relation, experience, and time factor (biological world time, subjective experience). Thus, in the "episodic memory" (Oerter / Montada 1987, 537 ff) experiences in life history are eidetically stored, and in the "semantic memory" language, rules, categories, contexts of meaning etc. "Other brain regions provide the meaning of the whole. Concepts of thought arise at the same time as feelings are activated in the interbrain" (Vester 1991, 148-152). This frame of reference is called "cluster" (Ebbinghaus 1971).

An engram thus contains: quantity, quality, structuredness, context information, subjective theory, interpretation patterns, etc. A trace of memory does not simply interact with a newly acquired sense stimulus (Becker-Carus 1981, 45), but (we conclude) with the whole biographical "cluster system" and the wholeness of the perceptual situation. This means that remembering attaches to many elements of a cluster (Krämer / Walter 1994, 32). Each element can theoretically be retrieved from multiple "addresses". The human brain has approximately 10+ Billion cells, with almost unlimited opportunities for trace formation.

The process is preceded by the "short-term memory" with an action time of about 30 seconds for memorizing, thinking, and imagining. Here again, a selection mechanism is built in. What is too weak, too difficult, and too unclear - in which stimulus quantity "sinks" or is disturbed by other stimuli - does not come into the long-term memory. We refrain from this and concentrate on the tracks in the long-term memory. The biochemical structure of long-term memory is still unclear in many aspects. What is certain is that certain biophysical and biochemical structures survive sleep and narcosis, and indeed last a lifetime. That can already confirm the everyday experience.

With biopsychology, we have another explanatory context for the proof of biographical trace formation. We conclude from this: The inventory in the unconscious consists of engrams, which build up their life history and intertwine into complex structures. Phylogenetically formed patterns, form the starting point or the "soil" on which engrams and engram intertwines, are impressed as "traces" early in the prenatal period. Gestalt theory speaks here of "dynamic wholes."

It can be assumed that emotion is also stored with the perceived experience situation. In addition, the conciseness of the tracks is consolidated with every repetitive experience. If the unconscious is "the forgotten and not remembered," then we find this in the biographical brain area. If the unconscious is what has not become objectified in perception, i.e., that escaped attention, we can identify it with the engrams. If the term "the unconscious" means instinctual, then we have the physiological correlate with the phylogenetic basic structures in the brain area.

The unconscious is thus essentially the clusters of structured and diverse intertwined biographical material, including the stored emotions and individual reaction patterns. Translated to life, this means that no human being can live outside his educated tracks. In other words, the engrams are the code program of life. Who wants to change his life, must change, form and expand his engrams.

We can examine this unconscious more closely from the point of view of social philosophy. What Schütz and Luckmann (1991, volume I) mean by the term " the world of life " reaches our use of the word "Inventory of the Unconscious". The "lifeworld" is the reality that man has in his consciousness or memory about the real outer world. Schütz and Luckmann call this the "natural attitude". "The everyday world of life should be understood as that realm of reality, that the alert and normal adult finds simple in the attitude of common sense" (Schütz / Luckmann 1991, I, 25).

The "experience" is therefore the intended reality, and not the real external conditions. Unquestionable in this attitude are: the physical existence of other people, the consciousness of other people, things of the outside world, the possibility of relationships, the possibility of understanding, and the social and cultural world. The personal situation is always partly created in person (Schütz / Luckmann 1991, 13, 27). However, this definition is not always conscious. The everyday social world, the natural world, as well as the dream and fantasy world are incorporated under this term (Schütz / Luckmann, 1991, I, 28, 47, 54, 59).

The term "memory" in Schütz and Luckmann refers to the biography of the individual. The consciousness and the situation arise from the history of the experiences (Schütz / Luckmann, 1991, I, 86).

In turn, experience is subject to the meaning of the subject. Experience, and therefore meaning, is always spatial-temporally structured in the social and material world. Experience creates a pool of knowledge, not only linguistically, but above all eidetic-biographical, as we would like to add (Schütz / Luckmann, 1991, I, 133-137). This brings us close to the concept of the "unconscious".

The "Inventory of the Unconscious" is the predominantly pictorial store of knowledge, composed from emotional sensory and value-experienced experiences, to which each new experience situation connects and draws. Three different types of time clash here: the time of the objective world, the subjective time of experiencing, and the time of previous experiences, which, with their typology and relevance, guarantee the continuing binding process of formation and remodeling of "traces" in the memory.
It results in "closed meaning areas", according to the principle of similarity. The world of the order of reality is therefore not constituted by given structures of objects, but by the very unity of units of meaning. We can insert these subjective sense-relevant experience units into our concept of the "unconscious". There may also be other sources of knowledge, but this is not significant for the characteristics of the unconscious, otherwise we would equate to long-term storage and the unconscious.

"Language, a system of vowels and signs, is the most important sign system of human society. The understanding of the phenomenon of language is therefore crucial for understanding the reality of the everyday world" (Berger / Luckmann 1970, 39). Language typifies experience and subsumes it according to meaning orders. "Language produces semantic fields or zones of meaning" (Berger / Luckmann 1970, 42).

We believe that these principles are also remembered in the construction of the imagery, in long-term storage. Lacan (1991, 136-137) understands the symbolism of the symptoms and the language of desire, and of the unconscious, as a language with a grammar like the verbal language. We doubt whether it makes sense or is useful to structure the inventory of the unconscious in this sense in terms of language theory.

Language is certainly an aspect of the "essence of being", but access to the unconscious is easier and more effective through meditation. Above all, the human being internalizes the world of life with images, expanded with all sensory receptors, based on the association principle. This is, firstly, socialization (Berger / Luckmann 1970, 139-185), secondly, ego education and, third, engram formation. With trace formation, man constructs his social reality, his personal reality, social relationships, his own identity (self-concept research), and above all - what we would like to emphasize - his progressive or regressive life course. All these areas are complex with each other.

There are many things in the world that human beings perceive, auditory and visual, that have no typical feature of the unconscious; so for example, names of rivers, natural conditions, mathematical formulas, all things of the world, which receive for the biography no specific emotionally toned meaning and value.

We do not want to operate sociology of knowledge (Berger / Luckmann 1970, Schütz / Luckmann 1991, volume 1, 293-392 and volume 2), but to crystallize those areas from the structures of the lifeworld that are constitutive for the concept of the unconscious. In the unconscious, subjective and objective truth are mixed. "Subjective" refers to the sense-relatedness and "objectively" to the real actual facts of the external life-world.

We cannot continue the train of thought of Schütz and Luckmann here. Our topic is the question of the internal structure, that is, the intertwining of the inventory in the unconscious. We can hardly find the answers in the analysis of knowledge structures and language structures. The experience and the images of the experiences are a much more comprehensive. The analytical reflexive and meditative experience, and the interpretation of the dream world, lead us to this inner subjective "truth".

"Man is biologically determined to construct a world and to inhabit it with others, and this world becomes a dominant and definitive reality" (Berger / Luckmann 1970, 195). Extend this reflection: just as man constructs the outer world, his psychic and social world, and his life course, so he influences the unimpeachable external (actual) reality and is influenced by it daily.

The more the internalized realities deviate from the facts, for example by means of simplification (or: verifying, dogmatizing, mystifying), the more his action in this reality becomes problematic, if not to say destructive.

If we also realize that these processes also occur physiologically (perception, storage, action impulses) and that emotional factors (also marked in the tracks) can make us ill or disturb us, then we may rightly assume that an optimal all-round balanced formation of the biological substrate (trace effects), the internalized reality of life (units of meaning and ego-identity), for the individual as well as for society, has vital significance on this holistic networked qualitative education as a necessity for survival (Vester 1991) and Cube (in Roth 1991, 122 ff.).

Man, as an "animal being", completely incapable of life at birth, needs this formation of his instincts (Luckmann 1970, 51, 56), an existing social order, and constructive activity in society. Thus, the formation of the unconscious receives highest priority in human education.

Basically, we have defined the so-called unconscious and explained the mode of action of the unconscious. One can critically argue: Many people remain healthy and successful throughout their lives, although their unconscious is full of one-sided images, life-deviant patterns and attitudes that are hostile to psychic life. In fact, there are many people who remain healthy all their lives with money, power, and reputation, despite the chaotically destructive unconscious. For that they create suffering in other people. They exploit others, suppress, and deceive others. You get in a rigid system (money or ideas) and in accordance with consistent action in balance.

You must put this situation in a bigger context. History is a cycle of the collective discharge of the unconscious of individuals. Here it also meets those who believed in a "healthy" balance. Or it hits her children. If one goes even further away as a philosopher and a wise man, the problem is shown in a wider perspective: Such people may live well materially, but they have not understood anything about life, except how to manipulate and exploit people, and how to cultivate their own egoism. They have no spirit and they lack the love. They are hollow, internally cold, and create in their environment a suffering that is hidden from everyone. It is ultimately not true that these people are "healthy" and happy.

Another aspect in this context is the meaning of the superego. For many people, the formed conscience seems to be without humanistic value. One then says that these people are "unscrupulous", meaning brutal, mean, cold-hearted, sadistic, exploitative, oppressive and so on. That is really the reality.
With a people-centered conscience - anchored in a multi-faceted growth process - one cannot do business in many sectors of society and not engage in successful politics.

"Homo homini lupus" (man is man's wolf) was said centuries ago. Leninism also teaches us how to deal successfully with people: lying, cheating, deceiving, intriguing, pretending, and getting the war financed by the enemy. We also find this human drama in the history of capitalism. People do not want the truth; they do not want the love and the mind. They want to be cheated. They want drugs. Those who do not sell drugs cannot do business anymore. The auto industry, the film industry, tourism, and everyone knows that, who are in the "big business" of capital and power. Plato has complained of the moral decline.

Every few centuries, the lack of conscience has always been a subject of debate. Conscience education is a central educational task of the educational system of a state. You get the impression that the superego has become ineffective. But the unconscious in the collective beats down terribly every few decades. No politics can "tame" the unconscious. No money can lift the destructive power of the repressed art inventory. The "Luxury Suite" on the Captain's Day of the WorldShip will end when the ship's journey ends. The unconscious of people sets the direction, not the mind. What almost everyone cannot (or does not want) see is that there are other forms of human destruction. Furthermore, hey are usually inconspicuous in public and quiet.

It is tragic today, and this is a judgment of our judgment that millions of people in Europe (we do not want to talk about the world) suffer because they have never learned how to cleanse their unconscious. Personality development can reduce a great deal of individual and social suffering here.

The first step is the problem of the inner order of the inventory, in the subconscious. Many thousands of pictures are in the subconscious. The pictures are as diverse as life itself. How can we create order? This can be done once by categorizing the image material content-analytically. Is there perhaps a dynamic of order directly from the subconscious? Through the casuistic exploration of the unconscious, we have found four main dynamic areas that may overlap. These four areas each have their own function.

The four functional units in the subconscious are:

1. Life experiences: On the one hand, these are pictorial patterns of all kinds, as they are described in the complex theories (Freud, Jung); on the other hand, expanded to the entire spectrum of emotionally experienced pictorial situations.

2. The superego: By that we mean the "conscience", as described by Freud and psychoanalysis in general. These are the internalized commandments, offers, norms, taboos and "judicial instances". The functions have a direct normative effect, and, depending on the impression, also "threatening-punishing".

3. Attitudes: In this way, we grasp all evaluative, and at first emotional, statements that contain an interpretation of life and man. Ideals are as much a part of it as are prejudices and beliefs,

4. The human images: We also call these "imagos". These are the pictures about husband, wife, father, mother, and child, as well as general picture patterns like businessman, pilot, salesman, teacher and so on.

For the "collective unconscious", we place as psychic reality separately and not within this personal unconscious.

In principle, the question arises as to whether the amount of image, in the subconscious can even be comprehensively processed and cleaned up. There are not only many one-sided and revision-needy single images available, but also internal interactions between the four areas, which create a significant energetic dynamic. The variety of interacting forces is a real mess of quality, strength, and direction of action. It really is a huge effort to dissolve these inner contradictions. We believe that it is possible to comprehensively revise the image inventory. But this process takes a long time.

In this understanding or construct of the unconscious, what is the relationship between consciousness and unconsciousness? For example, if an image is made aware of, what happens to the image afterwards? Or, If a complex is made aware of and processed - in the sense of reconciliation and cleansing or correction - what happens afterwards, with this image unit? Is the picture then dissolved?

We have found that the images are never "deleted" by becoming conscious and editing but remain as uncontaminated units in the unconscious. The image will then be freely available, so it can be reached by the ego, but remains autonomous. The psycho-energetic charge is according to the picture constructive, and largely relaxed. Even edited images are part of the "reservoir"; one must not overlook this with the term "the unconscious".

Let us take an example: During a conversation with his boss, Mr G. suddenly remembers his father - who he had talked so oppressively with when he was still a child. In his imagination, he sees his father and is very moved. After the "cleansing" of this image, Mr. G. can bring out and look at this memory image again and again, without being moved by it.

It has become energetically neutral, and above all, serves as an orientation unit. The new energetic charge of this picture is different. It is calm, stable, balanced, and more like a dynamic foundation. External conditions or memory can no longer "charge" this complex. By contrast, the image reacts energetically when the ego deviates from this orientation, i.e., it does not use this wealth of experience.

Let us take a further example: Mr. K. has been repeatedly cheated by real estate traders, during his business development. This almost ruined him. He has reconciled these experiences and these complex units are stored in the unconscious as adjusted units. Now, after many years, Mr. K. returns to business, with a real estate trader, who, with a client-centered method masterfully deceives him. Now the inner picture reacts and wants to warn the I: The picture creates a tensioning energy. Mr. K. deviates in his situation from his experience and lets himself be deceived. Mr. K. may feel it as a pressure on the chest or as a strange dull feeling in the stomach. Or he just reacts spontaneously. We then speak of intuition: Mr. K. is intuitively appropriate.

This interpretation of the inventory, in the unconscious, implies that, from prenatal time and onwards, man also absorbs many positive images into the unconscious that need no adjustment. However, it is always a gain in personality formation when the ego builds a conscious relationship to the inventory, in the unconscious.

How can we recognize the action of the unconscious, and at the same time provide proof that this unconscious really exists? The dreams are opened for the first time. We are working on this in the last chapter. Here we want to focus on the effects in everyday life.

Jung has proved this with the association experiment (Jung, 1904, and Meier 1968, 83-179). The experiment is based on the following: A conscious or unconscious emotion changes the water content in the skin. We can measure these changes with the psychogalvanometer. If one then presents an individual with a larger amount of words, he reacts to the individual words emotionally differently. Strong reactions suggest that – in the psychic system - the word or image is an emotionally charged entity. The stronger the reaction, the sooner it is a complex.

The second hypothesis means that the associations of the human being - to a specific (pictorial) word – results in an associative unit of images, which as a whole is interpreted as a complex emotional reaction.

Freud realized that so-called slip-ups and false reactions are expressions of an unconscious force, or that the repressed expresses itself through slips of speech and wrongdoing. The joke is based on the phenomenon that the unspoken contains something that can just be laughed out by the compact joke story.

Many mental disorders and psycho-somatic reactions are traceable to complexes. If these complexes are changed, the disorders and suffering disappear. The mate choice of a person is always based on the power play of the Images. It is often the case that, after a failed relationship, a person finds a new partner who at first appears as a "completely different character", but then suddenly proves to be a human being with the same basic dynamic. Relationship patterns and basic problems are repeated. Since a man can want to conclude with his past and emigrate for this purpose. He will have to experience that he also lives in a different cultural space, which is predetermined in images in his unconscious. You always take your own past with you.

If the psychodynamics of a person is chronically strained, and this is not due to external circumstances, internal factors must be hypothetically assumed. These factors can be in thinking, in unfulfilled needs, in growth blocks, or in the subconscious.

Projective tests, such as the Rorschach test, can demonstrate unconscious image structures, but also patterns of thinking and needs. We believe that the type, amount, and intensity of projecting a person generally indicates unconscious material. The analysis of the daily projections of an individual reveals the image inventory in the subconscious.

Strong ties to objects, to persons, to institutions and to ideas (especially ideological and dogmatic) also allow us to conclude that images from the unconscious express themselves here protectively. If the bonds are exaggerated and no longer objectively justifiable, then one must conclude on complexes.

Psycho-physical reactions such as blushing, cold hands or feet, sudden unfounded sweats, or increased pulse rates can be interpreted as a reaction to an addressed complex. If you change this imagery in the unconscious, then the psycho-physical reaction pattern changes as well.

The more intensively and frequently a person lives in defense, resistance and repression, the more intrapsychic powers are at work. These are images in the unconscious that threaten the ego and rarely only external factors. Also, acting and intriguing must be traced back to unconscious forces. They are never interpretable solely by the circumstances of the habitat or by conscious interests.

Life experiences: the present past

The term "life experience" encompasses an infinite field of general experiences that every person makes from earliest times. There are first the mother experiences, then the father, and sibling experiences.

The family environment offers the child the first life experiences. These relate to care, employment, and entertainment. Socio-economic environment components can already shape decisive impressions. Afterwards, the child expands the field of experiences in the school and in the environment of his schoolmates. The radius of action increases with age. Developmental psychology follows puberty and adolescence with the first sexual experiences as well as the field of vocational training and activities. The increasing independence increases the scope of experience.

A grown-up may think in retrospect that this is all past and therefore "over". But with a simple imagination exercise, everyone can see that many experiences are still alive in the unconscious. Already, prenatal experiences are influenced by concrete pictures about the first living environment. The entire psychodynamics in adulthood has its roots in the first years of life. According to Freud, the imprints are subdivided into phases: the oral, anal, and phallic phases (Freud 1961). Erikson (1974, 151) describes in his model how basic trust against mistrust, autonomy against shame and doubt, initiative against guilt, workmanship against inferiority, and identity against identity diffusion in the first years of life form up to adolescence.

In adulthood, the scope of experience is decisively expanded. Our own relationship with family, the professional life, and free time, all allow an immense variety of experiences. There are also cultural and political experiences. A consumer society which has been growing since the 1960s allows unprecedented expanded opportunities for experience. In particular, the media has made the world an extended living space for man. Everyone can experience the Pope, the King, and the statesman right up to bed. The intimate sharing of foreign worlds is possible today. Such experiences shape images in the subconscious.

Where man used to have experiences – only as a participant of a living space or event - today the individual can go out of the room, experience world travels, participate in wars, sympathize with poverty, take part in carnage and suffering, observe the people in love, and experience hate in a thousand situations. Such perceptions shape the unconscious, as well as personal suffering and tragic experiences.

The unconscious experiences the media in a specific way that was never seen before. The reality is often given boldly, simplified, realized, and unilaterally lifted out of context. Reality is then a corrected reality, in which the individual participates passively. There is a high level of labeling, stenciling and anonymity in this world. This creates distance and yet allows an active participation. The real, precise, and differentiated slips away in the plethora of striking requirements. This is how reality is distorted. The hero of bygone times appears with new magical powers. The illusion is imprinted: the good always wins. The media determine who should succeed. They are the "kingmakers", the new "popes" and the "mothers" who allow a bit of sexual pleasure to the viewer, colorful and symphonic, but never really real. They make passive participation options depersonalized. Almost everything is unaffected.

In fact, the live viewer cannot directly influence this reality. He cannot talk and negotiate immediately. Decisions, goals, specifications of the processes, and all active forces are at the moment of co-experience on television nothing but uninfluenced specifications of realities. Others think, direct, judge, solve, and answer. Therefore, the viewer learns no problem solving. He has no active confrontation. He cannot update himself in it. He has no room for spontaneity and initiatives. He is not called alive to co-responsibility. Man is small, not in demand, and as such, only an experiential consumer. Only as a recipient does he enjoy social recognition. Friendly words from the cigar box arouse at best a fake sensation of acceptance: "Good evening ... We wish you a fun evening ...". And then it goes directly to the advertising; life is made easy: The washing powder washes even whiter; again a new and even better car; enjoy life with chocolate; this 'cheese' is your new pleasure feeling; why not to try this new crème? this one?

The relationship between reality and the individual has a clear definition, like in the previous decades, the relationship between father-child: a one channel communication to obey and join and participate. Examples include:

Uncertainty	Doubt	Inner emptiness
Guilt	Secret enslavement	Irresponsibility
Thought block	Inability to live/ love	Irritation
Passivity	Illusions	Bill competencies
Isolation	Aggression	Blunting
Stencil perception	Manipulation	Inertia
Prejudice	Impotence	Convenience
Pseudo-knowledge	Inner emptiness	Value dilution
Feeling inhibitions	Superficiality	Lust for tragedy
Delusion	Indifference	Cultural consumption
Fear	Pseudo interests	Brutality of manners

The sum, of the effects of such life experiences, must be assumed that the traumatic effect is as strong as experienced suffering or, for example, educational misconduct of the mother in the anal phase. In addition to the Oedipus complex, andragogy today, for example, should place the "alienation complex" at the center of all relationship dynamics and the entire world relationship.

In this context, there is an important question about the unconscious. The "reincarnation therapy" (Dethlefsen 1978) implies that the psychic system, on the one hand, is an immortal psycho-energetic organism; yet, on the other hand, information about past lives is stored in the unconscious. The first hypothesis can be almost seamlessly be derived as a valid hypothesis from our theory about the psychic energy. It must be assumed that a subtle organization exists, to a certain extent, as the "vessel" for the versatile, malleable psychic energy in man.

Imagination is the main method (in addition to the interpretation of dreams), which can reach everything in the subconscious - up to prenatal time. The proof is the method or its result itself, as we have set out in examples in another work (see: Schellhammer 1987).

The reincarnation method is imagination. It is claimed that the material originates from the unconscious. But other theses are possible. Many research questions take up this point because the image material from reincarnation meditations cannot be logically interpreted as concrete subjective (that is, as previous life experience).

The Super-ego: the good and the bad conscious

The superego is a formed psychic subsystem. Man experiences this psychic power predominantly as a state of feeling. This is because the experience of conscience results from the tension between behavior and demands from this subsystem.

In 1923 Sigmund Freud wrote about the superego (1975, 296-306). We summarize some core ideas: On the one hand, the superego represents the social norms, from the conscience, and on the other hand, from the ego ideal. This includes the commandments and prohibitions of the parents (the representation of the parent relationship), especially of the father, but also of role models and authorities (religion, morality, and social feeling). The superego sets the strictest moral standard. In other words: Conscience and value building build in the parent relationship from birth.

Maier (1986, 14) takes another aspect: "Values become norms that want to be realized, and they push to move from an initially impersonal state to a state of subjective property."

Brezinka (educator) relativizes the power of the superego: "many talk of 'self-determination', 'self-realization', 'autonomy', 'maturity' and 'emancipation', but those same people cannot hide the fact that, although they are in highly industrialized societies, they still have the need for recognition from others, which leads to a strong feeling of dependency and extraordinary receptivity and willingness to follow for the actions and desires of others. Especially for the public opinion, which has been published itself and as a suggestion for others to set standards of valuation and norms that go beyond the existing vague similarities with the others or even contradict them. " (1978, 217).

Löwisch also qualifies the 'strict superego-education': "Kant's word that we are cultivated and civilized to the point of outrage, but still far from being moralized, is fully confirmed in the late 20th century: civil wars, tribal wars, wars of expansion, Race wars, racial fanaticism, ideological and prestige wars, disregard for human rights, the many tortures, hundreds of thousands of deaths through wars, flight, hunger, hundreds of thousands of misery and death by ideological fanaticism ... What is human life still worth today? " (1982, 161-162).

The pedagogy professor Oser briefly sums up this dark side: "No one can count how many people have been abused, injured or killed." (1994, 11). Oser therefore demands: "To learn virtue, one can only develop morality by trying to transform one's own justifications into action, according to the best knowledge. From this conviction emerges integrity. Today, we need people with backbone and moral courage." (ibid., 146). Also, "Moral education must lead into a holistic program of personality development and social competences. Moral education should not be limited to 'thought training' but must also promote moral sensitivity and moral capacity to act" (ibid., 331).

Blasi writes (in: Oser 1986, 80): "while lacking complete concern and personal commitment, there is a risk that morality will be abstract and sterile." If personal feelings and values are overemphasized, or more precisely, they are not depended on, then knowledge and reason are not guided by them. This will result in the individual nature of morality, and the feeling of obligation to be lost. ". (ibid., 358), "The core of immorality is that of not wanting to know, of blinding oneself to one's own knowledge, and of ignoring it in action."

The superego consists of several components:
1) Contents: Values and norms as well as commandments and prohibitions: "good", "evil", "one can do that", "one must not", "one should do that", "one should not do that".

2) Taboos: A taboo is a ban on thinking about something specific, questioning a matter, and, of course, a ban on doing something in this context. Taboos usually have unspoken social validity. In this prohibition the limit of the permitted is strict, absolute, rigid, and being "natural".

3) Judgment: An authority that judges in the sense of judging and just "speaks law". This instance measures the behavior in relation to the internal norms.

4) Claim: What has once been absorbed into the unconscious, acts from the inside on demanding, urging, authoritative and commanding.

5) Enforcement: The content acts as it is recorded, mostly strict, rigid, inflexible, uncompromising, unforgiving, and absolute.

6) Punishment: In conjunction with the internalized norms, the learned penalty is included. If a clearly defined sanction is lacking, "Fate punishes".

7) Guilt: School life is an experience of the difference between claim and action.

A good conscience is experienced as: relaxed, easy, safe, calming, satisfied, well, relieved, undisturbed, and innocent. A bad conscience is experienced or circumscribed with corresponding negative aspects: tense, difficult, uncertain, disturbing, dissatisfied, unwell, burdened, disturbed, and guilty.

From our general description of the unconscious results the subsystem "super-ego": All seven components of the superego are internalized through education, socialization, and enculturation. Conscience is not the "voice of God", but the voice from learned image of God. All commandments, prohibitions, norms, and judgmental-punitive powers are taken from outside. The internalized images work the way they were taken. It does not matter if the pictures are constructive or destructive to life and the person. It is irrelevant to the dynamics of the effect, or whether this internalized image of God is an image of a childish fantasy, a mythology, a nature religion, or invented by domineering fanatics. The valence of a picture is increased by binding to religious-mythical images, to state authorities, to punishment, and to devaluation of the person (in case of non-fulfillment of the norm).

The superego works positively and constructively when the recorded images are constructive and life-affirming in their value. If the norms are balanced on all sides, shaped by love and the mind, then internalized images as elements of conscience can control life. If the entire set of images in the superego contains the psychic organism and the process of psycho-spiritual development, but, above all, is centered on people in this orientation, then this conscience can take over its own function.

Without this orientation, the "bad conscience" is nothing but the discrepancy between behavior and internalized images. Even if the behavior may be so life-affirming and constructive, a superego with life-depraved and life-suppressing patterns subliminally creates a "bad conscience".

There are some important aspects to personality development. The knowledge about the functioning of the conscience, and the knowledge of the contents, is a prerequisite for a conscious progressive lifestyle. One can internalize thinking with such emancipated norms. The old prohibitions and commandments always come from the background. This is the victory of religion at the grave of a renegade: What was implanted in the superego, from earliest infancy, breaks out, even with the turning away of the "adult" ego in old age, when the individual does not consciously form personally.

Characteristics of attitudes and patterns of values

In the unconscious there is a sum of images that share a common characteristic: the attitudes. These are not just life experiences, not just human images or the prohibitions and commandments (superego). The attitudes are to be defined in the context of ideals, opinions, and beliefs.

Ideals are the pictorial embodiment of something perfect. They represent a supreme value and bring about a pursuit of realization, regardless of whether that value is realistic or not. Opinions are subjective, and mostly with limited information, with a judgmental undertone. Prejudices are opinions about how something is. Opinions arise from an experience, with little thought, or from a first (reflected) opinion. Attitudes are subjective, emotional evaluations, and divisions of the reality of life. They are also pictorial. Attitudes are preconceived judgments, with a value assignment, and often imperious. Beliefs are the highest level of a sentimental pictorial rating. Beliefs are views of life in a composite of thoughts and judgments, usually recorded in life situations, and often not reflected upon.

We can recognize different common elements from these definitions. They are all pictorial value patterns. They thereby regulate emotional affection and avoidance. They determine the acceptance range with their implicit weighting scale. Value patterns are also substantiating intentions and motivations. They influence the expectations of life. They provide orientation and direction. The value patterns can be realistic or life-distant and illusory. They work regardless of this life-related salary. If they are flexible, they also have a flexible effect. If the value patterns are rigid, then they act rigidly. If they are conciliatory, they also have a peculiar effect in life. If they are unforgivingly strict, they affect the ego as well.

Above all in life, people form ideals, opinions, attitudes, and beliefs. With value patterns, man encounters himself, the other human being, the goods, and the habitat. Billions of people around the world have different value patterns for all living conditions.

Value patterns regulate the inner relationship to people, goods, and in general to life. They regulate the interest, the commitment, the responsibility, as well as the kind and measure of action. The subjectivity of the value patterns is beyond doubt. Still, most people think their value patterns are the only correct ones.

The fact is that many attitudes and beliefs are unsuitable orientations in life. They do not promote the contribution of life or the integration of mental life. They are usually poorly thought out and based on superficial facts. They are subject to the subjective processes of perception, thinking, and feeling. Yet, people are at war for their beliefs. They punish others when they have different attitudes and they argue because their opinions diverge. Ideals are often untouchable.

During life, humans absorb an enormous variety of such images into their unconscious. There are many things that are contradictory and illogical. That does not interest the "vessel". Acts do these pictures anyway. They control perception, thinking, and emotions. They regulate the satisfaction of needs and daily actions. All life is captured with value patterns, even if the ego claims that it lives without value.

In many cases, the ego is not aware of which value patterns influence its thinking and acting. Sometimes a person believes that they know exactly which pictorial attitudes and beliefs direct them, what ideals they aspire to, and what opinions they have about this and that in life. But that is rarely the case. In the consciousness is usually only the "tip of the iceberg".

The real thrust comes from deeper emotionally and figuratively experienced contexts that come from the conscious element, i.e., the linguistic-rational form does not emerge directly.

The stability of the ego depends crucially on these value patterns. If you want to change a value pattern in a person, this causes a destabilization. This threatens the ego and learning processes are blocked. Defenses must be built up. In many cases, value patterns are rationally represented to achieve hidden interests. That makes life extremely complicated.

A reduction or a restructuring of values is only possible through the awareness of the history of origin or the embossed basic patterns, combined with a reflected way of life. This requires "work" on all psychic subsystems, and this is practical individuation.

Images about humans: Anima (Animus) and the innermost human

Every person has internalized images about: being the father, being the mother, being the child, being the man, being the woman. The life experiences with humans become human images in the subconscious. An image contains a large amount of image aspects. These can be both contradictory, positive, and negative at the same time.

The abundance of parts results in a concentrated overall picture. The images are emotional. The psychic forces influence the person - in his life - to grow as a man or as a woman. These human images also form the inner opposite sex: If the external man is a man, one speaks of "anima". If the external person is a woman, one speaks of: "Animus".

Anima or Animus are terms that Jung introduced to psychology (1971). But Jung himself had considerable definition difficulties. If he could still rewrite the "anima" as a variety of femininity in a man, the animus remains vague as the inner opposite-sex pole of the woman. A characterization with "Woman's Opinions" is unlikely to capture what Animus meant (Jung 1971, 100). No less problematic is the compensatory relationship between anima and persona - described by Jung. "Persona" is the "mask" of the individual, which each one uses to cover up his true "I." It can come to the ego identification with the mask (1971, 85-88).

Let's try to explain the images in this context. In the center of the basic images (of man, woman, mother, father, child) stands, to some extent, that image - which represents the opposite sex of the person. In the case of a man this is the "anima", in the case of the woman the "animus".

The more the individual basic images are fragmented in themselves, and contain an inner opposition, the stronger is this inner image of the anima (or the animus). The anima (or the animus) is to a certain extent the "theoretical logical consequence" of the five basic images.

The more unbalanced the individual basic images are, and act against each other, the more unbalanced the image of the anima (or the animus) is. Their parts are then: the alienated (for example Mother-God), the oppressed, and undeveloped girl (the nymph). And, to a certain extent the "avenging residual image" (witch). The man as a man then wants to live a life-alienated man's ideal but is himself partly an undeveloped and oppressed boy; and, also lives this third "evil" part. In women, the elements are corresponding. Dating is essentially based on this internal-external-dynamics. One then speaks more to aspects, that he interprets, as part of the ideal. Another experiences an attraction to the undeveloped of the other. The other parts of the person, as well as the inner picture, then gradually unfold their effect.

The "mask" can be used in this "game". Mask is an expression of the conscious or unconscious life lie. A role is what a person lives by their own and foreign expectations from their living environment in a specific situation. Role is something very self-evident and necessary in life. The mother at home does not have to live in the business nor the "mother role". The police officer at the workplace should not play the policeman at the family table either. But many people identify so much with a role that their whole life is dominated by it, until the ego is completely the role. Mask and role are not the same. But a role can become a mask. Rolls and masks, as an outer expression, are what Jung means by "persona". Both are not in a functional relation to the anima (or to the animus). In addition to role and mask, there are the different faces that are not expected and cannot be considered as covering in the sense of masks.

That is the diversity of the appearance of the individual. These are often an expression of what inside the opposite sex image has as an identically formed representation. So, a man is not just a man. He is also the undeveloped boy, the controller, and the illusion of the ideal.

The same applies vice versa for the woman: she is both the undeveloped girl, as well as the oppressor, and the illusion of the ideal. In a relationship these elements clash more and more clearly over the years. This results in various "forms of collusion" (Willi 1976) with all variants of pathology, or changes and growth. Without changing the inner images - in step with the outer behavioral change - profound changes are not possible.

The collective unconscious: Clarification and new orientation

Parapsychology teaches that psycho-energetic (PSI) energy can be recorded and transmitted by the psychologist as transmitter and receiver over any distance (Wolff, K. In: Wagner-Simon 1984, Rhine 1977, Bender 1973). Anyone who is "sensitive" can experience energy in rooms, from the previous people who have stayed in it before them. According to our experiments, this must be psychic shaped energy. There is always a stream of psychic energy flowing between people, which life partners and friends can observe in their personal lives. Psychoanalysis has not yet studied these phenomena in the context of transference and countertransference.

"There is only something mental and physical, both at the same time," writes Schultz-Hencke (1951, 12). He clearly rejects the existence of a collective unconscious. Our studies allow us to formulate the first theses on a new theory.

The so-called "collective unconscious", in the style of such parapsychic phenomena, is the sum of the individual psychic forces that energetically shape the space around the human being. Everyone radiates energies from their emotional thoughts, feelings, and unconsciousness. Depending on content and valence, these radiations reach other people over long distances. At the same time, humans are receivers, and, at the same time, integrated into this complex radiation field. We suspect that there are certain laws about the individual and collective attachments and the affectability.

We call this energy the "cosmic energy" outside of man. This cosmic energy is constantly being reshaped. Figuratively speaking, the air is polluted by pollution. This is what we call "psycho-smog". Parapsychology, with its experiments on telepathy and clairvoyance, has created theories that support our thesis. The extension of our hypothesis shows that over centuries and millennia, "residual particles" of human history have been preserved in the cosmic energy around the globe.

If we extend this thesis with the model of physical reality, for the air, then it has similar repercussions on the psychic system as the polluted air on the body. We can add further as a hypothesis, a cosmic-energetic power source in the universe, like the sun. The psychic "air" (the cosmic energy) needs this energy source. With increasing "psycho-smog" people create a kind of psycho-energetic ozone hole; we suspect a kind of "shielding". Thus, one day, the human being could mentally suffocate from the totally destructive cosmic energy. We have evidence for this model of energy that leads to the assumption that these "residual particles" from human history strongly influence the daily life of the individual. Collective aggression, and above all, wars also receive substantial psycho-energetic thrust from this collective "polluted" cosmic energy.

Our theses on the collective unconscious may seem "alien". The people - including the social scientists - will rethink how, centuries ago, the church needed to rethink its Galilean affairs. We have done numerous experiments demonstrating that there is this cosmic energy, and that man can shape that energy with his individually shaped psychic energy. Just as it is possible to psychologically relax, harmonize, purify, and center the psychic energy in a person by means of certain rituals, so it is possible to relax and "purify" the psychic (cosmic) energy in a room (see: Schellhammer 1986, 1987). The fact that these experiments lead to the same result, with thirty and more people, at the same time at different distances and directions, means that there is a psycho-energetic reality that psychology has scarcely explored until today.

Our core thesis on the collective unconscious means that the lived life of all people influences and determines the life of all subsequent generations through the formed collective unconscious. As a result, every human being is ultimately interweaving with other people and with the entire history of mankind.

This description of the collective unconscious does not coincide with the Jungian definition. What Jung means by this term is the "spirit" with the archetypes. Jung has included the access to human history in his definition. We propose that different conditions should not be taken under a term or a construct. Our construct also contains those aspects that Szondi calls "the repressed ancestors".

However, we believe that it is impossible to genetically identify this repressed material because you cannot reduce the mental and spiritual to physiological realities.

Grof (1993, 31, 49, 54, 75) defines consciousness with a subtle, transcendental, and absolute aspect. Man is more than mere material and biological consciousness. Grof's LSD research proves that, in addition to biographical material (including prenatal experiences), non-terrestrial worlds can be brought to consciousness. The consciousness can be extended temporally and spatially (transpersonal experiences). Encounters with deities, alien universes, and beings as well as the unveiling of the "holy grail" are possible (spiritistic-medial experiences). Earlier incarnations can be made aware. Furthermore, parapsychic phenomena can be produced, for example, precognition, clairvoyance, clairaudience, and time travel (Grof 1993, 178-221).

The distorted response patterns of LSD (symptoms, cognition, emotions, thinking, memory, psychomotor responses, sexuality, mystical experiences, etc.) may well explain the structuring principles (the intelligent working) of the massively disturbing, if not destroying, mind. The distortion dynamics also make an interpretation of the inner image or archetypes experience by LSD impossible. Whether one can even understand the global crisis as an expression of the dark archaic powers of the cosmos, the evil gods and ghosts from foreign universes, acting through the deepest layers of the unconscious, remains for us very doubtful (Grof 1993, 385-412).

The awareness of the most diverse stages of life, back to the prenatal time, can be achieved easily without LSD. There are the so-called "COEX experiences" as a trace, i.e., the systems of condensed experiences in the memory. Besides, in contrast to Grof's reports on treatment success, we do not see any therapeutic benefit from LSD sessions.

For everything that is enforced in this distorting way, there are simpler, gentler, and more rational ways of making man safe and stabilized.

We see from the research achievements of Grof, that, first and foremost, there is a paradigmatic gain, over the transcendental characteristic of consciousness and thus psychic life par excellence. Here we can develop theoretical models for the "world of archetypes", for the collective unconscious and for paranormal phenomena.
However, our own experiences give reason to leave open some conceptual associations, epistemological problems, concepts of depth psychology, and research methods. An example is presented for suggestion and explanation; a dream of its own: "I came into a large room, more of a far-reaching reality, containing thousands, perhaps a hundred thousand pictures. They are all images of my own life. Everything is well-adjusted, well-organized, and well-groomed. There were many different pictures. All so clear, colorful, and varied in forms. They were incredibly beautiful, partly humorous, and sometimes sublime to the "holy". The images were enormously impressive and showed a world full of archetypal images. This is a variety that is almost unimaginable on earth and absent in that richness. I thought, this is now the world of archetypes that CG Jung told us about, which is the source of life and the realm of ideas of Plato. This is the most valuable thing I can bring to people, and I plan to save it all on my PC to later publish it. " As soon as awakened, of course, these pictures, which were experienced, were no longer tangible. We acknowledge with this dream that in terms of archetypes, collective unconscious, and imagination, many questions remain unanswered. The sciences of human formation, psychology, psychoanalysis, philosophical, and anthropology have yet to open the deepest layers of human existence.

Let us briefly return to the personal unconscious. Here it can be demonstrated, without any doubt, how the circumstances in the unconscious of each forcefully influence the behavior in the living space - with individual as well as collective consequences. To give an example, I will mention the destruction of the environment. This problem can be interpreted as individual and collective unconscious forces. For what people do with their habitat is an expression of the vitality of their unconscious pictorial material.

We can therefore conclude that if a human being does not purify the unconscious, he destroys himself in the sense of regressive attachment, be it direct and individual, or indirect and collective. Following our reflections on the collective unconscious and the reality of the archetypes: what do we know about the impact of this reality on people's daily lives? Or, what do we know about all the possibilities of positive influences, and the evolutionary potentials of the collective unconscious, which humans do not allow through their burdened personal unconscious?

In the long term, we will not give the future of humanity any chances if pedagogy, andragogy, and above all private institutions of human education, do not pursue, explore, and practice these "depths" of psycho-spiritual existence. Because here are the traces of the past impressed. And these work through the patterns of behavior and experience into the present and the future (Piaget 1969). The history of the 20th century in Europe is neither reconciled nor comprehensively dealt with. On the other hand, in these depths of the unconscious, we can find and use inexhaustible sources of human evolution.

The Unconscious and the biography

The unconscious shapes itself through the life story. Therefore, we cannot leave the psychoanalytic conception of the unconscious detached from a theory of biography. Below, we present various aspects of observation, insights, and concepts for biography research.

Gudjons says of the biography (1994, 16), "We see biography as a life-long process of accumulating experiences that are consciously or unconsciously involved in our actions, not just as a cognitive dimension, but rather as a whole, including the body and the whole spectrum of sensual, preconscious, unconscious, and rational potentials.

Action ... Biography is not an ahistorical / unsocial 'private matter', rather experiences are acquired in concrete historical and social references. Furthermore, he learns to understand why he does what he does, and which influences have social conditions. In addition, the life story of a human being is the history of the formation, and of scenic experiential content. The personality is then the structure of this experience content, and the individuality of a person is the irreplaceable peculiarity of this structure in each social situation. "Finally, he says (ibid., 34-35), "The first goal is biographical self-reflection and understanding". The second main goal of biographical self-reflection is the development of change possibilities and action perspectives ". Biographical self-reflection allows, in a constant process (ibid., 37), "to acquire further 'pieces' of their life history and to continuously discover the mosaic of becoming one."

Heinze says of biographical self-reflection (1988, 366), "Previous experiences are reworked by the present state of consciousness and in the present forms of consciousness, thus gaining a new quality." "Each autobiographical document is both time visualized and remembered present (of I), as well as a draft into the future. The memory of past and completed events allows the autobiographer the subsequent 'smoothing' of his life story by integrating fractions, errors, bad experiences, and later by his interpretation and the selection of his memories, giving them a meaning in retrospect".

Steinbach (1985, 406), "Memory preserves primarily key historical experiences in life history, and only from this point of view can the lines of intersection between individual biography and collective history be recognized." Werner Fuchs writes in the same collective work (1985, 463), "... Certainly, this new interest (in the biography, author) is at the same time a sign of a new curiosity. In various attempts, individuals and groups want to know about their development, and to make their own clear to other members in that group. They was to tell each other about sorrow, disappointments, and opportunities for life, and to ask others about their hopes and decisions. Such biographical interest is not resignation, but the beginning.

"Meier and Rabe-Kleberg write (1993, 170)," Curriculum vitae is understood as a highly contradictory unity of individual action and socio-institutional requirements, and a result of negotiation and balancing processes to be constantly revised.

The authors cite limiting factors: poor starting chances, discontinuities in professional biography, and a lack of permeability in some occupational fields. For women, "... the creation of continuity and career is only possible if she behaves like a man, keeps free of family life, or at least freed from it" (ibid., 176-177).

Educational science has encyclopedically recorded the topic (Lenzen, 1992, Volume 1, Haan de / Langewand / Schulze, 316-321). We draw some central aspects from this: "What someone holds for himself does not result from what he was or is, but it expresses what he holds for what he was or is, albeit in biographical and historical limits." (ibid. 317) ... "The autobiography is the most perfect explication of the ascending self-conceptions and self-interpretations of life ..." (ibid., 318) "The levels of analysis in the autobiography are:

1) The objective level of material, cultural, and institutional realities.
2) The objective level of situational occasions, events, and actions.
3) The psychic level of experiences.
4) The psychic level of later memories.
5) The symbolic level of linguistic representation, with vague and incomplete memories (ibid., 319). "

In the transformation, selection, and reconstruction achievements, the possibility of deception, disfigurement, and repression is created, as well those for enlightenment and correction "(ibid., 319).

Biographical self-reflection is also important in the context of developmental psychological phases. Bock quotes Kampmann from 1966 (1984, 13). He states, "The existentially neglected childhood does not only burden the youth phase, but the adult stage and thus human life." The same applies to puberty, adolescence, and all other points of aging.

Even the matron can bear the stigma of an unresolved puberty. "Bock provides us with three anthropological approaches to biographical self-reflection (ibid., 140), " ... the personality of a person, which embraces both his uniqueness and his reference to the others. ...that man is constantly becoming, but that this is not happening as an endogenous development, but in dealing with the environment ...".

Whitebourne and Weinstock (1982, 138) describe the average developmental pattern of adult life. They state, "Early adulthood is characterized by willingness to experiment and by life force." In the first section of middle adulthood, adult roles and responsibilities are increasingly accepted, followed by the second section of middle adult life a questioning of obligations and reintegration - in each of these phases there is a connection between personal, family and professional development. " What an 'adult' is, however, is relative. "For example, there are enough 20 – 30year old's that we would not call 'grown-up' in their behavior. If you take the age of 65, as the end of adulthood, then some people retreat, some even become incapacitated, others remain as efficient as 55 "(ibid., 25).

Some theses by Kohli (in: Hurrelmann / Ulich, 1991, 303-317), and in short, it has been shown that the phase structure of life varies considerably in intercultural comparison and in the historical process. The development to modernity is a process of the temporalization of life. Away from statically / situationally ordered life form, there is today a standardized normal life course. There is a comprehensive process of individualization, i.e., liberation from (formerly) estates and local ties. The curriculum vitae is organized around working life in three phases: preparation, employment, and retirement.

Montada writes (1987, 68), "Every society has a system of age, has formal and informal norms for individual periods of life, and the environment responds to deviations, with outrage, punishment, or recognition." He goes on to say, "Man himself is seen as the creator of his development and is perceived as a cognitive and self-reflective being, who has a picture of himself and his environment and modifies both in the course of evaluating new and previous experiences." (ibid., 77).

The psychoanalyst Reich writes (1976 and 1933, 286-287), "... at the bottom of all reactions (of the human / psychic apparatus) there is not the opposite of love and hate, certainly not the eros and death instinct, but the antithesis of the ego (person, ego-pleasure-ego) and the outside world. Therefore, the first impulse of every living being must be an aspiration for contact with the outside world." This means that human development - and thus the biography - is always in the urgent touch of the ego and the outside world.

As a driving force of human development, we find in Adler, the inferiority (1977 and 1928, 57) He claims, "From the constitutional inferiority and from similarly acting positions of childhood, grows a sense of inferiority and a compensation in the sense of increasing the sense of personality. And, at the same time, the fictitious end of the striving for power comes to tremendous influence and pulls all psychic forces in his direction." In Human Knowledge, (1978 and 1927, 71) Adler says, "... at the beginning of every mental life there is a more or less profound sense of inferiority, which is the driving force, the point from which all aspirations of the child emanate, and develop to set a goal from which it expects all reassurance and assurance of his life for the future ... "

Olechowski writes about the stages of development. He states, "However, man never undergoes a psychic development that is solely conditioned by biological processes" (in: Zdarzil / Olechowski, 1976, 111-113).

The mental development in humans is always determined by learning and thinking processes. Therefore, development is not a process that is completed with the end of childhood or youth; rather, it lasts a lifetime. Mental development can be described by the following four features:

1. Differentiation (refinement).
2. Centralization (construction of higher-level central instances that act as control functions).
3. Consolidation (increasing limitation of possibilities).
4. Active design (the human being determines his future decisions to a certain extent through his decisions at a given moment. He can, in principle, freely dispose of this instrument of self-determination)

The problems of learning and developmental psychology are shaped by the examination of some (perhaps even most) of the following basic situations:

1. Situation of professional and economic competition.
2. Situation of the family.
3. To be aware of the imperfection of one's own existence.
4. Friction on the monotony of one's own existence.
5. To be aware of the finality of one's own destiny.
6. Confrontation with the limited nature of existence (Ibid., 124).

Inglehart, Professor of Political Science in Michigan, writes (1989, 487), "People live far more in the past than we know, for we interpret reality with concepts and worldviews based on past experiences. As we grow up, we build our interpretation of reality around certain concepts. That is why we're based on old maps". To discover their own life history Gudjons, Pieper and Wagner put together a broad spectrum of exercises (1994, 210-220).

Lenz offers us some theses on biographical development (1987, 157-162), from which we pick out some elements: "Man creates and is created by the world... Education is part of human development... The human way of life shows up because of cultural transformation... The development towards humanity and the approach to decent living conditions does not follow the course of natural evolution ... Education is located between reflection and action ... Education is based on the responsibility of the individual ". Prange (1988, 3) claims, "Education, and the offer of educational reflection, is the answer on crisis-experienced and epochal problem situations".

Already before birth, the biography begins. Doctor Verny writes (1981, 61), "A human being has a much greater chance of becoming an emotionally stable adult, when his mother is looking forward to the birth." Note: Every moral contains emotional components. After that comes, according to psychoanalysis:

1. The oral phase: ingest, clinging
2. The anal phase: retention, elimination, cleanliness
3. The Phallic Phase: Researching and Empowering (Flammer 1993, 80-82).

From the development model of Erikson, we mention the keywords: 1. trust; 2. autonomy; 3. initiative; 4. work sense; 5. identity; 6. intimacy; 7. creativity; 8. Integrity (Erikson 1974, 150-151, 214-215). And, "The smallest child lives in a community of life cycles that depend on him, as it depends on them ..." (ibid, 152). From our point of view then the individuation follows.

Overall, we conclude from these aspects to the importance of the biography: the clarification of the unconscious - in the psychoanalytic sense - must go hand in hand with a systematic biographical analysis from the prenatal period.

9. The Power of Love

Variations of love in the fields of life

Unusual and peculiar, it may seem that the power of love is declared as an independent psychic system. In fact, with some exceptions, psychology has not shown any significant scholarly interest in love until today. Of course, there was and still is much talk of the sexual urge (libido). Freud (1920) has decisively expanded his concept of pleasure in later years and juxtaposes Eros with the death instinct ("Thanatos"). Eros means "life drive". The life instinct is the force that pushes for development, works constructively, and synthetically. Eros is the principle of unification and synthesis. The death instinct, on the other hand, urges for destruction, dissolution, and aggression (Freud). The "libido" is the energy of this drive dynamics. Orthodox psychoanalysis still places the life instinct in the context of the sexual instinct. This is indeed an extremely important topic for every human and for andragogy. There is no consensus about the concept of life-drive in psychoanalysis (Schlegel 1975, II, 123).

Humanistic psychology speaks and writes about esteem, emotional affection, and trust. These are certainly expressive expressions that have something to do with love. But as an independent psychic power, love is not defined. Since time immemorial, love has been the central theme of human existence. Even Plato spoke of Eros, meaning the love of good and beauty. The pursuit of knowledge is also an expression of love here. Self-development and sensual happiness are not excluded.

The Greek word "agape" today contains a Christian understanding of love. First of all, this means the love of God for man. Man is the "sinner" and God gives him love, in a sense as an act of grace.

In common parlance, this Christian love predominantly means charity (Campbell 1990, 236-250). But in popular psychology dictionaries, this topic occupies a very modest space. In pedagogy the speech is predominantly about the love of the educator for the pupil. Philosophy "tastes" the subject much less than epistemological and metaphysical questions. Significant studies on love have Fromm (1956, 1979) delivered.

Surely, love is an essential condition for a person to grow healthily. If a child does not receive enough love from early childhood, then "narcissistic disorders" always develop. The whole society is ill in this regard (Battegay 1979, 34/35). We are breaking new ground, trying to define the power of love as an independent psychic system. For this we must look into life first.

When we talk about the love of mother and father, for their child, we generally have clear ideas about it. The parents take care of their child, take care of it, and protect it from danger as far as they can. Parents who love their children turn to them. They take their children seriously. They keep a certain care in all life matters. They express an inner interest in the life of the child. They try to understand their children and to promote their possibilities. They also have a special emotional affection that expresses an inner connection. In this sense, parents assume the educational and general life-related responsibility and duty. This is called the expression of "love".

When adults say, "I love ...", it is often associated with good food, a special wine, cars, home decor, clothes, perfumes, hobbies, and sometimes physical feelings. They mean that they like these things.

Some say it quite bluntly: "I love money". Yes, why not? Many people buy goods and claim that they are doing something good for them. One loves antiques. He is an antique lover. But looking closely you can see that this individual just likes the "size of Louis XVI" or the mood of the Biedermeier. Or the old rustic is a response to his rustic masculinity. The car is often used as a replacement. The owner can never work like a car, seldom has the "power" of his car and is never as free inside as he is when driving. That is something to keep in mind when someone says, "I love my car". "Be happy and love you" is the name of many of the philosophy of Lebenshilfe. This acts as an animation to buy and is a pure advertising slogan. Everyone wants to be happy, and yet many are not. "Day by day, I feel better and better". Everybody should speak this in front of the mirror three times a day, says the "art of positive thinking" as a life coach. But is that self-love?

What man "loves" in general is better understood by the term pleasure and selfishness. The beloved object is an extension of the self-image or ego. Goods and habitats are there to be exploited for themselves. Love is nothing else than the satisfaction of "quasi-needs". It is all about the self and not about the associated opportunities for life. The value of the ego is increased. This value is at the center of the interest in action. The ego identifies its being with the objects and with the amount of power of disposal. Control, domination, and power are the characteristics of this kind of love. The ego wants to have prestige, be popular and be loved as an attraction. This is a one-sided relationship to fellow human beings, to the objects and to the habitat.

When Hans says to his girlfriend Anna, "I love you," then the search for what he really means becomes problematic. Maybe Hans just has a good feeling. He feels moved and excited. He then says perhaps, "I feel pleasant pleasure when I am with you".

Sometimes this spell is just the ticket to the bedroom. It is also possible that he loves his Anna because she thinks like him, because she has the same attitudes toward life, because she is attractively dressed for him, because she is pretty - according to his ideas. We can look into the depths of the subconscious of Hans and then discover that his Anna has some similarities with Hans's mother when she was still young and Hans a baby.

Early childhood life pictures are revived in "I love you". In another subconscious corner, perhaps a woman's ideal image sits on a pedestal. Hans experiences this picture in Anna's face and unconsciously hopes to have found his "pure anima". Imagine, the two marry and then have children. Everyday life overtakes her. The kids tighten their love life enormously. Previously they could live love a whole weekend long. But today leisure is full of cleaning, cooking, washing clothes, caring for children and much more. Anna also has worries and problems with herself. She changes certain attitudes. She is moody and sometimes lazy, as everyone can be. Then it is missing, so we sketch, even on money. Hans may be successful in his career, climbing higher floors in the group and gaining a reputation in the community. He has to pay the mortgages of his house. That has priority. Love comes afterwards. And in general, Anna turns out to be more and more like his mother. This will sooner or later lead to crises. So, love quickly becomes a bleak light and gets lost in the gears of daily functioning.

"I love you" can mean, "I want to live with you"; or, "I want you". The longing for physical closeness and warmth, for intimacy and lust intensity all too often serves the purpose of covering up his own helplessness. The intense attraction can often mean a revival of the original prenatal mother-child unit. The feeling of intimate closeness is supposed to "fill in" the loneliness and the void of life. The outer togetherness conceals the existing self-estrangement.

It would be more appropriate in some situations to say, "I want sexual relaxation". This can happen without love, but it is not the same with love. One can (at the moment) create a satisfaction (relaxation), while the other means life-realization. Love surpasses the value and meaning of mere momentary pleasure life. Lusterleben is here in a growth and not just in an arbitrarily additive juxtaposition of coincidences and moments of experience without progression.

Many people make enormous social commitment. They are extremely helpful. They sacrifice their lives, put aside their own needs, and provide social or medical help wherever they can with the utmost dedication. They help people who are suffering, fight for the socially excluded, and toil for years in slums. They look after old people, drug addicts, prisoners, war victims, and or the poor.

One does that as a profession. Another helps wherever he can at leisure. This is called "charity". But what is the characteristic of "love"? Is not it perhaps so that the selfless, in many cases, has a deep fear of life (Lowen 1981) and is basically hostile to life? Is not it true that charity is often hidden behind this charity?

There is also the love of nature. Some like to spend their free time in nature, hiking, mountaineering, or traveling. You feel comfortable in nature. Or they have their own garden. Lovingly they cultivate their flower and vegetable garden. They feel good when they are busy with their gardening. But the critical eye may see a covert motive here: Mr. Gärtner simply likes to be alone. He wants to avoid his wife. He clings to his flowers, does everything he can for them just to avoid meeting himself. What does "nature love" mean here?

It is the same with animal love: Aunt Emma has a cat. She loves her cat very much. This is because she is always there, can almost always be caressed at will. The apartment is never left. It is good to hear the "meow",when you come in the door. The lady next door has a dog. That is already quite thick (overweight). The owner just cannot help but give this faithful dog's soul something to mouth whenever it makes a soulful sound. Uncle Josef has three dogs. He is dog lover. His faithful critters are always there and listen when he speaks to himself. However, he has a secret satisfaction when his dogs place their feces in front of other houses. "I shit on you" are the messages that his dear dogs distribute for him. The general comes home from the war. He greets his dog. He almost forgot his wife. From "dog love" or from "love of animals" is spoken there. But what does that have to do with "love"?

"Forgiveness", "reconciliation", "repentance", and "humility" refer to the power of love. There are "blows" in life that are difficult to process, for example, the effects of a financial crisis, a momentous meanness of another, a criminal act, a war and its consequences, or a dictatorship. The affected person is required to process the suffering, to free himself internally from the cause, to renounce revenge and acts of revenge, to reduce the pent-up anger and to live through grief.

You can do that too if the offender is still laughing. Conversely, for one cause of suffering to others, it can mean a tremendous inner challenge to understand and accept what they are doing, and at the same time, to change, to have true repentance, and to rejoice with the humility of the future. Here one can speak of an act of love, even if it must be done unilaterally.

Failures are part of life. The social psychodynamics of our western society is like a fighting arena. Always some winners and other losers. The majority remain spectators. They are always losers without fight. They lose their own lives. Losers are known to be ejected in all groups. That has nothing to do with love. Those who experience themselves, in such a situation, usually only overcome with the power of love and find an uplifting contribution to life.

Life sets facts: it has a beginning and an end. Generation and death are the limits of what gives our lives the frame. Man is separated from before and after. Man, as much as he tries to bind himself, is ultimately always alone. This separateness of what still is can never be abolished. Nobody can bring back what has been and lived. It is understandable if man clings to others and to things. This is because he does not know the inner reality as a stop. He did not find his roots in the mind. He did not reveal the secret of life. Only through love man can transcend these limits, the limits of his ego, of his consciousness, and of his world boundness.

Religious people say, "I love God". Many people who are especially ready for action unite spiritually with Jesus Christ and then say, "I love my Lord Jesus Christ most intimately". "God Almighty Father, we love you" is a prayer. Does anyone know what consequences such a prayer could have? Does he love God, or does he only fear him, and appease him with praise, as a child does his tyrannical father? Practiced religion predominantly proves to be an infantile relationship based on the pattern of childhood experiences.

What does a mystic say when he says, "Me and God are one... Through love I enter into God." (quoted from Fromm 1956, 109)? As you know, millions of people pray to God. Praying means: they talk. Heartfelt from love they ask for help.

Does anyone not notice that this is like talking in the telephone receiver without dialing a number? God must provide for every creature that is: praying to be listened to, for those who help raise money, those taking care of sorrow, those in need of comfort, those needing to be freed from grief, those needing help to solve a problem, those listening to a curse, those needing support to reconcile enormous sorrow, and at the same time, give strength to persevere in unconsciousness and denying self-knowledge. In it the love for God seems to have its motive. But God is not the "strict kind father with beard". This is an imprint of patriarchal society.

God can be pictorially illustrated only with the highest archetype. Through this, God can be experienced as: unity, wholeness, openness, life, being, creative power, value, meaning, spirit, and even love. We take a big step: realization of love is God's realization. In ancient Grail stories, love ("Cupid") is the power in man that develops as man goes on a journey to find himself (Campbell 1990, 249-250).

The word love also appears in the context of work, leisure and politics: "I love my work ... I love to play with the model train ... I love football ... I love jazz music ... I love the Sun and the sea ... I love Spain ... I love my homeland ... ". What does a person mean when he says this? He means entertainment, fun, or creative work.

If love also means activity, then the viewer and consumer, in this role, is outside of what love is. Longing for freedom and security can simply mean sentimental love. Memories move people and warm up earlier feelings. The love for another person, for a group, for an institution or for the state or one of its representatives is often only the expression of a regressively oriented love.

It is the deep desire of every person to be loved and to have a loving home. Conversely, politicians and institutions vie for the love of the people. Does that have anything to do with love? This is usually just a game with the emotion of love, based on interests that are beyond real love.

We also find this use of words in connection with art and culture. "I love the beautiful ..."; "I love how a message is artfully formed here ..."; "I love the harmonious ..."; "I love this symphony ..." Some people who have the money they need are collecting everything they love, filling their rooms or safes in banks, thus protecting what they love.

In psychotherapy there is often talk that the healing power is ultimately the experience of love (Frankl 1975, Battegay / Trenkel 1978). Siegel (1990) also points this out many times. By this is meant listening, understanding, showing interest, having patience, allowing, and accepting to help the client find and grow. In this love, the therapist is sometimes a projection field, sometimes a commentator, sometimes a father or mother, and sometimes a helper and a healer. But what he should be, too, is a human leader who says, "This is how we go on building forward, everything else is just a detour or an escape." Educating people on their way to life is an expression of love.

Characteristics and types of love

If we remain at the level of the linguistic use of this word "love," we can recognize some characteristics from these examples:

- ☐ Love contains an emotion.
- ☐ Love implies affirmation and affection.
- ☐ Love contains an experience of happiness.
- ☐ Love means caring, protection and care.
- ☐ Love means an inner relationship / connection to the subject / object.
- ☐ Love also means accepting responsibility.
- ☐ Love contains an interest in knowledge.
- ☐ Love causes actions, often creative.
- ☐ Love also contains an interest in the existence of what one loves.
- ☐ Love means a giving (the other or yourself).
- ☐ Love contains respect and consideration for the subject / object.
- ☐ Love contains a special value and meaning.
- ☐ Love is directed to a subject or object.
- ☐ Love is an extension of the person who loves.
- ☐ Love binds (and keeps free).
- ☐ Love is about truthfulness.

- Love creates unity and wholeness.
- Love contains individuality.
- Love implies a certain freedom.
- Love is an expression of active life.
- Love is meaning and value in itself, without purpose orientation.

From this overview we can extract what love means in essence: Love is the affirmation of life with the psychic wholeness. Love achieves the psychic wholeness as basis, way, and goal. Love is the realization of the psychic being in the habitat. Love uses the possibilities of objects and institutions.

It can be seen from the examples mentioned that there are obviously vastly different forms of love, and that some word uses are wrong - or man activates and lives love in false forms. We let ourselves be guided by the Christian guiding principle, which means: "Love your neighbor as yourself" (which was already a motto in Greek antiquity). Love has its starting point with the loving person. Therefore, it is always about this person first. If we put the person at the beginning of love and - in the target field - then we must include the entire psychic system. "Love yourself" may rightly mean that one should care for one's physical well-being and live pleasure. But man is, as we have explained, much more than just body and pleasure apparatus.

Genuine self-love implies the psychic life as wholeness and unity. Showing interest means learning about it. You cannot, as anyone should realize, love what you do not know. Care and protection require a specific way of dealing with the inner workings. The mental life receives a high value and demands responsibility. Self-love thus means to establish an inner relationship with oneself.

The search for happiness and meaning integrates the entire psychic life, which is never without truthfulness, obligation and affirmative taking care of it. In the overall overview of all the psychic subsystems, it is easy to see that true self-love requires work. It is not just a feeling, not simply an oral or sexual satisfaction, and much more than the care of the appearance. Self-love is one who works on himself fully and comprehensively.

In other words, "I love my feelings by taking them seriously, I love my intelligent power by using it, I love my basic needs by giving them a proper expression, I love my unconscious life by doing so, I love my ego powers by strengthening them, I love my mind by centering my life in it. I want to know, nurture, promote, protect, unfold and harmonize everything ".

This basis is, so we say, the starting point for all forms of love. Hans should love his Anna as much as he has to learn to love himself. And conversely, Anna first must learn to love herself to genuinely love her Hans. If both do, then their love power becomes a viable and fertile inner living substance.

Let us go to "Love Your Neighbor ...": The altruistic man is pushing himself to the limits of others. If he does not love himself in the sense in which we have just defined self-love, then he cannot really love those he helps. The motivation of altruistic help must then even be sought in that he wants to flee from himself. The help of the neighbor then becomes an activity, which at the same time psychologically makes one's own being insignificant, even destroyed. The helper ideal (Schmidbauer 1984) proves to be an accomplice in self-denial and as the main agent of a projective and unconsciously lived psychodynamic. In terms of psychic reality, the helping person then deals with the other person, as well as with himself. "I help you in your suffering, however I may, but your unconscious, your feelings, your intellect, your (psychic) needs but yourself and your spirit do not interest me".

We can now redefine the help to the next as an act of love: love integrates the whole person and all action is to serve that the psychic life receives the value and the realization that is given from the love. This is certainly not always easy to reconcile in practical work. The essential foundation is that all action springs from self-love. In other words, if the help is given to others without self-love, then this help cannot be described as love, but at best as an "altruistic attitude with a life-suppressing effect." If this help fosters escape from oneself and thus suppresses self-love, then one should not even call this "altruistic". It is not altruistic insofar as the dynamics of projection - to help obscure a certain form of life-lie.

Self-love means: being interested, caring, appreciating, affirming, protecting, unfolding, creating unity, forming freedom, taking responsibility, establishing inner connection, living truthfulness, respect, and binding meaning and happiness, to one's own psychic powers, such as: emotions, needs, intellect, unconsciousness, ego and self-control, defense, will, spirit or dreams, psychodynamics, and actions.

This love requires a lot of strength, which must first be built. There are obstacles to overcome. The zeitgeist does not promote this effort. Again, and again, you must accept circumstances that you really would rather not see. Before one has even approached the goal of such a self-love, without knowing what this means for a profit, one must set off on the way.

The self-love in the partnership live, promotes the love for the partner, and makes the love for the partner really possible. Life becomes interesting: the couple tells their dreams in the morning. They do exercises together to discover their unconsciousness. They discuss and seek their basic needs. They analyze together how they perceive and think.

They talk about their talking together. They look critically at their actions and thus at their role division. They meditate together and do relaxation exercises. They learn to understand their past together, to expand their present, and to prepare their future. They learn to meet each other with respect for the unformed and one-sidedly shaped psychic powers. They learn truthfulness in speaking, acting, and meeting. They perceive each other more and more holistically as the value and meaning of existence. Sexuality is then part of this complex love. Sometimes the couple must make a fresh attempt every day (certainly every month) to take the mental life seriously. This is how two trees of life grow side by side. In this way, both grow the love power.

However, determinants of the habitat often make such a way of life or love difficult. Sad experiences, unemployment, lack of money, disaster in the business, other people's meanness, family circumstances, social crises, and wars can seriously damage or even destroy the power of this love. The rampant refusal to take the psychic life and individuation seriously, is the real lie of life, and gives love almost no chance to grow in society.

There is no doubt that what we call "the power of love" has much to do with "meaning of life." Here we encounter two kinds of statements that often appear in connection with suffering: "Love is ultimately stronger than evil" and "The will in a sense, is the power to overcome suffering" (Frankl). There are difficult questions: what was the meaning of the suffering of those who, for example, did not survive Auschwitz?

What should be the meaning for the poor, the homeless, and the oppressed, who have neither education nor money to free themselves from their situation? Many are not even able to formulate their experience of life.
What is the meaning of the consequences of a car accident, when suddenly a family is without a father? Surely the cause cannot be "God's will"! What is the meaning of a cancer condition, when the affected person is unable to recognize the deeper psychic forces in the disease? What is the meaning of millions of victims of war and homeless, today and earlier?

We do not know any "ready" answer. But one thing seems certain to us: one cannot simply construct a "sense" from the stupidity, the brutality, the evil and the lie of the one, with the victims. One cannot simply make evil the purpose of love (as a duty) with the others. Nobody knows whether the power of love will ultimately "win" in the history of humanity.

Love and hate: Dedication towards life and rejection of life

In many forms of object love, animal love, and the love of institutions (we think of parties and churches, as well as of esoteric groups), it is characteristic that intrapsychic facts are projected outwards and the object of love becomes a substitute. Instead of loving oneself, or loving one's partner, or loving people (as explained above), people are bound to externalities. Dealing with objects and animals, but also with nature and with institutions, is a symbolic attempt to do what these people should do to themselves.

The external love wants to bypass the psychic life. Man loses the relationship to himself and to others. He can only express to the outside the power of love as an expression. Whether this power of love is lived and unfolded or not, the power is always there. But love can distort herself. She is destructive against the psychic and physical wholeness, and against the whole living space of man, because he does not shape this power and does not integrate it. At the same time, the psychic powers from the unconscious are increasingly active.

If the human being does not take an interest in his psychic life, then this force is directed outwards: objects, animals, power, etc. Since love is always also Du-directed and wants to find expression in relationships, these external possibilities serve as substitutes. This is easy to recognize with the dog and the cat. The pet receives a symbolic meaning that exceeds the meaningful. Instead of being a symbolic and creative possibility for personal enrichment, the animal becomes a substitute.

The love of objects, Fromm brought, from the perspective of "having instead of being" for discussion. But this should not be led into a dualism. We therefore say, "have for being" and interpret this from the viewpoint of self-love and love in general. If the object serves as an escape from oneself and one's own life, then man wants to "possess" in the sense of mastery and control. If the objects serve the design of love and if they generally promote a love for life, then credit has its value.

Anyone who clings to objects cannot live: he will fall as soon as the objects fall away. Who uses the object world for his life with love, is not bound to the objects, but to how he lives with them. Objects then have a "service function" and not a "function of being". Who equates his degree of inner freedom with his car mobility, is wrong. Many people, with a very small ego, sit in cars with a very strong engine. But if the symbolic meaning of the object coincides with the psychic reality of the person, then this is always a symbolic enrichment. This is the same with the money. Many people have a lot of money, but no love ability. They have not unfolded their abilities and do nothing with the possibilities of their capital, which would enhance their love ability.

The power of love wants to live. She wants to act. She wants to draw. She wants to do more of herself. She wants to implement herself. She wants to make the living space about love. She does not want to and cannot be locked in a steel safe. Otherwise, it will be destructive. Their energy is then available to the chaotic unconscious. Or she turns herself into the opposite. This always causes harm to the individual as well as society.

What love can live out of itself when it is integrated and grows with the other subsystems is its primary function in life. She represents life. She wants life.
She never speaks against objects, goods, capital, and institutions. When man is in the service of these things and circumstances, and this interplay is no longer guided by love, that is always the beginning of self-destruction. That is why we say: He who does not love himself ultimately destroys himself from within. In object love, humans also destroy their habitat in the long term. The "quasi needs" become dominant and keep the exponentially growing destruction gear in motion.

Why are people becoming criminal? Why do people develop into narcissists? Why do many people exercise harmful power? Why does a person become a sadist, exploit others, and oppress them? Why are there many forms of psychopathic personality? Why are many people violent? Why do people harm nature and primary life systems? Why do nations wage wars? The reasons are to be found in the psychic inner world. These are all expressions of collectively missing love. Love has perverted into hate, denial of life, and destructiveness wherever you look.

The psycho-social development stages of Erikson (1974, 150/151) can also be understood in the dimension of love and hate. This model of human development is an orientation for human education to live in the power of love. An age-specific developmental psychological classification is of no importance for personality development.

The aspects always apply:

a) Livelihood includes: basic trust, ego-identity, creativeness, intimacy, integrity, initiative, autonomy, and sense of purpose.

b) Aversion to life includes: distrust, ego-diffusion, stagnation, isolation, despair, guilt, doubt, and inferiority.

Jones (1978, 199) interprets hatred as a "guise of guilt and fear." The counterforce he calls "Liebestrieb". Against this power of love act: self-will, cynicism, coldness of the heart, insensibility to feelings, selfishness, and extreme individualism (1978, 252-261). Above all, these life-rejecting forces are an expression of the defense against the psychic inner life (1978, 258).

In everyday life, there are many forms that cannot be seen as diametrically opposed to love but are already recognizable in the "grey area". One exposes another. Everyone has heard devaluating sayings. Withdrawing recognition from those who no longer participate is a well-known pattern of group-dynamic processes. There are many forms of contempt. A mocking remark or a simple criticism with devaluing tone can get under your skin. Ignoring is sharp. Real is equal to a judge's verdict. Everyone knows what causes such behavior: fear, paralysis, powerlessness, aggression, anger, weakening, and injury in the psychic inner life. One can smile and hide the actual action behind his mask. In the sound, and often in the form, can be seen how people beat others. Taking blows is part of daily life training. This is the reversal of love in everyday forms.

Love is a power that also contains a value experience. It is the sense of those effects or forces of action that affirm or reject, build up or destroy, respect or disregard, promote or block mental life and therefore human life. Everyone knows that love can only do good and is conducive to inner well-being and happiness. It is not an empty saying, when it is said that love can heal.

Also, the reversal is a fact: missing love makes you sick, mentally, and often physically. Love is not just "eros", well-being, and joy in beauty. Love is the elixir of life. Without love, human beings will atrophy and ultimately destroy a state within themselves. Hate is like a cancer, in the psyche of the individual as in the state.

The power of love is the only power of the ego that can transcend one's own self and overcome the pride and injury that life can put over objects. In this sense, love is transcendental. It transcends the mechanical functioning of psychic powers. For Balint (1981, 230/231), the ultimate goal of psychoanalysis is not simply the abreaction of a trauma, but the "decision to restart love". The healing of early childhood traumas obviously leads to a "quality leap". Working through (repeating) cannot yet create love. The commitment to life is a new creative achievement, based on the inner reconciliation and resolution of sorrowful and development-inhibiting experiences. We call this the "transcendental achievement" of love. This contains a voluntary "yes" to the value and meaning of love itself, and without utilitarian interests (Frankl 1975).

The power of love and hatred can be grasped in a continuum (see Balint 1981, 151-169). Aspects or elements of the power of love and hatred are:

HATE: negation of psychic life; Life avert; regression; prevent; To neglect; Destructiveness; Lie; disunity; Occupy objects libidinally; Identification with externalities; Devalued psychic life; Disrespect for life.

LOVE: affirmation of psychic life; Life care; Progression; inner unity; turn; Care for; constructiveness; Truthfulness; holism; Objectively and symbolically use objects; Orientation to archetypes of individuation; Appreciation of psychic life; Respect for life.

If the goal of the "highest enlightenment" is to break away from all suffering, sensations, and bodily experience (Johari, 1979), then the hatred of life has nothing to do with the love for life. Love as "YES" to life involves accepting life the way it really is. And that is the everyday life of man.

"Critical" areas for love as a livelihood are:

☐ The daily household: keeping the cleaning, washing, shopping, cooking, washing dishes, cleaning shoes, budget planning, all in control.
☐ Work and earn a living. This also includes aspects such as sweat, exertion, hardships, duties and so on.
☐ Relationships with all the "banal" complexity that results from it: need for love, aggression, dishonesty, repression, power games and so on.
☐ Moods and feelings of all kinds that everyone has: listlessness, loneliness, emptiness, hope, yearning, fears, depression, boredom and so on.
☐ Problems and crises, conflicts and disturbances and difficulties with oneself, with others and with life in general.

☐ The suffering and misery of the world of billions of people, as it gets every day presented by the media in the room.

☐ Daily life also shows the losers and the broken, the weak and the helpless, the oppressed and the outlaw and the sick.

☐ Politics, business and religion as powers and gambling forces that are hard to understand.

☐ The cultivated habitat: streets, houses, factories (etc.) as anonymous, inhuman, cold, unpredictable, and decisively determining life.

☐ Millions of people and lives resemble each other like grains of sand by the sea: no special originality and outstanding achievements distinguish them.

☐ From everywhere the good news: "We have your luck", "Buy this", "Come to us for your happiness".

The ego is called upon to integrate everything into consciousness, to take it seriously, and to manage it. In it, man should build up his value and meaning. Responsibility should be assumed by man and fulfill his life's duties. The I want to live rather unconsciously, not looking, not feeling, not listening, and not acting responsibly. The ego wants to live outside this reality. Reality is so hard, so strict, so demanding, and it also scares you. And the actual abolition of life and negation of life begins: "I do not want this life"; or, "I do not want to be what I am." Man therefore tries to live without integrating this reality.

There are many attitudes that express no love power in our sense. They are not "evil" in the moral sense. But they nevertheless have a long-term effect on the individual, and the society is destructive. Because they have turned away from life in the origin of the psychic forces. The destructiveness of such attitudes can be recognized in depth psychology or introspectively and transformed with comprehensive personality development.

Conclusion: No one can claim that love is unimportant. It is at most, a private matter of the individual and is not a topic for the Andragogic or the formation of personality.

Love, relationship, partnership and sexuality

Mandel and Mandel (1971, 43-47) give the following orientations on the conditions for a satisfactory marriage partnership: "... equal partnership is the most important principle ...", "... communication should be as open as possible ...", "... Continuity (of the mutual exchange of information) throughout the marriage ... " , " Anything that matters to the relationship, such as: desires, as well as seemingly unfulfillable or embarrassing, or positive feelings for the partner, dependence fears, school experiences, own weaknesses and fear reactions, positive and negative observations on the partner, both sides with mixed feelings, anger and aggressive reactions, and embarrassing questions, should be successfully communicated with between partners. They should know that one open conversation is not possible at all times and not without interruptions ". This can cause a " demythologized and de-idealized partner and makes his reality visible, but heightens the critical self-perception and thus the ability to endure the other in its otherness and its problematic ... "

The psychotherapist Willi (1975) sees the central key to a good relationship. This being, "Partners should be more clearly differentiated, act independently, and not hinder their personal development. They should be capable of constructive conflict management, on partnership decision-making processes, and even distribution of privileges. " (ibid., 7) He mentions three functional principles: first, the principle of demarcation: A well-functioning dyad (couple relationship, author) must be clearly defined both externally and internally. The second principle of the operation states - that in marriage - regressive 'childlike' states need be addressed. The third principle concerns the balance of self-esteem, namely that in a functioning marriage, the partners should be in balance with each other (ibid., 15). According to Willi, a healthy marriage must observe the following boundaries: 1. The relationship of the spouses to each other must be clearly different from any other relationship. 2. Within the couple, however, the partners must remain clearly differentiated and respect clear boundaries between themselves. (ibid. 17) 3. In a mutually happy relationship, the partners stand by each other in the feeling of equality.

Later, Willi (1991, 238-243) expands on the terms of a good relationship. He claims, "more egoistic forms are characterized by the fact that give and take, profit and loss are continuously charged, and the partners demand short-term compensation. In satisfactory relationships, partners usually do not explicitly deal with the bookkeeping of merit and guilt. Making the partner happy is for many a form of love and happiness. In this sense, give and take cancel each other out, because giving can be a form of taking and taking a form of giving. A purely altruistic model of love is dangerous. There is nothing free in relationships regarding equivalency. Willi calls 'justice' the condition of a good marriage.

In the Christian-philosophical understanding (Brugger 1992, 73-74), marriage is defined as follows: "Man presents himself as man and woman as a woman. These presentations have differences, which are not limited to the physical, but shapes and manages their entire mental experience. Only in the polarity of the equivalent sexes does the fullness of the human come to full development, and in the special form of love, as it breaks out between man and woman. They are called upon to make a free decision to belong to one another and enter into a full communion of life, which also expresses itself in bodily-sexual devotion, and which is more primitive, more intimate, and deeper than all other forms of human community. "

Goldbrunner writes (Mainz 1994): "Love is a synthesis, an interaction of experience and action, which also means that the fate of a relationship depends on how the partners deal with the polarity, i.e., how they experience the space, the passive enjoyment, and the activity; who takes a more active and who takes a more passive role, which areas of experience and action are allowed or suppressed, etc" (ibid., 69). How early the couple's relationship forms as a pattern seems to become generally clear today. Goldbrunner notes: "Younger psychoanalysts are of the opinion that even in the first year of life the child unconsciously experiences the couple's relationship with parents, even if this perception is still very undifferentiated ..." (ibid., 109).

A woman in the 'Cinderella Complex' finds her true self-identity through liberation. Dowling describes the problem as follows (1984): "Nature does not give independence to men, it is acquired through training. Men are prepared for independence from birth, and women are systematically taught that they can expect something different: someday they will be saved in some way, that's the fairytale, the message that is sucked in with the mother's milk."

And further, "... the personal, and the psychological dependence (the deep-seated desire to be cared for by others) is the strongest force that oppresses women today. I call this the 'Cinderella Complex'. It is a network largely made up of oppressed attitudes and fears that keep women trapped in a sort of semi-darkness, preventing the unfolding of their full spiritual and creative powers ... "(ibid., 31).

From a feminist perspective, C.G. Jung's psychology is 'patriarchal'. For reflection on being a man and being a woman, we take a few passages from the poetry of Dorst's feminist critique (1995, 74-78): "According to Jung, the salient features of the feminine are illogical whims, resentment and irrationality, vanity and sensitivity. The anima is massless, capricious, uncontrollable, emotional, demonic, intuitive, ruthless, and mystical. She is the mistress of the soul and the angel of light. She shows an unbearable independence. This is full of pitfalls and trappings ... Female thinking, as this, is not valued by Jung, but is considered inferior, illogical, and unreasonable per se ... The ideology of a male world view with its ideas of the autonomy of the feminine, the degradation and annihilation of the feminine is determinant. Characteristic of the patriarchy, according to Erich Fromm's analysis, necrophilia, the capacity for death and violence are a power stroke of patriarchal masculinity, which was also reflected in myth and religious history ... In patriarchal imagery, the female is often split into opposites: the saint and the whore, Mary and Eve, the seductively young sex goddess, and the despised, sexless old woman ... "

Mary (1995) uses examples to illustrate that "man and woman experience love in different ways ... they live in the male and female worlds of love." (ibid., 22). The man is called upon to "develop feelings, show, and assert"; and the woman: "to turn to one's own needs, to gain safety from oneself". She finds this through her feminine identity in connection with the man (ibid, 207-208).

Fromm writes about erotic love (1971, 79-82): "Since sexual desire, in the view of most people, is related to love, they easily come to the misleading conclusion that one loves oneself when one wants to be physically one. Sexual attraction creates the illusion of union right now, but without love, strangers remain behind after this 'union'. Tenderness is the immediate expression of charity. if it really is love, erotic love has a presupposition: that I love from the nature of my being and experience the other in the nature of his being. Loving another is not only a strong feeling - it is a decision, a judgment, a promise. " Furthermore, Fromm writes: "... the notion of a bond that can easily be redeemed, if you do not succeed with it, is as erroneous as the idea that under no circumstances should this connection be resolved." (ibid., 82).

Bartholomew deals in detail with the diversity of sexual experience (1993). We take a few thoughts from his work: "The connection of sexuality with exciting pleasure or their integration into the relationship of love is ... a very young cultural-historical appearance." (ibid., 26) "Sexual pleasure, including sensual pleasure, is found in the whole of other person. It is in the beauty of his face, in the attractiveness of his body, in his exciting closeness, in the wildness of his movements, in the security of his arms, and his caresses. "(ibid., 29). "People who meet with relish recognize each other as a man and a woman and strengthen their sexual identity. They meet each other in the medium of their bodies and experience closeness and security. They grant each other and experience each other's excitement, and they give their community - if responsible also children - fertile life. Happiness has to do with the joyful and loving involvement in other people, which always includes suffering "(ibid., 108-109)" For most people, love remains the center. Who does not feel like love? Who does not long for lust for love? " (ibid., 234).

Lowen, doctor and psychotherapist, writes about love and orgasms (1993): "Sexuality is a biological expression of love." (ibid., 32) "One can separate the spiritual side of life from the physical only at the risk of destroying the unity and integrity of the whole person." (ibid., 32).

"So many women consciously or unconsciously reject their sexual nature because they think they are giving them a submissive attitude, and no woman wants to be an object, neither sexual nor otherwise." (ibid., 216) The search for pleasure is an expression of the life-force of an organism. "(ibid., 226)" Arousal and movement are energetic phenomena. The sexual drive is also an energetic phenomenon. "(Ibid., 227)" Love and sexuality are at the very core of every living organism. They give meaning to their lives and provide the strongest pleasurable motivations for their behavior. "(Ibid., 234)" The ability to attain satisfaction is the hallmark of a mature, integrated, and real personality. "(Ibid., 244).

York describes the child's sexual lust life "... for every child, nothing is more interesting than sex from birth and over long stretches of his development ... The way sexuality is treated (throughout childhood) has a decisive influence on the later life of the child. " In the same book, Schelling writes (ibid, 232): "The real life, the friendships of the young people, the way the parents relate to each other, their relationship with their children, and the emotional atmosphere in the family, all this ultimately has more weight (on the sexual Behavior, author) than what teenagers see on any screen (e.g. porn video, sex on TV). "

Alberoni says about erotism and relationship (1987, 171): "There is also a form of love that gradually emerges from eroticism and friendship.

Love does not show itself as a unique instant explosion, between two unknowns. It is only when two people encounter each other on the sensitive terrain of mutual esteem and confidentiality, that erotic desire begin ...

With "Sex with Love" (1990, 67) Useld-Baumanns: Lack of self-love, pessimistic thoughts, and exaggerated self-criticism, harm the health and thus the beauty.

Anyone who affirms himself and has fun with himself, signals this beautiful, pleasurable feeling through his posture. This relaxed and joyful life posture in turn influences the mental state. Self-esteem and beauty from within, radiate outward. "Other theses by the author are: "Body knowledge makes an orgasm capable." "Creativity makes one's senses." " Self-love makes one capable of love. "(ibid., 182-187).

Janov writes (1977, 228): "Basically, love means to be open-minded and free. It is to allow others this freedom, which means that the others naturally grow up and can articulate naturally." Primary theory defines love as follows: "let everyone be what they are. This can only happen if all needs are met. "

Sexuality and love are in a network with the 'whole' man. Beck (1992, 16-17) says, "the idealized portrayal of love - in the media - does not prepare couples to deal with disappointment, frustration, and friction. Very specific personal qualities are crucial to a happy relationship. This includes: commitment, sensitivity, generosity, consideration, loyalty, accountability, and trustworthiness.
Even among happily married couples, over 40% report the decline in their sexual needs. Beck sees the causes in various areas of life: changing roles (securing the family income), stress in the workplace, health problems and alcohol abuse. The most important factors, however, are psychological ones. These include: self-doubt, feelings of inadequacy, false ideals about one's own body, sexual anxiety, general interpersonal problems, different preferences about where, how, how long and how often (ibid., Summarized). 367).

In the Philosophical Dictionary of Brugger (1992), we find the following reference to "love": "Love is the value-affirming and value-creating primal force of the willing spirit." Essential and considered in its experiential core, it is an attitude of will, considered as an overall experience, the affirmative (appreciative, seeking creative unification),and total attitude of the spiritual soul towards persons as (real or potential) bearers of spiritual values and against these values themselves. Thus, it leads the individual personality out of its isolation and becomes 'we-become' in the different prototypes of human community. " (ibid., 224)

Dürckheim's view of love and erotica (1980, 73-75): "The personal sense of sexuality and eroticism is neither the biological, which is fulfilled in the production of a child, nor the unbridled lust, but rather the experience of a cosmic abundance, which is even more the experience of the divine. One in personal union with a du ... ".

Lowen (1976): "A human being is the sum of his life experiences, which are all incorporated into the personality and structured in the body - 'built-in'." (ibid, 44) "Life has a primary orientation: it flees the pain and strives for pleasure.

This orientation is of a biological nature, because pleasure physically promotes the life and well-being of the organism ... But when a situation promises pleasure and threatens pain, we feel anxiety. "(Ibid., 116) , 29): "The orgasm formula turns out to be the life formula par excellence, in reproduction, work performance, love of life, intellectual production, etc."

Freud (1976, 126): "... we consider the fact that the sexual drive of man does not originally serve the purposes of reproduction but has certain purposes of gaining pleasure". Furthermore, (ibid, 134-135): "The sexual behavior of one person is often exemplary for all his other way of reacting in the world".

Anyone who vigorously conquers his sexual object as a man, we trust similar reckless energy in the pursuit of other goals. On the other hand, those who renounce the satisfaction of their strong sexual impulses, for all sorts of reasons, will be more appeasing and resigned than energetic elsewhere in life. A special application of this phrase - of the model of sexual life for other functions - can easily be stated on the whole sex of women.

Education denies them an intellectual occupation, with the sexual problems for which they bring the greatest curiosity ... The prohibition of thinking reaches beyond the sexual sphere ... "

Vester (1993, 205) writes about the function of sexuality: "Unfortunately, in the realm of sexuality and erotism, only an intellectualized enlightenment is being carried out, which completely ignores the important moments of feeling. Such half-enlightenment, resulting in a little anatomy and some gymnastic exercises and exhausted techniques, unfortunately, in reality, often only supplemented by the fact that love and eroticism, in our cramped Civilization, coupled not with joy and beauty, but with fear, violence and crime. So, with the highest levels of stress, the suppression of a harmonious and pleasurable sexual behavior, destroys one of the biggest counterweights to stress, which makes it harder to deal with. "

We extend the considerations with the social and transcendental dimension of love. Our thesis: War and environmental destruction are expressions of lack of love. For this we have some authors to quote:

Freud: "The process of cultural development ... may lead to the extinction of the human species, because it affects the sexual function in more than one way ... The mental changes associated with the cultural process are conspicuous and unambiguous." They consist in a progressive shift of instinctual goals and limitations of the instinctual drives ... (most important characteristic of the culture): the strengthening of the intellect, which begins to dominate the instinctual life, and the internalization of the tendency to aggression, with all its advantageous and dangerous consequences. The mental attitudes - that the cultural process urges us to contradict - now war in the most vicious way; therefore, we must revolt against him, we must not tolerate him anymore. It is not just an intellectual and affective rejection, it is a pacifist constitutional intolerance, an idiosyncrasy (a very strong aversion). Indeed, it seems that the aesthetic humiliations of the war are not much less of a part of our rebellion than its cruelties. "(Letter to Einstein in September 1932).

Jung: "Yes, (the demonic) mind does everything to avoid having to see its own face, and everyone helps it to their utmost, but not psychology, because this debauchery could lead to self-knowledge. It depends on the free, i.e. the conscious decision of man, whether the good should not be translated into Satanic. His worst sin is the unconsciousness, but you indulge with the greatest devotion even those who should serve as a teacher and example to man. When will the time finally come when one does not simply presuppose man in a barbaric manner, but earnestly seeks ways and means to exorcise him, to seize from his obsession and unconsciousness and to make this the most important cultural task? "(Jung, 1951).

250

Roszak (California): "The great changes that our rampaged industrial civilization must make, if we want to keep the planet alive, will not come through the power of reason or the influence of the facts alone." What we need is one Psychological Transformation: What the earth needs to be felt in us, we need to feel it as if it were our most personal needs, facts, and numbers. Reason and logic can show us the flaws in our current way of living, keeping in mind which flaws, but they cannot motivate us, teach us any better way of life, not inspire us to lead a better way of life, or how we want to live. For my part, I would almost take it as a declaration of bankruptcy, believing the fate of ours living planet depends solely on the moral zeal of a small number of members of our species. Is there no alternative to scare tactics and guilt trips that lend the ecological necessity the fire of intelligence and passion? Yes, they exist. It is the intense interest that comes from a shared identity, from the fact that two people become one. The deep experience of this common identity we call love. Ecologically committed people must ask themselves where they can find it in themselves, and in others whose habits and wishes we want to change, as only love can change us. At the height of the industrial era, Gaia (the Earth) calls us back to the oldest philosophical task: Know thyself! ... The needs of the planet are the needs of the person. (1994, 46-47, 58, 440, 444) . What are the needs of a person? It's love.

In this context, Fromm speaks of "biophilia": the love of life (to the living). We quote some passages from his work (1979, 33-60): "The love of life represents a total orientation, an all-determining way to live. It manifests itself in the physical processes of a person, in his feelings, his thoughts and gestures. The biophilic orientation is expressed in the whole human being. It is a property inherent in any living substance, to live and to sustain itself. The living substance has a tendency to integration and union. It tends to unite, with different and opposing entities, and to grow according to a structure (in cells as well as in feeling and thinking). If you love life, you are attracted to the life and growth process in all areas: he can be astonished and he prefers to experience something new rather than seek safety in the affirmation of the old way of life worth as security. His attitude to life is functional, not mechanical. He sees the whole thing, not just his parts, he sees structures and not summations. He wants to shape and influence with love, reason, and so on ... "

The opposite is called "necrophilia". Their properties are summarized as: the truly evil; to glorify death; feels like diseases; love of funerals and violence; destroying life; despising the person and wanting them to be killed; master and control of life; having for the sake of having; only the memory, not the living counts; possession is everything; law and order are their idols; craving for certainty, prediction, control; fascination with killing and death; do not fear total annihilation; are indifferent to life; only profit and consumption count; mechanical pleasure (sex, happiness, food, drink, etc.); destruction of nature; fond of the tickle of death risk; misinterpretation of life; quantification / bureaucratization of all life; highly praising fight as beauty ... "

Teilhard de Chardin (theologian and philosopher), says to the lust for life (1967, 108-109, 112-113): "I understand that under 'lust for life' or 'love of life' here in the first approximation, and at the same time with the consideration of an intellectual and affective psychological disposition, that it is powerful, particularly for those, when an action seems altogether light, interesting, delicious to us, and with a disposition of joyful and a pleasing nature.

But one must not confuse this with a simple phenomenon of euphoria: firstly, because they are essentially dynamic, constructive, and adventurous. And then, because, they are capable, as they may surround themself with an atmosphere of exultation and intoxication.

At first glance, the presence, and the degree of this wanting to appear to have meaning and value only for individual health is nothing less than the energy of universal evolution. Therefore, the lust for life would ultimately be the basic driving force that moves and directs the universe on its major axis of complexity and consciousness. "

10. The Spirit in dreams and Imagination

Dream theories

Since immemorial time, the sages have dealt with dreams. Time and again, dreams have been taught as a crucial source of life. Even among primitive people - back to the earliest times - dreams have been understood as the voice of a spirit. Dreams are a revelation of God, as was taught in antiquity. They are the "messengers of the gods" (Homer). Dreams convey perceptions and have a healing function (trauma incubation). Our core thesis is: The dreams are created by a spiritual force, the so-called "spirit", or the "absolute (mental) intelligence".

The mind is a term with many meanings. The author has once set in the context of seminars, the task to indicate different terms, what they mean, and what the seminar participants have for associations. More than thirty subjective meanings or ideas and just as many different associations could be found for the word "spirit". The associations are in church, parapsychology, and otherworldly worlds.

We want to redefine the term "mind" and in doing so will achieve a novel transcendental dimension. We define the mind from the theoretical study of dreams. With this we have made a clear and unequivocal decision: dreams are a psychic force with a transcendental dimension.

To understand dreams as a psychic force is not a matter of course. It is a peculiar fact that most personality theories do not contain a word about dreams: not factor analysis, not behaviorism, not field theory, not life forms, not character models, attitude and motivation theories, nor in the behavioral theory. In humanistic psychology, dreams have no meaningful place and appear very marginalized here and there without any definite conception.

Even among the various psychoanalytic directions, there are positions that understand dreams very differently. For some, dreams are only just good enough to be analyzed as brain physiological phenomena. But dreams are as important a psychological subsystem as thinking or needs. Every person dreams every night several times. However, people have a very different memory. Let us look at the different points of view for a moment.

Firstly, we look at the suggestion that dreams mean nothing and are merely a physiological and brain-physiological phenomenon. Physical stimuli during sleep and automatic chemical processes in the brain ensure that remnants of life, which are sometimes remembered after awakening, come to consciousness during sleep. No meaningful message can be taken from the dreams. Dreams are often understood from this position as "morbid appearance" without specific meaning. Content-analytic processing of dream material can at most provide an overview of the life of an individual because the material always comes exclusively from lived life (Hall et al., 1972).

Freud commented on this position aptly for us: "The conceit of consciousness (he probably wanted to say" the people "), for example, the discreet rejection of the dream, is one of the strongest protective devices ..." (1919). In fact, those positions that discard dreams as an intelligent source of knowledge are ridiculous and mock those who seriously engage in dream life as something very essential to humanity.

"Interpretation of dreams is the Via regia (the king's way) to the knowledge of the unconscious in the soul life", Sigmund Freud wrote 1895. This dream theory is today no longer so acceptable. Many discoveries about psychic life have broadened the horizons of dream content, dream architecture, and dream-creating power, completely redesigning the entire analytic dream doctrine.

Jung wrote in 1934: "Certainly there are dreams that manifest desires or fears, but what else is not there? Dreams can be inexorable truths, philosophical sentiments, illusions, wild fantasies, memories, plans, anticipations, one's telepathic visions, irrational experiences, and God knows what else is. "

Jung: "A phenomenon that is hidden in the individual dream behind the respective compensation is a kind of developmental process in the personality. First, the compensations appear as respective adjustments and a balance of disturbed equilibrium positions. They can also be a deeper insight and experience. These seemingly one-off acts of compensation appear to be a kind of plan, which is seemingly interconnected and subordinate to a common goal, in a deeper sense. Therefore, a long series of dreams is no more than a futile juxtaposition of incoherent and unique events, but one in planned stages. I have described this as an individuation process "(1971, 155).

Jung writes on the spirit in man: "According to the original nature of the spirit (in ancient philosophy) it is always the active, invigorating, stimulating, provocative, which inspires man.

Aeppli, a disciple of Jung suggests, "Whoever deals with the dream in practice, comes to the idea of a superior, constructing and guiding authority, and we must not assume that the purpose of this dream-creator is to address our ego. The dream is the nocturnal statement of the soul. " (ibid., 27) "The dream, evidently, has the most complete knowledge of all psychic events and possibilities. It is as if it were living in a center from which the gaze goes beyond the nearest to the darkest humanity. It seems as if the following question arises again and again: How do I reconstruct the overall psychic situation of my human being in the material of personal experiences? In this library are the accounts of all events of our present life ... All that was once ours are in the magazines and pantries of the soul and in mind-bound storerooms. What we have experienced awaits us and when the dream needs its contents, its forms again. " (ibid., 28-29). "The primal wisdom of life is revealed in the dream. In it comes an answer, which says where one stands, and indicates the best ways to go." (ibid., 82).

The main characteristic of the psychoanalytic dream theory is that the dreams contain material from the conscious and unconscious life of the individual. Therefore, the dreams can be used diagnostically. Freud saw in dreams essentially the repressed material of the individual. (That is, the disguised instinctual impulses and the infantile desires.) These wishes are always defended unfulfilled instinctual wishes. Unfulfilled instinctual impulses are the creators of dreams. The dream is the result of a drive conflict.

There are also tendencies in the dream to recognize how the unconscious tries to solve such a conflict. After the dynamics of the defense mechanisms, the dream material must be reassembled into an original image: the misrepresented must be put right and the hidden is to be uncovered. The dream is a meaningful structure, Freud taught. The energetic force does the so-called "dream work". In a distorted form, she brings the repressed material back into consciousness, through the dream image. The pictures are the apparent dream material. The veiled units of meaning are the latent material. The purpose of dream interpretation is to reveal the latently hidden material from the obvious material.

Adler understands dreams as a variant of waking life. A dream is a "descendant of the imagination". His dream interpretation is based on the pursuit of power and the sense of community. A dream always deals with the solution of a current problem. In dreams, the individual thinks ahead and tries to reach a solution. These attempts to solve Adler are always self-centered. The dream images are based on memories. Just as the dreamer often likes to be a spectator, so in a dream he is often just a spectator. Adler rejects a theory of dream interpretation and sees dream interpretation as an artistic inspiration (Adler 1966).

Boss (1975) finds all the dream theories and dream interpretations of the deep psychological schools confusing, misleading, completely redundant, subjectivist, psychologistic, harmful, and completely out of the air speculations. All dream interpretations, since Freud, are "Dream UM interpretations. His approach is phenomenological. The dream reflects, in its own way, the relationship man has with life. Directly, the dream shows, one's own buried existential, and non-objective, behavioral possibilities.

The dream characterizes freedom and lack of freedom of the circumstances and the environment of the dreamer. Phenomenological dream interpretation wants to take the dream as an "own way or a modification of the human existence" (1972, 186). The understanding of the dream requires the understanding of existence analysis. We cannot call these essays by Boss a "theory." But they do emphasize what has often been neglected by the instinctual concept: Dasein as a certain mood of being in the direction of realization and unfolding.

Szondi (1963) also sets his own accents in his dream understanding. Above all, he separates "dream dreams" and "ancestral dreams". The dreamer is the "conductor of mentally ill ancestral figures" (1963, 79). These ancestral figures are stored in the unconscious and reach the consciousness of the dreams. In the dream, all unfulfilled life possibilities, as well as personal demands, wishes and experiences can be recognized. Recognition and working through is the central objective of interpretation. Szondi gives a whole series of warnings to all those who interpret the dreams of other people. One thought we want to pick out: "On the couch is a human and not a dream."

Neopsychoanalysis also teaches that in the dream, the inhibited driving life is expressed. However, according to Schultz-Hencke (1949), the instinctual life is interpreted more broadly, and not just as a sex drive. Dreams are compared to daydreaming. Dreams and daydreams are an important function in the psychic system. These are forms of coping with life. The danger of life (past and future) and death is an existential basic experience, that is reflected in both the waking dream and actual dream life.

According to Jung, not only the complexes are recognizable in the dreams. Dreams also manifest thoughts, judgments, moods, inclinations, plans and memories. In the dream, the entire material of the unconscious can be found. It also shows the so-called "archetypes", especially in extreme tension situations. The dreams have different functions. They reduce or enlarge in the sense of balancing the waking consciousness. Dreams can warn, design solutions to problems and conflicts, and prepare the future. Dreams contain material that is to be interpreted at the object level, that is, the information relates to objects of life. Subject level means that the dreams tell about the dreamer.

Jung calls the content that is neither subjective nor objective, and can be interpreted, archetypal dreams. Archetypal images are those characters that we know from mythologies and fairy tales. According to Jung, the fundamental direction of the dream is future-oriented: The psychic system is pushing for growth and development (individuation). On the one hand, the dream interpretation is based on the associations of the dreamer. On the other hand, one can also interpret a dream by adding archetypal motifs. He calls this activity "amplification". The thorough knowledge of the conscious life of the dreamer is a prerequisite for dream interpretation. Imagination has the same function as the dream. Imaginations are therefore like the dreams to interpret.

It is only marginally, that we can critically hold to the (orthodox) psychoanalytic theory, that "wish fulfillment" cannot possibly be the "driving force" or the "engine" of dream design. The content analysis of 50'000 dreams by Hall / Nordby (1972, 37-61, 83-101) shows a result that does not allow this conclusion. In most people's dreams are issues that can hardly be linked to sexuality (or "libido").

Based on our own experiences, with dreams or dream interpretation, in depth psychological counseling, we estimate the proportion of dreams that contain a (sexual or libidinal) wish fulfillment to max. 5 to 8 percent (based on around 50,000 heard dreams). Critical objections also arise from the analysis of REM phases (Becker-Carus, 1981, 296-298): "We seem to dream according to physiological rhythm and not according to latent psychological trauma".

Thus, the thesis that the instincts (the impulse) can be considered the fundamental force of the dream design is unnecessary. The theoretical assumption of a spirit principle, as a dream-shaping force, is the only appropriate way to work constructively with dreams on all sides.

"Psychosexuality" (Heim 1993, 451) can also not be the hinge point in which psychoanalytic insights on psycho-sexual and cognitive development are entangled. The "focal point" or pivot in the psychic system is the mind that mediates between all psychic subsystems and their potentials. In an organizational function, in the sense of individuation takes over, if the ego allows it.

We do not want to distract from the fact that man has emerged from nature, is subject to its laws, and is essentially "corporeal". Psychological and spiritual concepts, that move away from this "back-binding" in the sense of devaluation, create fatal consequences in individual as well as in collective life. Conversely, it is a massive anthropological limitation, if a human image, with instinctiveness and without spirit, is determined as a basis for education, analysis, or therapy.

Basic theses for a new dream theory

From this short overview, we can see various aspects that we want to discuss. Let us first assume that all dream theories contain "something true". Let us suppose that the different understandings of dream and dream interpretation are content based on the respective personality theory, and from the understanding of existing authors; therefore, we can record eight basic theses for a theory about the phenomenon "dream":

1) The images contain visual material that covers the entire spectrum of human life.

If you look at your own dreams, you will be able to recognize different inventories. First, there are those images that have a concrete connection to the life of the dreamer: other people, familiar objects, and places from the present and the past. Furthermore, figures and situations can be seen - time and again - that have no direct relationship to the dreamer. These are general figures (such as policemen, robbers, teachers, captains, pastors, professionals of all kinds) and places that are unknown to the dreamer.

There are also animals and houses in dreams that the person has never personally experienced, possibly from books or films knows. Teeth can fall out, rivers overflow their banks, birth and death occur to acquaintances and unknowns. The dreamer can be found in many variants of sexual acts that were never awake and perhaps never become reality. Then there is the weather, the plants, the earth, the water, and the fire. Also means of transport and accidents of all kinds occur in dreams. Goods in all the diversity of the given - such as food, clothes, money - can appear in dreams.

Peculiar symbols and symbolic actions can occur in dreams that are not directly related to the dreaming person. The dreamer can undertake journeys, which he never made concrete. The dreamer can be involved in ice and snow, war and criminal situations, as he never was. There are actions that the dreaming person would never do and to which he does not have his own direct experience (for example, flying). There are also dream images and scenes possible, which later become reality.

Obviously, one cannot say that in dreams only personal life inventory comes before. It should also be hard to interpret all this dream material in the context of drive or validity. To say that these are only brain-physiological remnants of human reality seems rather limited.

But if this material has a meaning, a specific meaning, then this sense may well be in the whole range of possible human experiences. The dream material is as rich as life.

2) Dreams contain meaningful messages about the dreaming person and their life.

Why does a human being at moment X just dream this and not something else? Why is hardly one dream the same as another, except for exceptions? Why is it almost never the case that another person has the same dream at the same time or at a different time? Just as two people can never have the same mental dispositions and the life of two people can never be completely identical, so too is the dream life always individual.

Obviously, we must assume that a dream always has a specific relation to the dreamer. This means that every dream has timeliness, which must be considered as individual. It therefore makes sense to assume that every dream has a meaning that is unique to it.

Regardless of whether we can identify meaning, we must assume that a dream always has person-centered actuality. It is also obvious that the message is meant for the dreamer and his life and should not be understood as something strange to those that it does not concern personally.

3) The messages of the dreams are usually veiled and therefore rarely directly understandable.

It is an inconvenient and incontrovertible fact that dreams can have a diverse form of presentation. Improbable becomes possible. Realities are displayed, enlarged, or reduced. Incompatible comes together. Things and circumstances are mingled that never occur together in life. Strange contrasts can appear. Past and present are sometimes mixed up. Certain elements can be neglected, where they usually have a share of consciousness in real life. Conditions are reversed to the contrary. Contrasts can shock and embarrass the dreamer.

The values in the dream by no means correspond to the conscious reality of the dreamer. Dream situations can bring about feelings that the dreamer has hardly ever experienced in his everyday life. Some dream stories are more like an allegory or metaphor.

We call this the "message types" of the dream. We can also pack and communicate our messages in concrete life. Literature and art, but also wit and irony are classic examples of this. In everyday life too, people often speak "distorted", disfigured and in many indirect ways with allusions. People put on masks, can lie and "beat the bag, but want to hit the cat in it".

People often allude in communication without directly speaking the message. How do you tell a person something that they do not want to hear and do not want to see? One makes hints, adds parables, simply says the opposite, exaggerates massively or understates massively. One can talk a lot about one thing, until the other one realizes the essence of the message. Many talks around what is usually not intended as the content of the message. We say now: The dreams reflect the most varied types of all forms of communication.

4) The nature of the manifest presentation and the types of communication are governed by specific laws.

If the human being packs his messages so diversely in his communication, then is usually has a reason. Likewise, we assume that dreams do not happen to have different types of message design.

First there are the resistors. What the ego does not want to see and hear directly must be made indirectly accessible. Then there are messages that can be conveyed easily and attractively as a parable. Some things can practically not be presented directly in pictures. An experience must be created for the message to be experienced. This applies to messages that belong to the experience area. Some things must be applied "thickly" to man if he has a "board in front of his head". Close up, many must feel in the dream, which he simply would not understand with objective communication. Some dreams are such an intense experience that you feel a change in them afterwards. This is often not about a message, but about an internal transformation of stored life inventory. Unconscious material is being restructured. Healing successes in psychotherapy - with dream interpretation - are usually accompanied by such dreams.

What in the dream can be called the manifest material is not just the superficial back drop. The very nature of the presentation or design of a message is part of the message. There cannot be a complete list of such laws. We are content with these examples to make it clear that the types of communication have specific reasons. Every interpretation of dreams must draw on this diversity and include the individual situation of the dreamer.

5) Dreams can be used in practical life.

Every image and every symbol - by which we also mean acts or events - has some meaning that is related to the dreaming person. We also said that the types of communication have specific causes. Therefore, it is obvious to say that dreams have a specific purpose. They want to inform, analyze, and explain. Dreams can warn. Dreams often just want to help process the inventory in the subconscious and restructure it directly. Dreams provide solutions to conflicts and problems. Dreams can confirm something where the ego is uncertain. Dreams can also "only" give suggestions to occupations of the dreamer in everyday life. Dreams can be understood as an impulse to reflect certain values, to consider the neglected, and to find "the right measure" for something. Dreams can have a direct healing effect, as the story of dreams shows in many ways. Some dreams are focused on development and growth. Such dreams can be understood in the context of the mental-spiritual growth process.

Esotericism and alchemy have finally taken their symbolic language from the dream world to depict psychic processes (Kessler 1977). Symbolic or archetypal experiences in dreams have not only one purpose - the information - but they are also an image of an inner fulfillment that must be integrated into the consciousness. There are dreams that can be understood as a direct experience of God. The parapsychological research on dreams has shown in many ways that telepathic or clairvoyant forces make a message. We can speak of "transcendental experience" here.

Once you start to systematically work with your own dreams, you will find that your dreams take on a life-giving function. Dreams should not only be interpreted. Dreams are there to be used. How can "experts" still claim: "a lot of dreams are unhealthy and even harmful, and an expression of neurosis"?

6) Dreams are produced by an intelligent force.

If our above analyzes are correct, then we must assume that a psychic force "produces" the dreams. This force works very intelligently in its own logic. It also has an extrasensory perception.

We call this power "mind" or "inner spirit". The ego may be able to silence that spirit, or simply not listen to it. But the mistaken notion of some "experts" are that one can manipulate dreams. This fails to recognize that this spirit never lets itself be controlled by the ego. Never can one command the mind and what it should communicate to the ego. Although one can ask for help, want clarification, and demand guidance, it is never possible to force this "intellectual intelligence" into an ideological or dogmatic system. The absurd and nonsensical idea that dreams can be mastered has already reached the field of managerial seminaries: "Let the Lord sleep in his own - program your dreams ... become the director of your dreams" (Czichos 1993, 214). Anyone who teaches this is an ignoramus who seduces and deceives people. Nothing has such dangerous consequences in human education as mental heresies.

Those who design their growth and their psycho-catharsis with dreams for a long time can see that this force also controls the process of the growth process. The mind has the "code program" of individuation. This spirit knows all the answers to the basic questions of being human and of existence. The spirit often evaluates the interests of life differently to both the ego and the superego. Therefore, we say: this mind is "absolute unrestricted". It is possible to impose a certain kind of thinking on a person, to shape the unconscious with unsuitable patterns of life, and to let the feelings "play" like a piano. Teaching and living values and attitudes of the most impossible dehumanization, but the mind always remains unmoved. In that sense, the mind is not malleable. Only man is malleable - in terms of his dreams - by learning the language of dreams and shaping his life with dreams.

We want to make it clear that the power of dreams is the Spirit of God in man, or in other words "the spirit of the universe." When God speaks to man, he speaks through dreams. God has no other direct communication with man than dreams, imagination, and contemplation. This spirit is the supreme intelligence in the creation of the universe.

As a side note, it should be pointed out that the systematic use of psychic energy (see: Schellhammer 1986 and 1987) always includes the communication with this mind, and that this energy with its own intelligence is active, if you know how to handle it.

7) Dreams are an independent psycho-mental subsystem

It is a fact that many people think little to almost nothing. But that is why no psychologist says that thinking as a mental function does not exist or as such does not belong to human beings.

Many people are hostile to feelings. Emotions only create difficulties and are irrational; therefore, to some extent eliminate. Access to the unconscious is difficult and exhausting. Yet no one who knows about this reality has said that the unconscious is not a psychic function.

However, because people do not understand their dreams and some psychologists find the conditioned reflex more interesting than the dream life, one cannot conclude that the dream life is not a psychic function. Although the psychoanalysts of the different schools often interpret the dreams very differently, it has been proven that at least eight different interpretations can be expected from ten different professionals.

Nevertheless, because the analysts have not yet sufficiently developed the dream theory, one cannot say that dream theories are fantasies or dreaming is not a mental function. Neither can it be said, that because people mostly have no access to their dreams, dreams are unimportant. Dreams are the most valuable asset in human life. Only dreams make the psycho-spiritual evolution of man comprehensively and holistically possible.

Here it should be clearly stated: dreams or the mind as the dream-creating agency is a psychic force that cannot be attributed to other forces. Thus, the mind is the central force in a psychic system of its own. We can call this system a "dream system". But since the imagination can be judged according to the same criteria and, moreover, this mind is the central active intelligent force, we speak of it as the "spirit system".

8) Imagination is structurally and functionally similar to the dream.

This thesis is practically represented by all experts. However, they handle the imagination as differently as the psychoanalysts interpret the dreams differently. In principle, everything that we have said about dreams, also applies to the imagination. There is one meaningful difference: we can direct and use the imagination.

Characteristic components, from which the "spirit" can be determined, are in the overall overview:

☐ Dream and imagination as a meaningful inner structured experience
☐ Pictures, symbols, and archetypes
☐ Extrasensory perception (also foresight)
☐ Human-leading (andragogic) function
☐ Code program individuation; completion of the transformation processes
☐ Processing power (partial healing effect)

- ☐ Own standard and value system
- ☐ Effectiveness in psychic energy in psycho-energetic exercises
- ☐ Dreams and contemplations on the transcendental reality

The language of dreams and dream interpretation with practical suggestions

Some characteristics, to the language of dreams, are recorded. We can divide the footage into three groups:

☐ The pictures and pictorial actions:

The images are those elements that have an obvious individual meaning from the personal life. The interpretation lies at the level of personal experiential associations. The picture is concrete, visually comprehensible, and individually and subjectively shaped. Images can be all experiences of the individual, such as, people, events, things, and places.

☐ The symbols and symbolic actions:

Symbols are pictures. They are from life. But they have supra-individual significance and are to be interpreted as being directly object-related, for example, independent of the individual experience. The associations are intersubjectively valid. These kinds of images can be understood as general living conditions of humans and thus they are relatively independent of time. Such symbols are concrete images of life and not formal abstractions (such as the circle or the pyramid). Symbols can be: a house, natural conditions, orchestra, forest, grotto, theater, transport, weather, human types, fruits, etc.

☐ The archetypes and archetypal processes:

Archetypal images can be concrete or abstract. But as a picture they are no longer completely life related. The figure of the wise man and the witch, all pictures of mythology and fairytale worlds are such pictures. They reflect basic motives of human life. Abstract images or symbols, such as the circle, the cross, insignia of all kinds, pyramid, sun, light source, and the like are among the highest forms of archetypes. We call the symbol of life the highest archetype there is.

Archetypes have a meaning that can no longer be expressed concretely. The associations have intersubjective validity. The archetypes are interculturally and universally valid, albeit differently designed. In particular, the abstract archetypes are time independent. The idea is hidden deeper than the pictures and symbols. Archetypes are: the life symbol, pyramid, cross, circle, hexagram, light, mandala (all sorts), the anchor symbol, crystal, precious metal, king and queen, priest and high priest, temple, travel, path and more.

For the interpretation of dreams this results in four aspects:

1. Images directly relate to the psychic system of man and his life. It can be a message about the dreamer or information about other people and circumstances.

2. Symbols expand the individual content to existential topics that have supra-individual significance. Such pictures reflect the general habitat of people. They have a personal message with their collective meaning for the individual.

3. Archetypes are transcendental experiences. They reflect the decisive transformation processes of individuation. They convey experiences about eternal humanity. What God is can only be approximately experienced through the inner fulfillment of the transformation archetypes.

4. In a dream, all three types of images can occur together. An example: Hans dreams: "He quarrels with his wife in a city theater while storming outside, his grammar school teacher is an onlooker, his wife's mother is hiding behind a curtain, and a wizard from far away land comes in and brings both a small stone that turns into a gem in one's hand. "

From the discussion of the function of dreams, we conclude the following core thesis for Andragogy: the most valuable source of all truths about man and life are dreams. Those who want to lead people to their being and to God, without dreams and without training for the interpretation of dreams, leads people away from the inner truth.

Dream interpretation must be learned like a foreign language. Dreaming can give useful stimulus but are rarely suitable for the direct adoption of an interpretation. For, the subjective experience of past and present can never be contained in a symbol dictionary. We want to give some hands-on work instructions and imagine the person taking their time.

☐ Practical work instructions:

Step 1: write down the dream
Step 2: decomposing into action units, for example: 1st act, 2nd act, etc.
Step 3: List the main elements separately: People, Things, Events, Places, Conflict Topics, Critical, Special, etc.
Step 4: Capturing your own location in a dream: viewers? Actively acting person? As? Feelings? Which values move?
Step 5: Capture special memories, and reference to the past and present: what was the day before? What events, thoughts, feelings?

Step 6: Which psychic powers and actions are addressed? Is it about correcting the view? Or about undeveloped or unilaterally developed psychic powers? Is a particular action (or omission) critically lit?

Step 7: Which general life topics are up to date? In which direction does the picture push? Should something be changed? Is there a concrete need for action due?

Step 8: Which other persons and circumstances are addressed?

Step 9: Are archetypes available? Which inner change themes are currently up to date?

Step 10: Link associations and reference elements together to form the message out of it. If necessary, distance yourself from the concrete picture and ask for general "wisdom", vices of life, guiding ideas and attitudes.

Step 11: Comparison with previous similar dreams or with earlier dreams that contain single identical elements.

Step 12: Extended interpretation and experience: relive the dream with imagination, talk to the characters, ask questions, and bring the situation to a solution or conclusion.

For people who want to promote their dream life, some general suggestions can be given as action orientation: It is essential to keep a dream book and to keep it ready on the bedside table next to the bed. This requires a positive attitude towards the dream life. Healthy sleep habits are beneficial. After awakening, you should not immediately turn on the radio or read the newspaper, but remain alone for a moment: "What have I dreamed now? ... Oh so ...". Then you should write down the dreams. After breakfast, dreams often "disappear" quickly. Because real life requires effort. Even inconspicuous little dream fragments can contain a message, even if only: "Pull on the red thread ... then you will find the topic already".

Even totally abstruse pictures contain a message. Nobody should be ashamed of a dream image, even if it says very clearly, "Man, look how you live, you cannot go on living like this." Of course, dealing with dreams means having a genuine interest in exploring and understanding yourself, your life, and growing inwardly. When working on a dream, one can orientate oneself to the question: what does the dream want? Let us keep, inform, explain, warn, process, unfold, advise, promote, change and prepare.

We want to enter the dream language in more detail. Core questions are:

a) Why does the dream not speak directly, openly, clearly, unmistakably, and simply?

b) Why does the dream often speak in obscure, indirect, similar, mysterious, metaphorical, and complicated ways?

c) Why are pictures the main elements of the dream language and not words and thoughts?

We can answer these questions in many ways and present here an overview as a basis for discussion:

☐ Man has not only the intellect with speech ability, but also an eidetic, i.e. the ability of visual representations and processing.

☐ The inventory in the subconscious consists mainly of images; possibly linked with words with a clear pictorial idea.

☐ Man also experiences many images in concrete life that cannot be reduced to language. Pictures are a part of life.

☐ A single image can often convey a complex message, while long speech would be necessary.

☐ There are also versatile, complex, metaphorical and equable forms of expression in language and communication.

☐ In real life, too, the ego can often only be indirectly, suggestively, postponed, and paraphrased.

☐ Images activate a much stronger energy than thought can. The entire psychic organism is psychic energy.

☐ The dream-creating force, i.e. the inner mind is not an absolutist and authoritative authority to which it must be obeyed literally.

☐ The ego has the freedom to respond to this spirit or not. If a person wants to communicate with the spirit, he must learn the dream language.

☐ The mind behaves in an andragogical way, i.e. restrained, wise, clever, skillful, and often easy and often demanding, without taking the autonomy from the ego.

The relationship between the ego and the mind, as it can be analyzed from the position of the dream language, illustrates how great the freedom of the people is with respect to this transcendental divine power. The responsibility, on the other hand, is enormous for humans. If man does not enter this power, then he always remains a prisoner of his unconscious and can never be guided by his spiritual source of life.

Psychic-spiritual evolution is not possible. In the end, humans develop regressively. Another question is whether in the spiritual world (after death) it has consequences if man does not enter this cooperation with the spirit. We cannot clarify that here.

Meditation, imagination, and contemplation with practical suggestions

In addition to the dreams, we want to get closer to the imagination and, above all, give ideas for the practice. First, we want to do something with the conceptual salad. There are many words that all mean only one thing, namely, imagination; to following are some imagination synonyms: visualization, katathym pictures of life, autogenic training school, healing meditation, conscious dreaming, symbol drama, repatriations, daydreaming, contemplation, psycho-cybernetics, spiritual healing.

We define imagination: Imagination is inner picture viewing. You can passively run the pictures or control the pictures. You can enter pictures and change pictures. The language of the images and their functions are to be understood as well as the language of dreams. The pictures have a meaning and generate emotions. With imagination, one can gain insight into one's own psychic subsystems and grasp other people "medially"; thus, learn to understand better. The psychic energy of the imagination can also have healing effects.

Contemplation is a special form of imagination. In contemplation, archetypes are imaginatively experienced. One can immerse oneself in the image event to understand or experience the power of an archetype. Contemplation is always an intense inner viewing and working of archetypes, a introspective contemplation and spiritual immersion in "ideas" (see Plato). One does not contemplate on concrete life circumstances. One imagines it. Imagination and contemplation together we call meditation.

There are the following types of meditation:

1. Concrete Imagination: See past and present life situations inwardly; to pass through a critical situation imaginatively.

2. Symbolic Imagination: A tree means the growth of life. Imagination calls a tree to show what life's own growth is like. In a warehouse is the entire inventory of the subconscious. Imagination then deals with the unconscious material, as it turns out.

3. Contemplation: inner color vision or simple conditions from the habitat (lake, tree, spring); archetypes like the life symbol, pyramid, the ancient wise, experience the sun inside.

4. Merging is possible. The implementation can take place in two variants: a) Active meditation: the image process is actively directed, be it by the meditating person himself or by a third person.

b) Passive meditation: the person passively surrenders to the course of the picture and then breaks off after a few minutes.

Die Practice of the imagination in the German psycho-esoteric market is like a rampant landscape with Babylonian speeches. There is often a lack of a clear systematic approach. Imagine and meditate without clear goals, without clear structuring of images, simply with the intention to create a sensational experience, or a nice feeling. There is talk of transcendence experience, where the meditating person does not even approach the sun with the exercise. Above all, the healing meditation sector makes the experience of pictures much more than the substance can do. A corresponding spiritistic atmosphere replaces the technical competence.

Like one can have a limited concept of personality, so can they have with the concept of meditation. But without open-mindedness, one cannot achieve. The most absurd of all opinions is the idea that one can become enlightened through pleasant imaginative experiences. We therefore give some basic rules for everyday use. We cannot enter into the techniques of spiritual healing, although this opens interesting perspectives, but far from what the market offers in terms of practices or promises in general.

Meditation is basically something simple if you do not want to storm the Himalayas right away. We provide a practical scheme below.

General scheme of meditative imagination:

Step 1. Target decision and symbol selection
a) Relaxation: choose appropriate images that can be fluid or static. Here are some suggestions:

☐ Colors: note the different effects of blue, red, orange, green, brown.
☐ Experience landscapes: green meadows, lakes, rivers, streams, mountains.
☐ Experience the sun.

b) Take a look at one's own psychological relationships: there are general symbols for each subsystem; we give some suggestions:

☐ The overall system: an orchestra plays.
☐ Ego System: the captain with his ship is at sea.
☐ The unconscious: a warehouse full of pictures and inventory.
☐ Feelings: a color spectrum.
☐ Intellect: a computer room in operation.
☐ Needs: the pets on a farm.

☐ The love power: the warming eternal fire.
☐ The spirit: the wise woman.
☐ Actions: stage with acting figures in costumes.

c) Experiencing archetypes: It makes sense to first check and decide what you really want to experience and what it should serve. For example:

☐ Wisdom: talk to a wise person.
☐ Wholeness of the psyche: experience a mandala (circle-cross symbol).
☐ Process of individuation: take a journey, go a pathway.

Step 2. Processing

☐ First, always a short relaxation.
☐ Focused on the image or images.
☐ Concentrated control in the sense of "staying with the picture".
☐ Slowly indulge in and / or control the changes.
☐ Try to understand, if necessary, the meaning inside / directed: "what does this image mean? Change so that I understand better!"
☐ We recommend a maximum duration of 5 to 8 minutes per exercise.

A purely passive imagination is at best adapted to relaxation intentions. Otherwise, it is always creative and enriching to work with the footage at the same time. For example, you can talk to the characters. It is interesting to explore the places and spaces more closely. You can talk to animals: "who are you, what do you want to tell me?" In difficult situations, one can look for solutions and ways out. It is always a win to mediate (reconcile, accept) between characters and to arrange a situation. While meditating, one can linger as a spectator or intervene in the event as a co-actor.

Everyone has their own inclinations and different requirements for this kind of meditation. It is never profitable to have pictures in abundance. Then you should slow things down or even break off. Sometimes it suffices, when the pictures appear only tentatively, to speak as vague shadows. This is enough for first experiences on a specific topic. Anyone who is a little anxious should never make an imagination longer than two to three minutes. Absence and inattention are first broken down by general relaxation (Autogenic Training). Resistors are normal. It also takes some courage to open the psychic inner world.

Sometimes the pictures are based on andragogic patterns. The intelligent force may say through a picture constellation, "Do you really want to see that?" Or, "Now I show you how good and big you are." Or, "What, you want to see God and you do not want to recognize yourself, I will not open this gate for you." Or, "Now I show you first what you do not want to see."

Sometimes this intelligent force can relentlessly show a mental state directly: chaos and filth appear before the "third eye". Logical arguments and conceptual abstractions are ineffective in the imagination and therefore useless. Imagination as a picture event follows the logic of the picture world, not the linguistic (thinker) rationality.

The imagination also has a clairvoyant ability, in the same way one can gain insight into the psychic life of another person through inner concentration at any distance. One can ask institutions about mental worthiness. The pictures often take "no mince words". You can only show your own illusions because you want to see what is real only superficially. Some pictures do not give a full answer, but only allow you to get started. After that should be sought further. Pictures are more effective than words and thoughts. The more vivid the pictures are, the more intense they are experienced. Archetypes can have an enormously powerful effect, although they are not as vivid as concrete images of life in the same way. Images that have an individual emotional occupation activate these emotions first.

About the so-called "symbolic operations" should be given some hints. Meditation should reach a goal. It can hardly be the meaning of an imagination exercise to see any pictures, just to experience "beautiful pictures" or ecstatic feelings. That would be like running a compact disc or a video for entertainment.

It is therefore necessary to become aware of what you want or intend to achieve with each imagination, for example: relaxation, strengthening of strength, inner energetic centering, catharsis of the unconscious, psycho-hygiene, knowledge about the state of the feelings or the power of love, finding solutions for a personal difficult situation in life, understanding archetypes and so on. We consider active imagining an indispensable technique for reshaping intrapsychic powers and fully exploiting the intelligence of the "third eye".

Incidentally, it should be pointed out briefly that the autogenic training elementary school is not an imagination. Here mental ideas are practiced and applied with a slightly affective tint to psychophysiological conditioning.

As in all life matters, exercise is necessary to make meditation effective. We refer to a broad spectrum of exercises that we have set out in other works.

The author has always worked in his depth psychological career with dreams and meditations. This certainly diverse experience is not a guarantor of scientific interpretation of dreams. But the dreams were - and always are - a big challenge to reveal more and more the mystery of the dream language. Because here, are the deepest secrets of being human. So far, all experiences in working with dreams show so much: dreams are indispensable for a comprehensive personality development and for individuation.

Note: After completing this chapter, the author has written, step by step, the new work on Dreams and Dream Interpretation "In Somnis Veritas" based on 20 years of material collection. The current presentation will be deepened in this work and processed in even more detail as a new andragogic conception.

Needs for a New Education for all ages

Commentary

In our study we have discussed various aspects of the comprehensive psychic life and the development of the psychic organism. Any practical training in this area begins with the initial situation. Every educational process must be able to evaluate the achieved intermediate goals in stages.

With increasing progress in the process of individuation, the psychic forces can be rolled up and grasped more and more differentiated down to the details.

Education in the classroom and in individual counseling needs a clear grid for understanding the educational needs and success of educational achievement.

The following 10 units are an attempt, according to our study, to capture the key basic aspects of the psychic subsystems, the psychic individual forces, and the process of individuation.

This questionnaire can be the starting point for an educational program (course) as well as for individual counseling.

The questions provide the student / client and the andragogen with an orientation aid, for the analysis of the situation, in the determination of objectives, and in the decision on the measures necessary for the implementation or course of education.

We believe that we have dealt with enough aspects in our study so that the andragogen can interpret a processed questionnaire on a work-related basis.

This questionnaire also allows the scientists and practitioners of pedagogy and andragogy to discuss professional issues, and to lay down standards for the personality development of the andragogen (in science and practice).

In addition, this questionnaire for a research project can cover very broadly the educational needs of people. The formulation of a clear education policy and the development of graduated education programs. Andragogic education, as well as for andragogical human education, are further applications of this questionnaire.

Methodological reflections and theoretical discussions on the realization and analytical processing of a survey are not the subject of this study but are of course essential for a scientific research project.

1. The Individuation

The process of psycho-spiritual development contains a variety of small steps and can be interpreted as a "pathway". With some elementary steps we can grasp the educational needs. Make a note of what applies to you:

6 = complete, 5 = very, 4 = predominantly, 3 = medium, 2 = partial, 1 = little, 0 = not at all

- ☐ I practice relaxation techniques.
- ☐ I know my projection dynamics.
- ☐ I practice mental hygiene.
- ☐ I know my resistance / defense.
- ☐ I practice mental training.
- ☐ I can systematically imagine.
- ☐ I can express my experience in language.
- ☐ I practice contemplation.
- ☐ I have a clear view of my actions.
- ☐ I interpret my dreams.
- ☐ I systematically turn to my psychic powers.
- ☐ I integrate my weak psychic powers.
- ☐ I recognize the interaction of my psychic powers.
- ☐ I have thoroughly edited my life story.
- ☐ I can fully affirm the psychic life.
- ☐ I have an overview of the interplay inside-outside life.
- ☐ The power of the Spirit is an important backbone for me.
- ☐ I have inner support through the formation of my psychic powers.
- ☐ Archetypes are life oriented.
- ☐ I live value / meaning from within.
- ☐ I work my inner life thoroughly.
- ☐ I practice psycho-catharsis.
- ☐ I experience new humanity in me.
- ☐ I experience attachment to love.
- ☐ I accept spirit as a guiding principle.
- ☐ I extend human consciousness.
- ☐ I experience more and more inner dissolution of opposites.
- ☐ I live more and more clearly the essential basic needs.
- ☐ I pay special attention to building the power of love.
- ☐ I can distinguish well between masks and the reality behind them.
- ☐ I experience clearly what freedom and duty within mean.
- ☐ Spirit and love are stronger in me than all other powers.
- ☐ I can handle masks / facades.
- ☐ I cooperate with the spirit.
- ☐ I can fit into my destiny.
- ☐ I experience myself inwardly free.

☐ I know the collective unconscious.
☐ I practice imagination competently.
☐ Even in the most difficult situations, I experience inner support.
☐ I have differentiated and networked experiences with archetypes.
☐ In the inner feedback you can rely on me.
☐ I experience my dream interpretation as reliable and valid.
☐ I can live the transcending power of love.
☐ My life is a comprehensive expression of acquired self-education.
☐ I am increasingly experiencing my living image of the main archetype.
☐ Life has formed me comprehensively with dream and meditation.
☐ I experience the positive images in my unconscious as carrying.
☐ I constantly train my newly acquired powers in daily life.

2. The "Critical Actions"

Educational needs in actions are given when a person experiences their own action as "critical". "Critical" means: goal of action not achieved, action blocked, undesired side effects, uncertainty in action, consequences of conflict, lack of motivation, lack of understanding of the action, lack of clarity about internal pressures, mental interference factors, unrealizable intentions to act, and acting power. From the many thematic "life systems", we select those that mean a daily reality for many people, be it in person or in the consciousness of the media. In which life systems do you experience your actions as "critical"? Make a note of what applies to you:

6 = complete, 5 = very, 4 = predominantly, 3 = medium, 2 = partial, 1 = little, 0 = not at all

☐ Personal relationship / marriage / friendship
☐ Parenting
☐ Colleagues, acquaintances, relatives
☐ Free time
☐ Holiday / vacation
☐ Personal housing
☐ Personal environment (place of residence)
☐ Nutrition, food
☐ Health
☐ Alcohol and / or tobacco
☐ Medicines
☐ Consumption in general
☐ Households

- ☐ Conflict with superiors
- ☐ Divorce / separation
- ☐ Diseases
- ☐ Mental suffering / disorders
- ☐ Life crises of all kinds
- ☐ Religious practices, faith
- ☐ Self-living (fear, inferior value)
- ☐ Education, training
- ☐ Sexuality
- ☐ Day planning
- ☐ Media consumption
- ☐ Money, cost of living
- ☐ Furniture, appliances, car, clothes
- ☐ Leisure activities (hobbies)
- ☐ Victims (theft, fraud, etc.)
- ☐ Work / workplace
- ☐ Politics, parties
- ☐ Economy, business life
- ☐ Art, culture in general
- ☐ Institutions of religions
- ☐ Traffic, transportation
- ☐ Nuclear waste, nuclear power plant
- ☐ Public finances, taxes
- ☐ Pollution
- ☐ International conflicts
- ☐ National, regional conflicts
- ☐ Cultivated habitat
- ☐ Nature destruction
- ☐ Animal husbandry
- ☐ Crime
- ☐ Pornography, prostitution
- ☐ Alienation
- ☐ Banks, insurance
- ☐ Authorities
- ☐ Marginal groups
- ☐ Extremism, fundamentalism
- ☐ Waste (garbage, wastewater)
- ☐ Environmental destruction
- ☐ Poverty (in Europe, in your own country)
- ☐ Wars, genocide, oppression
- ☐ Old people, retirement
- ☐ Communication between people
- ☐ Drug situation

☐ Unemployment
☐ Death

3. The Psychodynamics

Everybody experiences a psycho-energetic state every day. It is usually variable and sometimes almost constant over a longer period. Different aspects can be used to formulate a picture of the educational needs. Not every aspect requires the same measures. Make a note of what applies to you:

6 = complete, 5 = very, 4 = predominantly, 3 = medium, 2 = partial, 1 = little, 0 = not at all

☐ I feel tense
☐ I am inwardly restless
☐ I live hectic
☐ I feel disharmony in me
☐ I eat hastily
☐ I have sleep problems
☐ I feel pressure in me
☐ I'm easy to upset
☐ I have tension (of all kinds)
☐ My stomach is sensitive to feelings
☐ My basic condition is "disunity"
☐ I experience myself heavy and dull
☐ I tend to be more depressed
☐ I feel tight
☐ I'm not very happy in terms of mood
☐ I am unstable
☐ I'm quick to "skid"
☐ My daily rhythm is unstable
☐ I quickly feel insecure
☐ I am missing in many situations "inner state"
☐ I move strictly as I want
☐ I feel stiff
☐ My inner life is armored
☐ I am difficult to approach
☐ I can react quite rigidly depending on the situation
☐ I tend to be lethargic
☐ I feel powerless
☐ I have little purposeful energy

- ☐ My energy is lame
- ☐ I miss the desire to do something active
- ☐ I mostly react moodily
- ☐ I feel "angry"
- ☐ My energy is more life-less
- ☐ I can be inexplicably destructive
- ☐ I am easily infected by the moods of others
- ☐ I experience mostly introverted
- ☐ I tend to be extravert
- ☐ I cannot control intro / extra version
- ☐ I am changeable intro / extrovert
- ☐ Together with others, I quickly "lose" my energies

4. The I and is Control Mechanisms

The ego with its auxiliary functions is a complex system. We can ask many questions about each subsystem to identify educational needs. We want to limit ourselves to essential aspects. Make a note of what applies to you:

6 = complete, 5 = very, 4 = predominantly, 3 = medium, 2 = partial, 1 = little, 0 = not at all

- ☐ I experience valuable / rich.
- ☐ I experience my health healthy and strong.
- ☐ I fully experience myself.
- ☐ I experience intensely that I live.
- ☐ I clearly experience my psycho-physical identity.
- ☐ My willpower is differentiated.
- ☐ I experience myself strong-willed.
- ☐ I have differentiated action goals.
- ☐ My determination is strong.
- ☐ I clearly experience motivation in my actions.
- ☐ I regulate my life clearly.
- ☐ I am very focused.
- ☐ I fight against obstacles.
- ☐ I consciously lead myself in everyday life.
- ☐ Even after work I control myself consciously.
- ☐ I do not displace / cover anything.
- ☐ I have no projections.
- ☐ I do not disfigure a reality.
- ☐ I do not deny facts.

- ☐ I do not suppress anything in me.
- ☐ I mediate between interests.
- ☐ I work on what to expect.
- ☐ I have an active basic interest.
- ☐ I consider new things balanced.
- ☐ I can make a relationship with too much.
- ☐ I live well towards my goals.
- ☐ I have many good skills.
- ☐ I live consciously and differentiated.
- ☐ I realize my personality.
- ☐ I have a differentiated knowledge of my psychic life.
- ☐ I see others psychologically differentiated.
- ☐ I have a lot of clarity about people.
- ☐ I recognize the inner life of others.
- ☐ I have processed experience.
- ☐ I see others with their life story.
- ☐ I have complex knowledge of society.
- ☐ I have differentiated knowledge about the earth.
- ☐ I cover the earth as a habitat.
- ☐ I experience the world differentiated in a big time dimension.
- ☐ I see the collective in the complex networks.
- ☐ I have clear inner experiences of God.
- ☐ I know differentiated the power of the mind.
- ☐ I have experiences about the transcendental.
- ☐ I clarified my religious attitude meditatively.
- ☐ I have a lot of experience about archetypes (Symbols).

5. The main Functions of Intelligence

The process of thinking is embedded in a process from perception to the creative learning outcome. These include language and thought processes. For all aspects we can look for educational needs. We want to limit ourselves to essential excerpts. Make a note of what applies to you:

6 = complete, 5 = very, 4 = predominantly, 3 = medium, 2 = partial, 1 = little, 0 = not at all

- ☐ I can easily read difficult texts.
- ☐ My vocabulary is rich.

- ☐ I am skilled at language.
- ☐ I can express myself well.
- ☐ I often weigh up what words to use.
- ☐ I can disassemble complex text well.
- ☐ I think purposefully.
- ☐ A conclusion does not bother me.
- ☐ I can easily arrange meaningfully.
- ☐ I am thorough in analyzing a problem.
- ☐ I often have creative ideas for solutions.
- ☐ Intuition is often a help to me.
- ☐ I have a good empathy.
- ☐ I easily feel connections.
- ☐ I often "see" the thinking before I can put it in words.
- ☐ My perception is clear and alert.
- ☐ I see quickly in complex spatial interdependencies.
- ☐ I perceive many things from a temporal perspective.
- ☐ I deliberately control what I want to perceive.
- ☐ I can easily see the complexities of a thing or a person.
- ☐ I have a good memory.
- ☐ I easily remember names.
- ☐ I can easily study a thing for a long time.
- ☐ My memory is fresh and alert.
- ☐ I can easily summon memories back to childhood.
- ☐ I think through my ideals and goals for life exactly.
- ☐ I think free of dogmas and ideologies.
- ☐ I reflect my values and norms.
- ☐ My settings are thoroughly reflected.
- ☐ Every now and then, I test my beliefs profoundly.
- ☐ I can easily distinguish between describing and evaluating.
- ☐ Before I make a judgment, I use my thinking on all sides.
- ☐ When I talk, I distinguish between facts and ratings.
- ☐ I can justify my debts.
- ☐ I explain why I rate something negative.
- ☐ I am agile in grasping something new.
- ☐ I can also think the "never thought".
- ☐ I can think in foreign cultures.
- ☐ I can also look at opportunities that are new to me.
- ☐ I can also reflect improbable claims.

6. The Emotions

We can grasp the educational needs of emotions with general questions about the existence of certain emotions. Since the subjective experience of a certain feeling always contains interpretations and personal elements, we therefore consider dynamic aspects. Make a note of what applies to you:

6 = complete, 5 = very, 4 = predominantly, 3 = medium, 2 = partial, 1 = little, 0 = not at all

- ☐ I am free from inner turmoil.
- ☐ I experience emotional flexibility.
- ☐ I experience myself freely, when dealing with others.
- ☐ I am very diffused.
- ☐ I do not experience a dull weight.
- ☐ I do not experience compulsive.
- ☐ I can handle feelings easily.
- ☐ My feelings are rarely blocked.
- ☐ Rarely I have changeable feelings.
- ☐ I experience life.
- ☐ My feelings are reliable for me.
- ☐ I experience inner peace.
- ☐ I experience myself free from my lived life.
- ☐ My feelings are fluid and easy to control.
- ☐ I feel completely harmonious inside.
- ☐ I experience my feelings constructively for daily life.
- ☐ I experience my feelings as predictable.
- ☐ I intensively sense in my life.
- ☐ I experience a lot of love .
- ☐ I hope.
- ☐ Am I am cheerful.
- ☐ I experience life.
- ☐ I enjoy what I am.
- ☐ I experience a sense of life all around.
- ☐ I am happy.
- ☐ I experience inner peace.
- ☐ I can integrate tenderness well.
- ☐ I am a satisfied person.
- ☐ I experience my life's fulfillment.
- ☐ I feel safe and valuable.
- ☐ I experience myself and life with pleasure and well-being.
- ☐ I have mostly positive feelings.
- ☐ I have no fears.
- ☐ I am rarely sad.
- ☐ I do not have depression.

- Envy is alien to me.
- I am free of aggressive mood.
- I am rarely depressed for a long time.
- I have no doubt about my life.
- I have no hate and / or revenge feelings.
- I have no vague, unclear guilt feelings.
- I do not feel helpless.
- I have no grief.
- I am not a jealous person.
- I rarely experience frustration.
- I feel no hostility in me.
- I'm angry.

7. The Basic Needs

The clarification of the basic needs can address different aspects with questions: the experience of the needs, the satisfaction of the needs, the subjectively experienced meaning of the needs, the "artificial" needs and so on. We limit ourselves here and select a question to determine educational deficits: To which needs do you experience a deficit of satisfaction? Write down how much you experience deficit:

6 = complete, 5 = very, 4 = predominantly, 3 = medium, 2 = partial, 1 = little, 0 − not at all

- Hunger, thirst, warmth
- Sexual relaxation
- Sex with a partner
- Protection against diseases
- Physical exercise
- Acting in everyday situations
- Designing one's own living space (home)
- Designing the living environment (neighborhood / neighborhood)
- Live relationships
- Group affiliation
- Co-determination
- Friendship / marriage / partnership
- Having own children
- Safety and stability
- Work and performance
- Experiencing and shaping culture

- ☐ Game and entertainment
- ☐ Autonomy and self-assertion
- ☐ Truth and truthfulness
- ☐ Tenderness
- ☐ Well-being, joy
- ☐ Mental health
- ☐ Physical health
- ☐ Take possession
- ☐ Knowledge and thinking
- ☐ Growth and development
- ☐ Love life
- ☐ Living meaning and values
- ☐ Realize inner potentials / talents
- ☐ Experience of God
- ☐ The experience of transcendence / otherworldly reality
- ☐ Being carried and being guided by the Spirit (God)

8. The Unconscious

To be able to find the educational needs for the unconscious life, one first must grasp the mode of action of the unconscious. Based on the indirect and usually hidden activities of the inventory in the unconscious, we can recognize what must be done with the inventory and what other psychic forces should co-operate and be formed there. Make a note of what applies to you:

6 = complete, 5 = very, 4 = predominantly, 3 = medium, 2 = partial, 1 = little, 0 = not at all

- ☐ The relationship with my father is negative.
- ☐ My relationship with my mother is negative.
- ☐ I have not worked much of my life experiences yet.
- ☐ Some memories are sometimes embarrassing for me.
- ☐ I do not want to remember certain phases of my life.
- ☐ Memories of the past can move me a lot.
- ☐ I still have a considerable amount of anger for certain people.
- ☐ I still see certain teachers as punitive people before me.
- ☐ I long for a good father.
- ☐ I do not like problematic people.
- ☐ I long for a good mother.
- ☐ I have negative feelings about sex.
- ☐ Fairytale pictures about witches bother me.

- [ ] I experience a kind of "child" in me.
- [ ] A Napoleon figure in a picture activates me.
- [ ] I like pictures like "Mother of God" or "saints" or "heroes".
- [ ] I have a clear picture of the "right" man.
- [ ] I have a clear picture of the "right" woman.
- [ ] I like to see pictures about the "good mother" and the "good father".
- [ ] I do not question religious authorities.
- [ ] I have inexplicable remorse.
- [ ] I think the politicians are brave.
- [ ] There are inviolable beliefs.
- [ ] Orders and prohibitions from my childhood still arouse feelings.
- [ ] Sometimes I punish like my father and / or like my mother.
- [ ] I have clear ideals about the "religious man".
- [ ] I am angry about the needs that I could not fulfill.
- [ ] The church points the way to God.
- [ ] There will always be wars.
- [ ] Too much thinking only creates problems.
- [ ] Environmental damage is not that bad.
- [ ] Traffic accidents are "fate".
- [ ] "Giving speed" is good.
- [ ] You should not think too much about yourself.
- [ ] I'm just talking about what's necessary.
- [ ] A woman should become a mother and do the household work.
- [ ] Career and earning well is the ultimate goal for a man.
- [ ] I have diffuse vegetative complaints.
- [ ] I have sleep problems.
- [ ] I'm claustrophobic (tunnel, lift etc.).
- [ ] I smoke / drink / eat too much.
- [ ] I have sexual disorders / trouble with my sexuality.
- [ ] I am overly conscientious, obsessively order-minded.
- [ ] Baseless, diffuse feelings of fear can move me.
- [ ] I blush easily / have sweaty hands quickly.

9. The Power of Love

We can discover the power of love in all walks of life. In doing so, we find the educational needs. Make a note of what applies to you:
6 = complete, 5 = very, 4 = predominantly, 3 = medium, 2 = partial, 1 = little, 0 = not at all

- [ ] I live in life with a built up sense of life.
- [ ] I experience myself with inner freedom.
- [ ] I take my feelings seriously.
- [ ] I experience inner development.
- [ ] I care differentiated.
- [ ] I experience myself with a clearly original expression.
- [ ] I live with low accident / disease risk.
- [ ] I am attentive to my basic needs.
- [ ] I can give meaning to my life.
- [ ] I develop my life with all my psychic powers.
- [ ] I experience sustainable positive feelings.
- [ ] I do not suppress feelings.
- [ ] I can meditate on life well.
- [ ] I am open to truthfulness.
- [ ] I experience responsibility for intrinsic value.
- [ ] You can rely on me.
- [ ] Loving life is more important than receiving love.
- [ ] I am open to my inner life.
- [ ] I am open to learning / ready for change.
- [ ] My life is a journey of discovery,
- [ ] I have internally reconciled experienced malice / experienced suffering.
- [ ] I live so that mental growth is possible all around.
- [ ] I can reconcile grievous humiliations in me.
- [ ] I take care of the environment.
- [ ] I rarely have projections.
- [ ] I consciously live many situations creatively.
- [ ] Life is more important to me than having.
- [ ] I experienced the love of God through meditation on archetypes.
- [ ] If I judge important things, then I weigh thoroughly with love.
- [ ] I experience other people with their psychic wholeness.
- [ ] I also base important decisions on my dreams.
- [ ] I use the possibilities of my goods for life.
- [ ] I can accept challenges.
- [ ] I face the realities.
- [ ] I positively integrate the household work.
- [ ] I am responsible for quality of life.
- [ ] I can share my love with others.
- [ ] I live flexible role sharing.
- [ ] Life has "forged" me to understand other people.
- [ ] I appreciate the "good things"; I'm still anchored in the spirit.
- [ ] I can take action to protect love, if necessary.
- [ ] I use all my life-shaping potential.

- ☐ I can update myself and versatile in my free time.
- ☐ I live solidarity with psycho-spiritual values.
- ☐ I live my "destiny" in devotion to the inner unfolding process.
- ☐ I handle life conflicts balanced.
- ☐ I accept challenges of high intrinsic value.
- ☐ I experience my work as a "life expression".
- ☐ I can live a relationship with the opposite sex.

10. Dreams, meditation and the inner Spirit

The educational needs of what we call "mind" can be seen in the field of dream and meditation experiences. Make a note of what applies to you: 6 = complete, 5 = very, 4 = predominantly, 3 = medium, 2 = partial, 1 = little, 0 = not at all

- ☐ I know my dreams on awakening.
- ☐ I can interpret my dreams.
- ☐ Dreams are important guides for me.
- ☐ I talk to others about dreams.
- ☐ Certain dreams have influenced me.
- ☐ I notice dreams to life.
- ☐ I have learned that a spirit principle works in dreams.
- ☐ I build my personality with my dreams.
- ☐ Certain dreams have moved me deeply.
- ☐ I am alert in the interpretation of dreams.
- ☐ I read / read about dream interpretation.
- ☐ I write down my dreams.
- ☐ I meditate on my life.
- ☐ I discuss meditations.
- ☐ I try to understand myself meditatively.
- ☐ I learned to meditate.
- ☐ I search in my dreams for all my psychic powers.
- ☐ My dreams have repeatedly made my resistance clear.
- ☐ I thoroughly work on my life themes with my dreams.
- ☐ I focus on problems / conflicts in my dreams.
- ☐ I meditate on my unconscious inner life.
- ☐ I am critically open in my differentiated inside show.
- ☐ I live so that meditation is possible on a regular basis.
- ☐ I know what "new birth" means.
- ☐ I check my projections accurately.
- ☐ I have experienced psychic changes with meditations.

- ☐ I approve the contribution of life and find deepening in meditations.
- ☐ Catharsis of psychic life is important to my development.
- ☐ I edit my unconscious inventory regularly and thoroughly.
- ☐ I meditate on symbols and archetypes.
- ☐ I know my resistance to the inner life exactly.
- ☐ When I think about important things, I consider introspection.
- ☐ I take intuition seriously.
- ☐ I live reflected wisdom.
- ☐ I am interested in spiritual values.
- ☐ I experience meaning / value in the spirit principle .
- ☐ I care for my development carefully.
- ☐ The inner growth is important to me.
- ☐ I experience an inner force that pushes for development.
- ☐ I agree with the entire psychic life of man.
- ☐ I always see the other people with their inner life as well.
- ☐ I can connect my lust with spirit.
- ☐ I know what "wisdom" is.
- ☐ I take extrasensory perception critically serious.
- ☐ I am capable of solidarity with mental and spiritual values.
- ☐ I experience responsibility for inner values.
- ☐ I see differentiated behind the masks and facades.
- ☐ I can well distinguish between "faith" and "experience".

Bibliography

Adler, A.: Praxis und Theorie der Individualpsychologie. Frankfurt 1978 (1930)

Adler, A.: Menschenkenntnis. Frankfurt 1978/1966 (1927, 1947)

Adler, A.: Über den nervösen Charakter. Frankfurt 1977 (1928)

Aebli, H.: Denken: Das Ordnen des Tuns. Kognitive Aspekte der Handlungstheorie. Band I. Stuttgart 1993 (1980)

Aebli, H.: Denken: Das Ordnen des Tuns. Denkprozesse. Band II. Stuttgart 1993 (1980)

Aepli, E.: Der Traum und seine Deutung. Erlenbach 1977

Aquilera, D.C./Messinck, J.M.: Grundlagen der Krisenintervention. Freiburg 1977

Alberoni, F.: Erotik. München 1987

Alexander, F.: Psychosomatische Medizin. Berlin/New York 1985

Arnold, R.: Deutungsmuster und pädagogisches Handeln in der Erwachsenenbildung. Bad Heilbrunn 1985

Assagioli, R.: Psychosynthese und transpersonale Entwicklung. Paderborn 1992

Balint, M.: Die Urformen der Liebe und die Technik der Psychoanalyse. Frankfurt 1981

Bandler, R./MacDonald W.: Der feine Unterschied. Paderborn 1991

Bartholomäus, W.: Lust aus Liebe. München 1993

Barz, H.: Psychopathologie und ihre psychologischen Grundlagen. Bern/Stuttgart 1977

Battegay, R.: Narzissmus und Objektbeziehungen. Bern 1979

Battegay, R.: Die therapeutische Beziehung unter dem Aspekt verschiedener psychotherapeutischer Schulen. Bern/Stuttgart 1978

Bauer, W. u.a.: Lexikon der Symbole. Wiesbaden 1982

Beck, T.A.: Liebe ist nie genug. Köln 1992

Becker-Carus, C.: Grundriss der physiologischen Psychologie. Basel/Stuttgart 1982

Becker, P.: Psychologie der seelischen Gesundheit. Göttingen 1982

Bender, H.: Telepathie, Hellsehen und Psychokinese. München 1972

Berger, P.L./Luckmann T.: Die gesellschaftliche Konstruktion der Wirklichkeit. Frankfurt 1970

Biller, K.: Bildung - integrierender Faktor in Theorie und Praxis. Weinheim 1994

Blasi, A.: in: Oser, F.: Moralische Zugänge zum Menschen. München 1986

Bock, I.: Pädagogische Anthropologie der Lebensalter. München 1984

Bonin, W.F.: Lexikon der Parapsychologie. München 1976

Boron, R. de: Merlin. Der Künder des Gral. Stuttgart 1980
Boron, R. de: Die Geschichte des heiligen Gral. Stuttgart 1979
Boss, M.: Praxis der Psychosomatik. Bern 1978
Boss, M.: Der Traum und seine Auslegung. München 1974
Bosshart, E.: Christliche Symbole. Zürich 1970
Bourdieu, P.: Zur Soziologie der symbolischen Formen. Frankfurt 1974
Bourdieu, P.: Entwurf einer Theorie der Praxis. Frankfurt 1979
Bourdieu, P.: Die feinen Unterschiede. Frankfurt 1984
Bradshaw, J.: Creating Love. London 1992
Brezinka, W.: Metatheorie der Erziehung. München 1978
Bronfenbrenner, U.: Die Oekologie der menschlichen Entwicklung. Frankfurt 1989
Brüderl, L. (Hrgr.): Belastende Lebenssituationen. Weinheim 1988
Brugger, W.: Philosophisches Wörterbuch. Freiburg 1992
Buela-Casal G./Caballo, V.E.: Manual de Psicologia clinica aplicada. Madrid 1991
Burisch, M.: Das Burnout-Syndrom. Theorie der inneren Erschöpfung. Berlin 1989

Campbell, J.: Der Heros in tausend Gestalten. Frankfurt 1953
Campbell, J.: Der Flug der Wildgans. Mythologische Streifzüge. Basel 1990
Chardin de, Th.: Die lebendige Macht der Evolution. Olten 1967
Cattell, R.B.: Description and measurement of personality. 1946
Chertok, L.: Hypnose. München 1973
Chrestien de Troyes: Perceval der Gralskönig. Stuttgart 1983
Condrau, G.: Angst und Schuld. Bern 1962
Cranach von, M. (u.a.): Zielgerichtetes Handeln. Bern 1980
Czichos, R.: Creaktivität und Chaosmanagement. München 1993

Dethlefson, T.: Das Erlebnis der Wiedergeburt. München 1979
Dieterich, R.u.a.: Psychologische Perspektiven der Erwachsenenbildung. Bad Heilbrunn 1987
Dorsch, W.: Psychologisches Wörterbuch. Bern/Stuttgart 1987
Dorst, B.: C.G. Jung und die feministische Kritik. Zeitschrift 'DU'. Nr.8, 1995
Doucet, F.W.: PSI-Training. München 1975
Dowling, C.: Cinderella-Komplex. Frankfurt 1984
Drewermann, E.: Tiefenpsychologie und Exegese. Band I: Die Wahrheit der Formen. Olten 1987
Driesch, H.: Parapsychologie. München 1975
Düker, H.: Untersuchungen über die Ausbildung des Wollens. Bern 1975
Düker, H.: Über unterschwelliges Wollen. Göttingen 1983

Dürckheim Graf, K.F.: Meditieren - wozu und wie. Freiburg 1976
Dürckheim Graf, K.F.: Vom doppelten Ursprung des Menschen. Freiburg 1983

Eckensberger, L.H. (Hrgr): Entwicklung sozialer Kognition: Paradigmen, Theorien, Ergebnisse. Stuttgart 1981
Eckes-Lapp, R.: Psychoanalytische Traumtheorie und Trauminterpretation. Göttingen 1980
Eggebrecht, A.: El antiguo Egipto. Barcelona/München 1984
Eissler, K.R.: Todestrieb, Ambivalenz, Narzissmus. Hamburg 1980
Eliade, M.: Mythen, Träume und Mysterien. Salzburg 1961
Ellenberger, H.F.: Die Entdeckung des Unbewussten. 2 Bde. Bern 1973
Erickson, M.H. (u.a.): Hypnose. München 1978
Erikson, E.: Identität und Lebenszyklus. Frankfurt 1974
Eysenck, H.J./Eysenck M.W.: Persönlichkeit und Individualität. München 1987
Eysenck, H.J.: Die Ungleichheit der Menschen. Frankfurt 1989

Ferenczi, S.: Zur Erkenntnis des Unbewussten. München 1978 (Texte 1908-1929)
Filipp, S.-H. (Hrgr.): Selbstkonzept-Forschung. Probleme, Befunde, Perspektiven. Stuttgart 1979 (1993)
Filipp, S.H. (Hrgr.): Kritische Lebensereignisse. München 1981 (1990)
Flammer, A.: Entwicklungstheorien. Psychologische Theorien der menschlichen Entwicklung. Bern/Göttingen 1993 (1988)
Foppa, K./Groner, R. (Hrgr): Kognitive Strukturen und ihre Entwicklung. Bern/Stuttgart 1981
Frankl, V.E.: Anthropologische Grundlagen der Psychotherapie. Bern/Stuttgart/Wien 1975
Frankl, V.E.: Der Mensch auf der Suche nach Sinn. Freiburg 1973
Frankl, V.E.: The unheard cry for meaning. New York 1985
Freud, A.: Das Ich und die Abwehrmechanismen. München 1973 (1936)
Freud, S.: Drei Abhandlungen zur Sexualtheorie. Frankfurt 1976/1961, (1904/05 sowie verwandte Schriften 1906-1931)
Freud, S.: Die Traumdeutung. Zürich 1972 (1900)
Freud, S.: Sexualleben. Zürich 1972 (diverse Schriften 1898-1932)
Freud, S.: Das Ich und das Es. Psychologie des Unbewussten. Zürich 1972 (diverse Schriften 1911-1938)
Freud, S.: Fragen der Gesellschaft - Ursprünge der Religion. Zürich 1977 (Aufsätze 1915-1938)
Freud, S.: Bewusstsein und Unbewusstes. 1923

Freud, S.: Über Psychoanalyse. 1919

Freud, S.: Brief an Einstein im September 1932. In: Ds Unbehagen der Kultur.

Fromm, E.: Analytische Charaktertheorie. Band II der Gesamtausgabe. Stuttgart 1980

Fromm, E.: Die Kunst des Liebens. Frankfurt 1971 (1956)

Fromm, E.: Die Seele des Menschen. Stuttgart 1979

Fromm, E.: Märchen, Mythen und Träume. Konstanz/Stuttgart 1957

Fuchs, W.: Biographische Forschung. Eine Einführung in Praxis und Methoden. Opladen 1984

Fuchs, W.: Möglichkeiten der biographischen Methoden. In: Niethammer 1985

Gage, N.L./Berliner, D.C.: Pädagogische Psychologie. Weinheim 1986

Garma, A.: Tratado Mayor del psicoanálisis de los sueños. Madrid 1990

Garz, D.: Sozialpsychologische Entwicklungstheorien. Opladen 1994

Gehlen, A.: Moral und Hypermoral. Frankfurt 1969

Geue, B.: Entscheidungstraining in der Erwachsenenbildung. Baden-Baden 1993

Gloger-Tippelt, G.: Beiträge einer Entwicklungspsychologie der Lebensspanne zur Erwachsenenbildung. In: PAD 1993, 98-118

Goldbrunner, H.: Masken der Partnerschaft. Mainz 1994

Gregory, R.L. (ed.): The Mind. Oxford/New York 1987

Grindler, J./Bandler, R.: Therapie in Trance. Stuttgart 1991

Groddeck, G.: Krankheit als Symbol. Frankfurt 1990 (Aufsätze 1889-1934)

Grof, S.: Geburt, Tod und Transzendenz.München 1985 (1993)

Grof, S.: Topologie des Unbewussten. Stuttgart 1993 (6)

Gudjons, H./Pieper, M./ Wagner, B.: Auf meinen Spuren. Die Entdeckung der eigenen Lebensgeschichte. Reinbek 1986

Guilford, J.P.: Persönlichkeit. Weinheim 1964

Haan de, G./Schulze, Th.: in: Lenzen, D. 1993

Hacker, F.: Aggression. Reinbek 1973

Hall, C.S./Nordby,V.J.: The Individual and his dreams. New York 1972

Halsig, N./Schröder, A.: in: Brüderl, L.

Hare, R.M.: Die Sprache der Moral. Frankfurt 1972

Harris, Th.A.: Ich bin o.k. - Du bist o.k. Reinbek 1975

Hartmann, F.: Mysterien, Symbole und magisch wirkende Kräfte. Calw (ohne Jahr)

Hartmann, F.: Die Symbole der Bibel und der Kirche. Calw (ohne Jahr)

Hartmann, H.: Psychoanalyse und moralische Werte. Stuttgart 1973

Hartmann, H.: Ich-Psychologie. Stuttgart 1972

Haseloff, O.W./Hoffmann H.-J.: Kleines Lehrbuch der Statistik. Berlin 1971

Heckhausen, H.: Motivation und Handeln. Lehrbuch der Motivationspsychologie. Berlin 1980

Heim, R.: Die Rationalität der Psychoanalyse. Basel 1993

Heinz-Mohr, G.: Lexikon der Symbole. Düsseldorf 1976

Heinze, Th.: Interpretation eines (auto-)biographischen Dokuments. In: Gruppendynamik 19/4, 1988

Helmchen, H./Linden M./Rüger U.(Hrgr.): Psychotherapie in der Psychiatrie. Berlin 1982

Hempel, C.G.: Typologische Modelle in den Sozialwissenschaften. In: Topitsch 1970

Herder: Lexikon der Symbole. Freiburg 1978

Hertz, A.: Moral. Mainz 1972

Herzog, W.: Pädagogik und Psychologie. In: Zeitschrift für Pädagogik Nr.3/40.Jg. Weinheim 1994

Heursen, G. (Hrgr.): Didaktik im Umbruch. 1984

Hilgard, E.R./Bower, G.H.: Theorien des Lernens. 2 Bde. Stuttgart 1970

Höffe, 0. (Hrgr.): Klassiker der Philosophie. 2 Bde. München 1985

Hoffmann, N. (Hrgr.): Grundlagen kognitiver Therapie. Bern, Stuttgart, Wien 1979

Holzkamp, K.: Kritische Psychologie. Frankfurt 1972

Homfeldt, H.G. (u.a.): Sinnliche Wahrnehmung, Körperbewusstsein, Gesundheitsbildung. Weinheim 1993

Homfeldt, H.G.: Anleitungsbuch zur Gesundheitsbildung. Baltmannsweiler 1994

Hull, C.L.: Principles of behavior. New York 1943

Hull, C.L.: A Behavior system. New Haven Yake 1952

Hurrelmann, K./Ulich, D. (Hrgr.): Handbuch der Sozialisationsforschung. Weinheim 1980

Hurrelmann, K.: Persönlichkeitsentwicklung als produktive Realitätsverarbeitung. In: PAD 1993, 155-175

Hurrelmann, K.: Sozialisation und Gesundheit. Weinheim 1994

Inglehart, R.: Kultureller Umbruch. Frankfurt 1989

Illich, I.: Entschulung der Gesellschaft. München 1970

Izard, C.E.: Die Emotionen des Menschen. Weinheim 1981

Jacoby, R.: Die Verdrängung der Psychoanalyse. Frankfurt 1990

Jacobi, J.: Komplex, Archetyp, Symbol. Zürich 1957

Jacobi, J.: Der Weg zur Individuation. Zürich 1965

James, W.: Die Vielfalt religiöser Erfahrung. Olten 1979 (1901/1902)

Janov, A.: Der Urschrei. Frankfurt 1977

Jones, E.: Die Theorie der Symbolik und andere Aufsätze. Berlin 1978

Jung, E./von Franz A.-L.: Die Gralslegende in psychologischer Sicht. Olten 1983

Jung, C.G.: Aion. Olten 1978

Jung, C.G.: Psychologie und Alchemie. Olten 1972

Jung, C.G.: Über Grundlagen der analytischen Psychologie. Frankfurt 1975 (Die Tavistock Lectures 1935)

Jung, C.G.: Über die Psychologie des Unbewussten. Frankfurt 1975

Jung, C.G.: Bewusstes und Unbewusstes. Frankfurt 1977/1957

Jung, C.G.: Die Beziehungen zwischen dem Ich und dem Unbewussten. Olten 1971

Jung, C.G.: Typologie. Olten 1972

Jung, C.G. Symbolik des Geistes. Zürich 1951

Jung, C.G.: Das persönliche und das überpersönliche Unbewusste. 1916-1936

Jung, C.G.: Über die Entwicklung der Persönlichkeit. Olten 1972

Jung, C.G.: Mandala. Olten 1977

Jung, C.G. Die Individuation. Olten 1971

Jung, C.G.: Zur Empirie des Individuationsprozesses. Band 9. Olten 1976

Jung, C.G.: Die Archetypen und das kollektive Unbewusste. Olten 1976

Jung, C.G.: Zur Psychologie westlicher und östlicher Religion. Olten 1973

Jung, C.G.: Die praktische Verwendbarkeit der Traumanalyse. 1934

Jung, C.G.: Über psychische Energetik und das Wesen der Träume. Olten 1972

Jungk, R./Müllert, N.R.: Zukunftswerkstätten. München 1994

Kaufmann, H.: Struktur und Dynamik menschlichen Verhaltens. 1970

Kegan, R.: Die Entwicklungsstufen des Selbst. München 1986 (1994)

Keller, W.: Was gestern noch als Wunder galt. Zürich 1979

Kerényi, K.: Antike Religion. München/Wien 1971

Kessler, H.: Das offenbare Geheimnis. Freiburg 1977

Klupp, A.: Planen. Managen. Trainieren. München 1992

Kohli, M. (Hrgr.): Zur Soziologie des Lebenslaufs. Darmstadt 1978

Kohli, M.: Lebenslauftheoretische Ansätze. In: Hurrelmann, K./Ulich, D.: Sozialisationsforschung. Weinheim 1991

Kohut, H.: Narzissmus. Frankfurt 1973

Kruse, L./Graumann, C.F./Lantermann, E.-D.: Ökologische Psychologie. München 1990

Laaser, U. (u.a.): Prävention - Gesundheitserziehung. Berlin 1987

Lacan, J.: Grundlegung der Psychoanalyse. Frankfurt. 1973

Lacan, J.: Schriften I. Weinheim 1991 (1973 bzw. Paris 1966)

Lantermann, E.D.: Interaktionen. Person, Situation und Handlung. München 1980

Lazarus, A.: Multimodale Verhaltenstherapie. Frankfurt 1979

Langen, D.: Kompendium der medizinischen Hypnose. Basel 1972

Landmann, M.: Philosophische Anthropologie. Berlin 1969

Leinfellner, W.: Einführung in die Erkenntnis- und Wissenschaftstheorie. Mannheim 1967

Leirmann, W./Pöggeler, F. (Hrgr.): Erwachsenenbildung in 5 Kontinenten. Handbuch der Erwachsenenbildung. Bd. 5. Stuttgart 1979

Lenz, W.: Lehrbuch der Erwachsenenbildung. Stuttgart 1987

Lenzen, D. (Hrgr.): Enzyklopädie Erziehungswissenschaft. 12 Bde.Stuttgart 1984

Lenzen, D.: Handbuch und Lexikon der Erziehung. Stuttgart 1992

Lennhoff, E./Posner, O.: Internationales Freimaurer-Lexikon. Wien 1932 (1980)

Léon, A.: Psychologie der Erwachsenenbildung. Stuttgart 1977

Lersch, Ph./Thomae H. (Hrgr.): Handbuch der Psychologie. Göttingen 1960

Lersch, Ph.: Aufbau der Person. 1970 (10)

Leuner, H./Schroeter, E.: Indikationen und spezifische Applikationen der Hypnosebehandlung. Bern/Stuttgart 1975

Leuner, H. (u.a.): Katathymes Bilderleben mit Kindern und Jugendlichen. München/Basel 1978

Leuner, H. (Hrgr.): Katathymes Bilderleben. Bern/Stuttgart 1980

Lewin, K.: Feldtheorie in den Sozialwissenschaften. Bern 1963

Lowen, A.: Angst vor dem Leben. München 1981

Lowen, A.: Bioenergetik. Bern/München 1980

Lowen, A.: Liebe und Orgasmus. München 1993

Löwisch, D.J.: Einführung in die Erziehungsphilosophie. 1982

Lück, H.E. (u.a.): Einführung in die Psychologie. Leverkusen 1986

Lurker, M.: Wörterbuch biblischer Bilder und Symbole. München 1978

Mader, W.u.a.: Zehn Jahre Erwachsenenbildungswissenschaft. Bad Heilbrunn 1991

Mandel, K.H. (u.a.): Einübung der Liebesfähigkeit. München 1975

Mandel, A./Mandel, K.H.: Einübung in Partnerschaft. München 1971

Marcuse, H.: Der eindimensionale Mensch. Luchterhand 1968

Mary, M.: Schluss mit dem Beziehungskampf. München 1995

Maslow, A.H.: Motivation und Persönlichkeit. Olten 1977

Maslow, A,H.: Psychologie des Seins. München 1973

Mayer, K.E.: Grundriss moralischer Erziehung. Bad Heilbrunn 1986

Meek, G.W.: Heiler und Heil-Prozess. München 1980

Meili, H.: Analytischer Intelligenztest (AIT). Bern 1971
Meili, R./Steingrüber, H.-J.: Lehrbuch der psychologischen Diagnostik. Bern 1978
Meier, C.A.: Die Bedeutung des Traumes. Olten 1979
Meier, A./Rabe-Kleberg, U.: Weiterbildung, Lebenslauf, sozialer Wandel. Neuwies 1993
Menninger, K.: Das Leben als Balance. München 1968
Merleau-Ponty, M.: Phänomenologie der Wahrnehmung. Berlin 1974
Miers, H.E.: Lexikon des Geheimwissens. Freiburg 1980
Miller, G.A./Galanter, E./ Pribram, K.H.: Strategien des Handelns. Pläne und Strukturen des Verhaltens. Stuttgart 1991 (1973 bzw. 1960)
Montada, L.: Entwicklungspsychologie. München 1987
Müller, R.: Wandlung zur Ganzheit. Freiburg 1981
Murphy, G.: Personality. 1947
Murray, H.A.: Explorations in personality. Oxford Wiley 1963

Neue Helvetische Gesellschaft (NHG): Anno 709 p.R. Aarau 1973
Neumann, E.: Ursprungsgeschichte des Bewusstseins. Olten 1971
Nickel, E.: Die Erfahrung der kosmischen Dimension. In: Resch, A. (1973)
Niethammer, L. (Hrgr.): Lebenserfahrung und kollektives Gedächtnis. Stuttgart 1985

Obrist, W.: Die Mutation des Bewussteins. Bern 1980
Oerter, R.: Psychologie des Denkens. Donauwörth 1972
Oerter, R./Montada L.: Entwicklungspsychologie. München/Weinheim 1987
Omkarananda Swami: Stufen zur Selbstverwirklichung. Schopfheim 1968
Olechowski, R./Zdarzil, H.: Anthropologie und Psychologie des Erwachsenen. Stuttgart 1976
Opaschowski, H.W.: Einführung in die Freizeitwissenschaft. Opladen 1994
Oser, F.: Das Gewissen lernen. Olten 1976
Oser, F./Althof, W.: Moralische Selbstbestimmung. Stuttgart 1992 (1994)

PAD (Pädagogische Arbeitsstelle des DVV: Beiträge der Bezugswissenschaften zur Erwachsenenbildung. Frankfurt 1993
Perls, F.S. (u.a.): Gestalttherapie. Stuttgart 1979
Petzold E./Reindell, A.: Klinische Psychosomatik. Heidelberg 1980
Pfniss, A.: Die Zukunft meistern. Graz 1988
Piaget, J.: Das moralische Urteil beim Kinde. Olten/Freiburg 1973
Piaget, J.: Das Erwachen der Intelligenz beim Kinde. Stuttgart 1969
Piaget, J.: Die Equilibration der kognitiven Strukturen. Stuttgart 1976
Piaget, J.: Der Aufbau der Wirklichkeit beim Kinde. Stuttgart 1975

Plutchik: Emotion. A psychoevolutionary synthesis. New York 1980

Poeppig, F.: Ursymbole der Menschheit. Freiburg 1972

Pongratz, L.J. (Hrgr.): Psychotherapie in Selbstdarstellungen. Bern 1973

Prange, K.: Bildung in dürftiger Zeit. In: Zeitschrift für internationale erziehungs- und sozialwissenschaftliche Forschung. 5/1, 1988

Preiser, S.: Kreativitätsforschung. Darmstadt 1976

Ravenscroft, T.: Der Kelch des Schicksals. Die Suche nach dem Gral. Basel 1982

Reich, W.: Charakteranalyse. Frankfurt 1976 (1933)

Reich, W.: Der Krebs. Frankfurt 1976

Reich, W.: Die Entdeckung des Orgons: Der Krebs. Köln 1974

Resch, A. (Hrgr.): Der kosmische Mensch. Bd. 4. Paderborn 1973

Richter, H.E.: Lernziel Solidarität. Zürich 1975

Riemann, F.: Grundformen helfender Partnerschaft. München 1974

Ritzl, M.: ASW-Training. Genf 1976

Rogers, C.R.: Die klientenzentrierte Gesprächspsychotherapie. München 1972

Rogers, C.R.: Entwicklung der Persönlichkeit. Stuttgart 1973

Rohracher, H.: Einführung in die Psychologie. Wien/München 1971

Rosemann, H.: Intelligenztheorien. Reinbeck 1979

Roszak, T.: Öko-Psychologie. Stuttgart 1994

Roth E.: Persönlichkeitspsychologie. Stuttgart 1969

Rothacker, E.: Die Schichten der Persönlichkeit. 1952

Ruprecht, H./Sitzmann, G.H.: Erwachsenenbildung als Wissenschaft. Weltenburger Akademie 1986

Sader, M.: Psychologie der Persönlichkeit. München 1980

Schäfer, H.W.: Kelch und Stein. Frankfurt 1983

Scharfetter, Ch.: Allgemeine Psychopathologie. Stuttgart 1976

Schellhammer, E.: Menschsein in der Zukunft. Der Prozess der Individuation. Zürich 1987 (4)

Schellhammer, E.: Seelische Innenwelt im Alltag. Traum. Imagination. Psychische Energie. Zürich 1986 (3)

Schellhammer, E.: Der innere Mensch. Das eigene Schicksal gestalten. Zürich 1987

Schellhammer, E.: Unsere Zukunft in Ihrer Hand. Bildung für Umwelt und Frieden. Zürich 1988

Schellhammer, E.: Evolutionäre Menschenbildung. Allgemeine Andragogik. 2001

Schellhammer, E.: Individuation Grundstufe. Werkhefte Nr. 1-5. Zürich 2001

Schellhammer, E.: Individuation Oberstufe. Werkhefte 1-10. Zürich 2001

Schellhammer, E.: Handbuch der Traumdeutung. 2001

Schlegel, L.: Grundriss der Tiefenpsychologie. Bde 1-4. München 1972

Schramml, W.J./Baumann, U.: Klinische Psychologie. 2 Bde. Bern 1974/75

Schultz, J.H.: Hypnose-Technik. Stuttgart 1976

Schultz, J.H.: Das Autogene Training. Stuttgart 1973

Schultz-Hencke, H.: Lehrbuch der analytischen Psychotherapie. Stuttgart 1951

Schultz-Hencke, H.: Lehrbuch der Traumanalyse. Stuttgart 1968 (1949)

Schütz, A./Luckmann, Th.: Strukturen der Lebenswelt. 2 Bde. Frankfurt 1991

Schwarz-Winklhofer,I./Biedermann, H.: Das Buch der Zeichen und Symbole. Graz 1980

Selye, H.: Stress. Frankfurt 1982

Senzky, K.: Selbstreflexion als Zielperspektive wissenschaftsorientierter Erwachsenenbildung. In: Ruprecht/Sitzmann 1986

Siebenthal von, W.: Die Wissenschaft vom Traum. 1953

Siebert, H.: Aspekte einer reflexiven Didaktik. In: Mader 1991

Siebert, H.: Das Interesse der Erwachsenenbildung an der Psychologie. In: Dieterich 1987

Simon, F.B. Der Prozess der Individuation. Über den Zusammenhang von Vernunft und Gefühlen. Göttingen 1984

Sommer, A.: in: Knörzer, W.: Ganzheitliche Gesundheitsbildung in Theorie und Praxis. Heidelberg 1994

Steinbach, L.: in: Niethammer, L. (Hrgr.): Lebenserfahrung und kollektives Gedächtnis. Frankfurt 1985

Stelter, A.: PSI-Heilung. Bern 1973

SVEB: Aus dem Leben lernen: biographische Ansätze. Education permanente 1992/1

Szondi, L.: Schicksalsanalytische Therapie. Bern/Stuttgart 1963

Szondi, L.: Schicksalsanalyse. Basel 1965

Tart, Ch.T. (Hrgr): Transpersonale Psychologie. Olten 1978

Thomae, H. (Hrgr.): Die Motivation menschlichen Handelns. Köln/Berlin 1969

Thomae, H.: Persönlichkeit. Eine dynamische Interpretation. 1955

Thomae, H.: Das Individuum und seine Welt. Göttingen/Zürich 1988

Thomas, A./Chess, S.: Temperament und Entwicklung. Stuttgart 1980

Tietgens, H.: Erwachsenenbildung als Suchbewegung. Bad Heilbrunn 1986

Topitsch, E. (Hrgr.): Logik der Sozialwissenschaften. Köln 1970

Tress, W.: Das Rätsel der seelischen Gesundheit. Göttingen 1986

Useld-Baumann, Ch.: Sex und Liebe. München 1990

Vaitl, D./Petermann, F. (Hrgr.): Handbuch der Entspannungsverfahren. Band I: Grundlagen und Methoden. Weinheim 1993. Band II: Anwendungen. Weinheim 1994
Vallejo-Nagera, L.A. (u.a.): Guia practica de Psicologia. Madrid 1991
Verny, T.: Das Seelenleben des Ungeborenen. München 1981
Vester, F.: Unsere Welt - ein vernetztes System. München 1991 (7)
Vester, F.: Phänomen Stress. München 1993
Vester, H.G.: Soziologie der Postmoderne. München 1993
Vester, F.: Phänomen Stress. München 1993 (13)
Von Eckartshausen, K.: Über die wichtigsten Mysterien der Religion. Freiburg 1978

Wagner-Simon, Th./Benedetti, C.(Hrgr.): Traum und Träumen. Göttingen 1984
Wagner-Simon, Th./Benedetti, C.(Hrgr.): Sich selbst erkennen. Göttingen 1982
Watzlawick, P.: Die Möglichkeit des Andersseins. Bern/Stuttgart 1991
Watzlawick, P. (u.a.): Lösungen. Bern/Stuttgart 1979
Watzlawick, P. (u.a.): Menschliche Kommunikation. Bern/Stuttgart 1974
Weber, H.: Das Stresskonzept in Wissenschaft und Laientheorie. Regensburg 1987
Weber, H./Knapp-Glatzel, B.: Alltagsbelastungen. In: Brüderl (Hrgr.) 1988, 140-147
Weidenmann, B.: Ambivalenzen empirisch-analytischer Weiterbildungsforschung. In: Mader 1991
Whitbourne, S.K./Weinstock, C.S.: Die mittlere Lebensspanne. München 1982
Whorf, B.L.: Sprache. Denken. Wirklichkeit. Hamburg 1974
Willi, J.: Die Zweierbeziehung. Reinbeck 1975
Willi, J.: Was Paare zusammenhält. Reinbeck 1991
Wurmser, L.: Flucht vor dem Gewissen. Heidelberg 1993

York, U.: in: Nitsch, C. (u.a.): Sexualität im Familienalltag. München 1992

Zdarzil, H./Olechowski, R.: Anthropologie und Psychologie des Erwachsenen. Stuttgart 1976

For the Study of Individuation
The most Advanced Concept
Dr Eduard Schellhammer, Swiss

☐ The human being is differentiated under the aspects of action theory, psychoanalysis, psychology, biography and life worlds.

☐ A newly structured dream theory, an evaluated methodology of meditation, and an expanded understanding of the unconscious are further foundations for a step-by-step conception of personality formation and individuation.

☐ The most thorough and meticulous processes of individuation like nowhere else.

☐ An indispensable guide for those who teach individuation and accompany others in this psychic-spiritual process.

☐ A study book for those who want to achieve the goal of individuation.